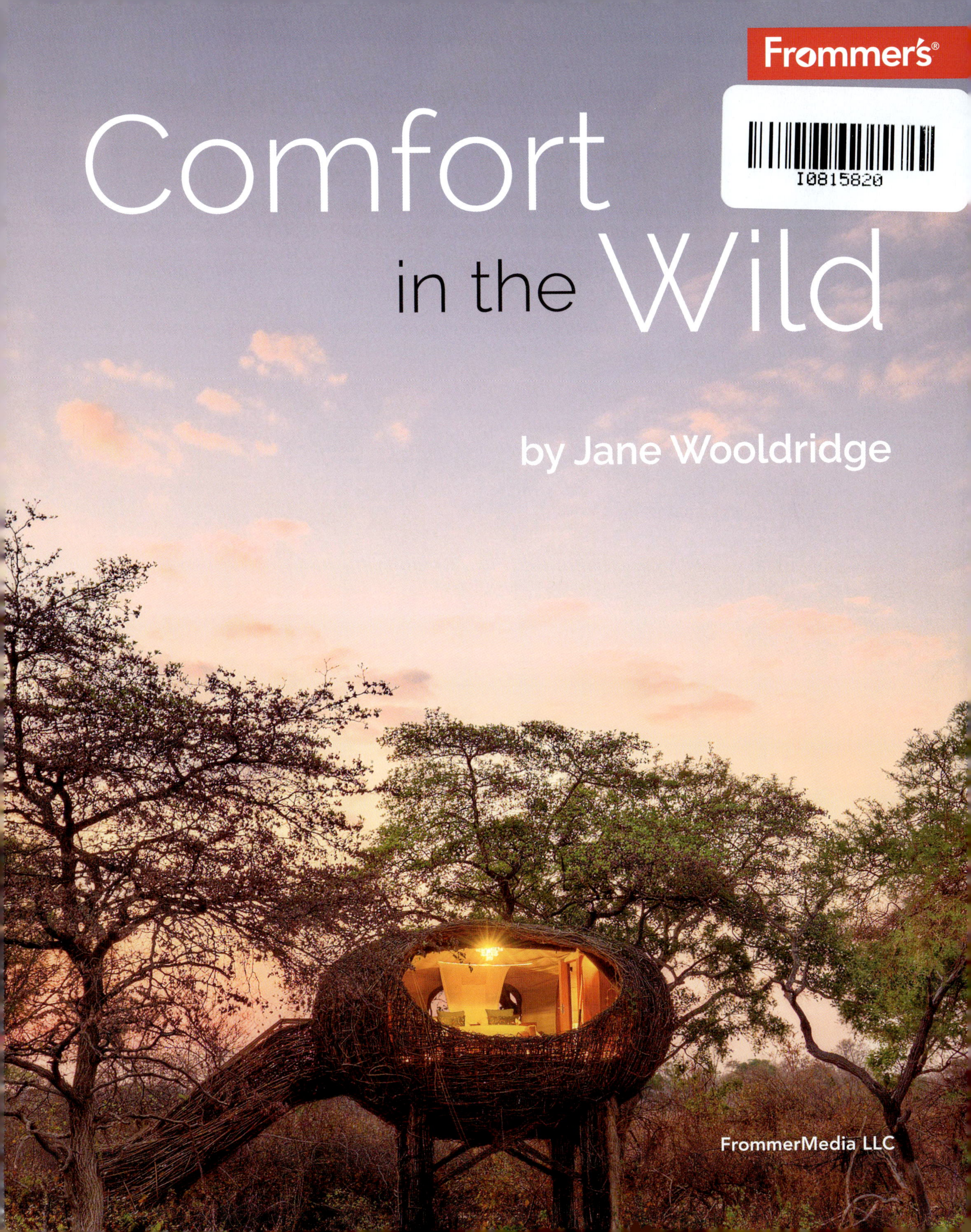

Comfort in the Wild

by Jane Wooldridge

FrommerMedia LLC

Frommer's

Comfort in the Wild: 100+ Idyllic Nature Destinations, No Roughing It Required

Published by:
FrommerMedia LLC

ISBN 978-1-62887-639-0 (paper), 978-1-62887-640-6 (ebk)

Editorial Director: Pauline Frommer
Editor: Pauline Frommer
Production Editor: Heather Wilcox
Compositor: Lissa Auciello-Brogan
Photo Editor: Meghan Lamb
Indexer: Cheryl Lenser
Cover Designer: Dave Riedy

Front cover photo: Nest at Green Safaris Chisa Busanga Camp.

Back cover photos: (top) White Desert in Antarctica; (middle) Misool in Raja Ampat, Indonesia; (bottom) Bubble room at Finn Lough.

For information on our other products or services, see www.frommers.com.

FrommerMedia LLC also publishes its books in a variety of electronic formats. Some content that appears in print may not be available in electronic formats.

Manufactured in Malaysia

5 4 3 2 1

HOW TO CONTACT US

In researching this book, we discovered many wonderful places—hotels, restaurants, shops, and more. We're sure you'll find others. Please tell us about them, so we can share the information with your fellow travelers in upcoming editions. If you were disappointed with a recommendation, we'd love to know that, too. Please write to: Support@FrommerMedia.com

CONTENTS

ABOUT THE AUTHOR

Jane Wooldridge's passion for travel has taken her to more than 100 countries on seven continents, from Montana to Mongolia to Mali. An award-winning travel, arts, and business journalist, her many honors include the prestigious Lowell Thomas Travel Journalist of the Year. She is a past president of the Society of American Travel Writers and former travel editor at the *Miami Herald*, where she has also served as an executive, business editor, columnist, arts writer, and Pulitzer Prize–winning team member. She has written for *Travel + Leisure, Virtuoso Life, Business Traveler*, and *National Geographic Traveler*, focusing on cruising, soft adventure, and upscale travel.

A WORD FROM JANE

"Writing a book is hard work," commiserated a fellow author during a chance meeting in an airport. He's written a dozen and knows. With 1½ books spewed from my computer, I'll add this: Writing a book is impossible without cheerleaders.

Thank you to my squad: Forever friends Elizabeth Brown, Kate Gilhuly, and Jose-Valdes Fauli, on whose sofas I have slept so often. ("Get her married and off my couch.") Robert Brewer and David Highfill, with whom I survived junior high and those early years in New York. (Remember the frozen Thanksgiving turkey bobbing in the bathtub?) My first roommate, my late brother Bob Wooldridge, his wife, Cathy, and family. (You're still with me, Brother.) The gang at the Miami Herald, *where some of this material was first published. (Support Local Journalism. It really matters.) My co-author on another book, Larry Bleiberg, and all my colleagues at SATW, the Society of American Travel Writers. (Note to self: Never allow a pandemic while you're president of a travel organization.) My editor and publisher, Pauline Frommer, without whom this book wouldn't exist. Travel pros Kathy Bernstein, an advisor with ProTravel, and her sources Ian Swain of Swain Destinations and Catherine Heald of Remote Lands. Eliza Bailey of This Is Beyond and Misty Belles Ewing of Virtuoso for their support. Laura Davidson of LDPR, Geoffrey Weill of his namesake firm, and Julie Earle of Luxury Lodges of Australia, who generously shared their amazing knowledge.*

And most especially, my cheerleader-in-chief and pilot-racer-husband, Stetson Glines. This book started out as a means to shared adventures; little did we imagine they would include a fractured pelvis, emergency room visits in multiple countries, a totaled Airstream, and a frantic afternoon looking for Ziggy, lead investigator of the Dogged Detectives. (We love you, too, Coconut.) Here's to the next adventure.

INTRODUCTION

Connecting with nature makes people feel better.

If your own COVID lockdown didn't convince you, studies by the National Institutes of Health, the Mental Health Foundation, and scientists across the globe provide proof that spending time outdoors decreases stress and increases general happiness.

A walk in a park is a good start. But in a chaotic, tech-crazed world, an afternoon is a temporary tonic. A deep detox requires days of breathing fresh fir-scented air, staring at the stars, and watching great herds of wildlife amble by.

The good news for comfort-craving travelers: These days, immersing in nature doesn't require pitching a tent, sleeping on hard ground, or eating canned meat and freeze-dried peas.

Glamping resorts, treehouses, expedition cruise ships, and nature lodges immerse us in forests, jungles, dark skies, and ice caps with the comforts of snug beds, en-suite bathrooms, hot-and-cold showers, and, sometimes, even Michelin-worthy dining.

I firmly believe that nature brings solace in all troubles.
— Anne Frank

Dock at Finn Lough on Lough Erne.

For me, camping has never really been an option. (My mother shuddered at the very idea of dirt.) Though I spent several years in Girl Scouts, the skills and appreciation for camping never took hold.

Still, my inherent passions for adventure and travel drove vacation decisions. For years in the pre-Internet age, I lived without a TV. Every time I had the money to buy one, I bought a plane ticket instead.

Since then, I've traveled from Montana to Mali to Mongolia—more than 120 countries at last count. I've traveled with friends, my husband, alone. Many trips were for pleasure; others were part of my job at the *Miami Herald,* where some portions of this book were first published. Through them, I've become intensely aware of the delicate balance between man and land. Trekking with gorillas, hiking in the Himalayas, and sitting high in the trees reminds me that there's more to life than my laptop.

I've also come to appreciate the value of a great mattress, an en-suite bathroom, thoughtful design (I'm married to an architect), and a fresh, finely crafted meal.

This book highlights experiences where nature meets creature comforts. Some of the places featured here have delivered extraordinary adventures for generations of nature lovers; others opened just recently. Some cost about the same as a chain motel; others are priced for the well-walleted and special-occasion splurgers.

To narrow the list from the hundreds—no, thousands!—of options, I consulted years of notebooks and dozens of experts. I raided my frequent-flier accounts and flew tens of thousands of miles.

Over two summers, my husband and I drove an aged SUV and vintage Airstream 6,742 miles from Portland, Maine, to Portland, Oregon, along a zig-zag route, then another 1,500 or so miles to California, Arizona, and Colorado. Our two handsome-but-shaggy Westies, Ziggy's and The Coconut, helped research glampsites, lodges, and inns. Along the way, we encountered elk, elephant seals, bison, crowned cranes, a hailstorm, and remarkable people whose kindness restored our faith in a divided America.

Like all adventures, our road trip came with challenges. Medical centers tended to kidney stones (The Husband's), stomach distress (Ziggy's), and chiggers (mine). AAA aided with mechanical failures of six tires, three sets of brakes, an automatic wench, and an Airstream refrigeration panel.

Then came a windy August day, when an 18-wheeler flew past us on a California highway, creating a draft too fierce for even The Husband, a one-time pilot and racecar driver. We fishtailed, spun, and flipped like a turtle onto our back. Our meticulously restored 1980 Airstream and VW Touareg were totaled. People pulled over to help; the police and rescue were alerted.

Fortunately, The Husband, dogs, and I were unharmed. But the accident was a reminder that life happens. Change can flare at any minute. Joy is ephemeral—and to some degree, the wilderness is too. Extreme weather events, climate change, and city sprawl have diminished untouched lands and the creatures that live in them.

I'm going to go while I can.

Jane Wooldridge

CHAPTER 1

IN THE TREES: TREEHOUSES & FOREST COTTAGES

Mirror Cube room at Treehotel (p. 21).

Trees are poems that the earth writes upon the sky.
— Kahlil Gabran
Blessed is she who clearly sees the wood for the trees.
— Incubus
After a whole day in the woods, we are already immortal.
— John Muir

VERMONT, USA

Maple Country

GREAT FOR	COST	WEBSITE
COUPLES, SMALL FAMILIES	$$$	MOOSEMEADOWLODGE.NET

The road turns off a road off a Vermont road, and you may well wonder just where it's heading. The drive leads up a hill to a lovely log house. But instead of heading up the stone steps to the B&B, your host leads the way through ferns and maples in back. There, at the edge of a pond, is a childhood dream come to life.

The two-story Treehouse at **Moose Meadow Lodge** sits on stilts overlooking a pond and dozens of forested acres beyond. Inside, a sitting room of smooth finished wood is set with a table and two chairs, a bench by the heating stove, and a shelf of books. A curved set of steps leads to the dormered bedroom and the deck around it.

Unlike some "treehouses" that simply sit amid trees, this log house really does hang from the pair of mature pines growing through its deck and sheltering overhang. While big windows provide wide views, the point is to get outdoors on the two broad balconies. An artfully carved stone sink sits outside on the lower deck; just beyond it are the toilet room and outdoor shower. Both are screened from view.

The decor reflects its New England country setting. Lights are made from deer antlers. A taxidermied beaver hangs on the wall, a trout is displayed above a window, a duck "flies" in a corner: In the woods, hunting is a way of life. But the moose that greets you from the pillow is a plush toy; the real thing would never fit.

From the deck, guests can hear the thrush trill, hang in the canvas chair swing, and watch the trees wave in the wind. They can walk through the forest to the gazebo atop the mountain or head to Waterbury for a beer at Prohibition Pig. Or just gaze through the treehouse's 31 windows and take in the views.

Planning a Trip

Moose Meadow Lodge is open from late May to October. The treehouse sits about 200 yards from the main lodge and offers plenty of privacy. The main house operates as a B&B, with three rooms with private baths. Stays at both include breakfast. (Treehouse guests can get theirs delivered.)

The lodge sits about 10 minutes from Waterbury, Vermont, and about 45 minutes from Burlington, home to the closest airport. Visitors come to the region for corn mazes, farmer's markets, artisan galleries, scenic drives, biking, fishing, and canoeing. Ben & Jerry's Ice Cream and Cabot Creamery were born in Vermont, and the region's signature red barns and cows can still be found throughout the countryside. Locally made maple syrup is a prized souvenir.

Treehouse at Moose Meadow Lodge.

TOP: Exterior, Seth Peterson Cottage.
MIDDLE: Dining area.
BOTTOM: Living room.

WISCONSIN, USA

A Wright-Designed House in Nature, Yours for the Night

GREAT FOR	COST	WEBSITE
COUPLES	$$	SETHPETERSON.ORG

The **Seth Peterson Cottage** is deceptively plain, a single open room with a bedroom and a bath tucked behind the stone hearth. But with Frank Lloyd Wright as its architect, the house is anything but simple.

Inside, these 880 square feet make use of every inch without appearing crowded. Here are spaces for living, dining, cooking, reading, and entertaining. An L-shaped sofa sits against a stone wall, a square oak table close enough for visitors to rest their drinks. A pair of sleek easy chairs with footstools flank the stone hearth. The stovetop, counter, and sink are set in the kitchen alcove, lit by a skylight. Two tables can accommodate four each for breakfast or dinner, or they can serve as desks.

The sloped shed roof shelters 12-foot-tall windows, aiming the focus where Wright intended: at the oaks and pines of Wisconsin's Mirror State Park, in harmony with nature.

Today, the Seth Peterson Cottage is one of a half dozen Wright-designed homes in the Midwest available for vacation rental, and the only one in a state park. It is the smallest of Wright's so-called Usonian homes, envisioned as moderately priced housing.

When it was commissioned in 1958, the client was 22-year-old Seth Peterson, who originally sought to study with Wright but couldn't afford to do so. Just months before the house was finished in 1960, Peterson took his own life. The house was sold and then sold again to the state of Wisconsin but left unoccupied. In the late 1980s, a group of local preservationists restored the cottage, which opened in 1992 for overnight rentals.

More than a mile of woods separates the park entrance from the cottage. The odd deer or fox may amble past, but otherwise, guests are blessedly on their own. Mammoth water parks are only a few miles away, but visitors rarely see or hear them from this bluff above the lake.

Planning a Trip

Mirror Lake State Park is located in the Wisconsin Dells. The park's 19 miles of trails facilitate hiking, biking, and snow-shoeing for views of the lake and sandstone cliffs. Fishing, canoeing, and no-wake boating are allowed.

A 15-minute drive takes you to the lively town of Baraboo, where the Ringling Brothers started their circus in 1884. Today, the town is home to the Circus World Museum. Ten minutes outside its limits, the conservation-oriented International Crane Center is open May to October. In summer, visitors may spot sandhill cranes in fields along the roads.

CALIFORNIA, USA

The Giants of the Forest

GREAT FOR	COST	WEBSITE
COUPLES	$$$$	ARTISTREEHOME.COM

The redwoods all around sway ever-so-slightly in the wind, groaning in the way that any 2,000-year-old earthling might. There's no need to feel anxious; the steel supporting the house is securely fastened in a massive sequoia and braced from the ground with more steel.

Guests lounge in the hot tub on the wooden deck cantilevered over a hill, sipping a Patz & Hall pinot noir crafted in the nearby valley. Tomorrow, they may head to Sonoma's the girl & the fig for duck confit and heritage pork wrapped in cabbage. But a quiet moment, pâté picked up at a farmer's market, and air freshened with the scent of hundreds-foot-high redwoods can serve as well.

When the sun dips lower, it's time to slip inside the cozy conical home and watch the sky darken through the floor-to-ceiling window. The giant bed, snug kitchen, and en suite bath are all that's needed for a serene evening in the forest. Measuring 465 square feet, the spyglass is larger than many a city apartment.

"The Spectacular Spyglass Treehouse," as it is called on the Airbnb website, is the brainchild of Will Beilharz, founder and president of **Artistree Home.** He designed the spyglass shape as an eco-sensitive guest rental. The cylinder is fabricated in Tennessee, then installed on-site with finishes chosen by each owner. In the redwoods, the interior is finished in a smooth pale pine, with matching cabinets and wood floors.

Will inherited his love of nature from his mother, Amy Beilharz, whose family opened the first U.S. canopy tour in Spicewood, Texas, in 2005. "The goal was to share nature with other people and get people outdoors. People would do the zip lines and want to spend the night on the platforms," she said, and the treehouse business was born.

Since then, Artistree has built treehouses in Texas, Hawaii, and Mexico that serve as short-term rentals. Another "spyglass" rental located nearby, outside Sebastopol, overlooks a vineyard. It's less secluded than the redwoods but comes with a private sauna with an outdoor shower and a giant bathtub on the spyglass deck. Guests may want to soak until their skin prunes, but it will be worth it.

Bathtub at Spyglass Sonoma.

Exterior, Spyglass Sonoma.

Planning a Trip

The **Spectacular Spyglass Treehouse** in the redwood forest is a short drive from the Northern California coast at Salmon Creek and Bodega Bay, the cozy towns of Occidental and Sebastopol, and more wineries than you could possibly visit in a day. A museum showcasing the work of Charles Schulz, the beloved *Peanuts* creator, lies 30 minutes away in Santa Rosa. The town of Sonoma lies an hour to the south. No stairs are involved.

Spyglass Sonoma overlooks a vineyard and grove near historic Sebastopol, home to a Sunday farmer's market. In the nearby town of Barlow, the market is open daily and hosts a brewery and several farm-to-table eateries for takeout or dining in the courtyard. Entry at Spyglass Sonoma involves a short staircase.

The Beilharz family also offers vacation rentals at a wide range of treehouses at Cypress Valley near Austin, Texas. Most involve climbing steps. *cypressvalley.com.*

FACING PAGE, TOP: *Exterior, Spyglass Redwoods.*
BOTTOM: *Bedroom, Spyglass Redwoods.*

MONTANA, USA

The Enchanted Forest of the green o

GREAT FOR	COST	WEBSITE
THE GREEN O IS ADULTS-ONLY. CHILDREN ARE WELCOME ELSEWHERE AT PAWS UP.	$$$$	THEGREENO.COM

This can't be glamping.

That is our first thought when we arrive at our modernist house in the pines. A fireplace sits between giant windows that bring the forest inside. The bath is tiled in forest green; the tub for two sits in a separate wet space lit by a malachite-shaded porthole. On the deck, we can sway in a padded basket swing or soak in the outdoor hot tub, with trees all around. From the four-poster wooden bed, we look through the skylight that, come night, envelopes us in a soft blanket of stars.

When it opened in 2005 on these same 37,000 acres, **Paws Up Montana** launched American "glamping." Roomy African safari tents featured heated floors, en suite bathrooms, climate control, and camping butlers. Massage and hot-stone treatments were delivered in open-air tents to the soothing sounds of bird calls and a bubbling brook. Magazine awards soon followed.

The **green o** debuted in 2021, with 12 forest houses for adults-only that go far beyond glamping, with Wi-Fi, TV, and an award-winning design by Dave Lipson and Pieter De Liagre Bohl. The Tree Haus sits on three levels, with a hot tub on the ground floor and king bed up the spiral staircase leading to the top. The Round Haus offers 180-degree views of deer that occasionally amble by. The Green Haus, where we stay, welcomes pets, including our two Westies, who are mesmerized by the sheep statues emblazoned with a giant green "O"—a clever nod to the resort's mailing address in Greenough, Montana.

But the big surprise is the **Social Haus,** combination meeting point, lounge, and gourmet restaurant so remarkable that its chef, Brandon Cunningham, is a James Beard Award finalist. Despite that honor, he chats easily with us at the open kitchen while he creates our next meal. After indulging in the six-course tasting menu featuring albacore tuna topped with thin-sliced roasted squash and salmon with slivered fennel, we're sure he should win.

To burn off the calories, Paws Up offers horse-riding, ponies, fishing, hiking, and shooting—all part of daily life on a working cattle ranch, but adapted for guests. On a clear day, my private guide and I drive beyond the jagged mountains and wide green valleys to the Blackfoot River, renowned for brown, cutthroat, and rainbow trout. A flock of ducks lands on water so clear, you can see the outline of the rocks below.

***TOP:* Living room at green o.**
***MIDDLE:* Exterior of green o in the snow.**
***BOTTOM:* Bedroom, green o.**

Chef Brandon in the kitchen at green o.

Our raft goes into the river, a fly on my lure. I expect a fish to glide past at any moment. One does, but it isn't interested in my line. I cast again, getting my fly stuck on a rock, and start over. My guide takes over, hooking a couple of trout on my line so I'll feel successful. But the fish have figured out that I'm less interested in them than in watching the cliffs and sky and trees slip by. After too many texts and emails in days past, this quiet moment is my reward.

Planning a Trip

The green o is located at Paws Up Montana, a 35-minute drive from Missoula International Airport. Meals at any of Paws Up's resort venues are included, along with some activities.

FACING PAGE, TOP: *Cowgirl cattle drive at The Resort at Paw's Up.*
MIDDLE: *Spa treatment tents at The Resort at Paw's Up.*
BOTTOM: *Buffalo at The Resort at Paw's Up.*

MINNESOTA, USA

A Treehouse Made of Magic

GREAT FOR	COST	WEBSITE
COUPLES, FAMILIES WITH OLDER CHILDREN	$$	HOPEGLENFARM.COM

The cottage looks like a movie set. *Where's the film crew?* I wonder as I walk up the steps beneath the 150-year-old burr white oak tree.

I open the treehouse door and gasp. Crystals dangle from the chandelier hanging beneath the peaked roof of the living room. Kitchen counters are marble, the full-size refrigerator stainless steel. Wooden staircases lead up and down to a library, outdoor decks, and two bedrooms. The bathroom sink and the Jacuzzi-style bathtub are set in hewn stone. Floors have radiant heat plus two fireplaces—so cozy in winter. From the observation tower on top, a telescope enables guests to see the heavens.

At 1,200 square feet, this seven-room treehouse is bigger than many city apartments. But the real magic isn't the secret room, which I eventually discover: It's the story of **Hope Glen Farm.**

For years, Paula Buschilla admired the 100-year-old homestead as she drove to Minnesota's Twin Cities. In 2001, the woman who owned it—the grandmother of a friend—sold it to Paula and her husband, Michael, who restored its seven buildings and ran it as a hobby. When the recession hit in 2011, their printing business collapsed, and they were forced to put the farm up for sale. The bank was just days from foreclosing on it when a frantic bride called, asking to hold her wedding at Hope Glen; she'd be happy to pay for the privilege.

A local newspaper wrote up the story, and the phone started ringing. By 2015, the Buschillas were hosting 100 weddings each year, using the barn for cocktails, the vineyard for ceremonies, and a newly built pavilion for dining.

The treehouse came in 2016. Michael crafted it from 12 species of wood, with 12 doors, 12 steps from ground to front door, and 12 stairs inside to the upstairs level—all by serendipity rather than plan. The result was fairylike—and perfect for a honeymoon suite.

But you don't have to be newlyweds to stay here. Sitting in front of the fireplace on a cool evening brings romance of its own.

Planning a Trip

Hope Glen Farm is located in Cottage Grove, Minnesota, about a half-hour southeast of Minneapolis. The Tree House is heated and air-conditioned and sleeps four. A second comfortable suite is located in the barn.

Guests are welcome to stroll the grounds and visit the resident goats and chickens. Cottage Grove Ravine Regional Park is within walking distance. Its 500 acres include forest trails for gentle hikes and bike rides and a lake where visitors can fish from a pier or sit in their kayaks.

TOP LEFT: *Dining area.*
TOP RIGHT: *Living room.*
BOTTOM LEFT: *Hope Glen Farm cabin in the snow.*
BOTTOM RIGHT: *Bedroom.*

TOP: Aerial view of Entre Cîmes et Racines.
BOTTOM LEFT: Hobbit House at Entre Cîmes et Racines.
BOTTOM RIGHT: Kitchen in Entre Cîmes et Racines.

At Home with Elfin Folk

GREAT FOR	COST	WEBSITE
COUPLES, FAMILIES UNTETHERED FROM DEVICES	$	ENTRECIMESETRACINES.COM

A long gravel road through a forest of firs leads to a timbered tower straight out of a fairy tale. Drawings on the reception wall offer a hint of things to come. A giant owl flies away with a two-story cabin. A stone cottage rests on the generous antlers of a moose. A massive beaver wraps its tail around a peaked thatched roof. All are the work of local artist Marc Simard.

At last, I'm standing at the door of the cottage that drew us here. Since I first read *The Lord of the Rings,* I've wanted to stay in a hobbit house. Now, here it is, a vaulted stone house tucked into a hillside and covered with vines, complete with a round door and windows. Inside, a pair of cozy red leather chairs sit near a dining table, the wood kitchen counter, wood-burning stove, and bunked double beds. An outdoor fire pit and picnic table surrounded by pines offer plenty of privacy.

Prefer Fred Flintstone's cottage? It's down a path and through the forest, its curved ceiling carved into rock.

A gingerbread house? It's tucked into another copse. Up the hill, the two-level Love Nest is waiting for Rapunzel to throw down her braid.

Entre Cîmes et Racines—"between roots and treetops"—grew out of love for the forest. In the 1960s, local villager Bernard Berger began buying land and reforesting it. Some 20 years later, he moved to what was then 175 acres and started making sugar from the surrounding maples. In 1998, his three sons took over, and in 1999, they opened their forest retreat, now home to 14 individual ecolodges.

All cabins offer private outdoor space and are available in summer and winter. Each has an indoor toilet, but only a few have electricity. To charge devices, hook into Wi-Fi, and take a shower, guests need to head back up the path to the office building.

The forest is meant to be admired, from one's deck cottage or an Adirondack chair around private fire pits, on a hike or scavenger hunt, or while the kids check out the pint-sized play houses. The scent of pines is a kiss on my wounds. After a few days in the woods, I'll be healed.

Planning a Trip

Entre Cîmes et Racines is located in Quebec province about an hour east of Montreal and about 40 minutes north of the U.S. border near Newport, Vermont. It is open year-round except April. The Hobbit House books out well in advance.

Guests need to bring their own sheets, towels, and food. Ice, candles, and wood are available for sale.

WASHINGTON, USA

At the Foot of the Mountain

GREAT FOR	COST	WEBSITE
COUPLES, SMALL FAMILIES	$$	IRONANDVINETREEHOUSE.COM

It's August, but the snow falling on the road to Mount Rainier's Jackson Visitor Center is so thick that we've set the windshield wipers to top speed. We decide to turn back, but by the time we've cleared the national park gates, the snow has been vanquished by sunshine. Mount Rainier's fierce microclimates are serious business.

When you can see it, the namesake mountain is an impressive sight. The volcanic cone rises 2½ miles into the sky. Though its glaciers are shrinking, the mountain is still dappled with white year-round, tempting mountaineers as it has since the 1800s. Millenia before that, Indigenous people gathered fruit, fished, and hunted in the surrounding meadows, and while hunting is no longer permitted, visitors can still cast a fly for trout and whitefish.

Outside the park and within it, the land is thick with evergreens. Just a few miles outside Rainier's boundary lies the town of Ashford, population 300, give or take. The GPS leads us up a side road on a hill to our destination: a treehouse set in four massive Douglas firs.

The iron steps lead to the door of **Iron & Vine Treehouse.** It feels like I'm actually inside a tree. Walls are finished in cedar. The rolling stools at the breakfast bar are topped with wood. The kitchen counters are topped with wood. The windows are trimmed in bark-edged wood. Even the bathroom (save for the shower) is lined in cedar. It's all clear, varnished, warm, smooth wood—except for the stone surrounding the cozy electric fire, next to the leather sofa.

The stair-step ladder—yes, wood—leads to the second level overlooking the main room. A queen bed is tucked into a nook. One section is slung with a hammock, inviting a nap.

Creating this 400-square-foot sanctuary took owners Chris and Emily Gregerson 4 full years. Though they grew up here and knew the area well, finding just the right trees in just the right location took months. Then, the design and engineering phase kicked in. With the help of treehouse engineer Charley Greenwood—yes, such experts exist—they figured out how to bolt and secure the house onto the four trees. Friends and family helped mill the wood, mostly from trees already on site. Finally, in 2022, they opened Iron & Vine Treehouse to overnight guests.

The sanctuary that resulted was made for world-weary adults. While children are welcome—the Gregersons' first arrived during the project—there's nothing fanciful about it. Decor nods to nature: dried flowers, a leaf preserved in glass, a shadow-box forest cut from wood. Here, I'm a squirrel ready for rest, however long it may be.

Planning a Trip

Ashford, Washington, is 6 miles west of Mount Rainier National Park. The drive takes about 90 minutes from Seattle and a little over 2 hours from Portland, Oregon. Bookings are accepted 9 months in advance via Airbnb.

TOP LEFT: Iron & Vine Treehouse in the snow.
TOP MIDDLE: Fishing on Mineral Lake in Mt. Rainer National Park.
TOP RIGHT: Sleeping nook, Iron & Vine Treehouse.
BOTTOM LEFT: Hiking in Mt. Rainer National Park.
BOTTOM RIGHT: Interior, Iron & Vine Treehouse.

HARADS, SWEDEN

High Design, High in the Pines

GREAT FOR	COST	WEBSITE
COUPLES, SMALL FAMILIES	$ GUESTROOM, $$$ TREEHOUSES	TREEHOTEL.SE

One looks like a bird's nest, another like a cartoon UFO. The stairs of another seem to disappear altogether into the sky and trees.

Each of the eight houses of Sweden's **Treehotel** qualifies as a unique architectural marvel. Looking at it now, you would never imagine that this design-centered celebrity getaway started as a B&B in a dilapidated 1920s retirement house.

Britta Lindvall, a nurse, and her husband, Kent, a school counselor and fishing guide, grew up in Swedish Lapland in the 500-person village of Harads. Initially, they set out simply to restore the historic house. Then, they thought to make it into a guest house. But getting tourists to come proved a challenge.

A fishing trip to Russia changed everything. One evening, Kent and a trio of friends turned their conversation to *The Tree Lover,* a 2008 Swedish documentary. The three, all architects, were soon debating the qualities of the ideal treehouse. Theorizing wasn't enough, and they decided to build their designs in the forest surrounding the guest house.

In 2010, the first four treehouses opened. The Mirrorcube, a retreat for two designed by Bolle Tham and Martin Videgård, reflects the surrounding forest and seems to disappear inside it. Bertil Harström's Birds Nest looks exactly like its name and can be reached only by a ladder. Mårten and Gustav Cyrén's Cabin features a deck with long views across the nearby valley. Sandellsandberg's ironically named Blue Cone is as red as Santa's hat and sits near the ground off a gentle ramp.

The original guest house remains the heart of the hotel. It's a cozy, eclectic place where guests dine in front of a hand-painted fireplace on delicate venison tartare and seared arctic char. Upstairs, six guest rooms with shared bath offer a price-wise alternative for guests who want to take a husky-pulled sled or horse sleigh into the snow, visit a Sami reindeer herder, or kayak under the summer's midnight sun.

But most come for a tree room, and the Bjake Ingels–designed Biosphere it is. On this crisp March day, I stand at the windows and peer across the pines to a cerulean sky—a memorable view. But what lingers months later is the profound silence of snow on treetops. When chaos threatens, it's this moment that brings me peace.

Planning a Trip

Treehotel is located in Harads, about an hour's drive from the airport in Lulea.

***TOP:* Birds Nest room, Treehotel. *MIDDLE:* Reindeer in front of the UFO Treehotel room. *BOTTOM:* Room 7, Treehotel.**

NEW ZEALAND

Of Whales & Wine

GREAT FOR	COST	WEBSITE
COUPLES, FAMILIES WITH OLDER CHILDREN	$$$	HAPUKULODGE.COM

Some 60,000 pounds of humpback whale pirouette out of the sea, then splash back into the chilly water. In the Southern Hemisphere winter of June to August, you're here to see it poke its head above water and breach again and again, framed by the peaks of the Southern Alps. Your Kaikoura-based tour boat stays at least 150 feet away—which means you'll stay dry, even if the temps drop to the 40s Fahrenheit.

For whale-watchers, Kaikoura is the mecca. Throughout the cool season, from May to November, you can spot Southern Right whales right from the beach. Between November and March, blue whales come to visit. And just about any time of year, visitors find the permanent locals: male sperm whales, dusky dolphins, and fur seals.

New Zealand prohibits swimming with whales, but visitors can snorkel with dolphins and fur seals on organized excursions or view them from lookout points. They can stretch their legs on the coastal walking path and even trek with llamas.

Despite its appeal, Kaikoura remains a fishing village with a human population of about 4,000. Long before it was trendy, food trucks along the beach began serving up crayfish, mussels, and barbecue. More than half of Kaikoura's visitors are day-trippers; those who overnight sleep in motels and small B&Bs.

The exception lies 15 minutes to the north, at **Hapuku Lodge + Tree Houses.**

Opened in 2003, Hapuku Lodge + Tree Houses features five wooden stilt houses set 30 feet above ground in a grove of Kanuka trees. The climb is worth the effort. Picture windows set into wooden frames meld indoors with the outside, so guests feel like they're in nature even when they're snug. From the lounge chair beside the gas fire, the snow-dusted Southern Alps rise to the west, behind a large meadow that's home to red deer and sheep. From the generous bathtub, you can look to the east over a grove of olive trees to the sea. Three of the treehouses are designed for couples; two feature a pair of bedrooms for families.

The Olive House—once home to olive presses—offers a three-bedroom suite, suitable for a large family or three couples. The lodge presents another alternative, with three rooms with soaking tubs and views to the deer paddock. One room is wheelchair-accessible.

The fields and treehouses are part of a 1,000-acre farm. A garden provides herbs, asparagus, tomatoes, artichokes, leeks, berries, and citrus used in the kitchen in the multicourse

TOP: Treehouse Lounge at Hapuku Lodge + Tree Houses.
MIDDLE: Exterior, Hapuku Lodge + Tree Houses.
BOTTOM: Spa soaking tubs, Hapuku Lodge + Tree Houses.

evening meal. The antlers of the red deer visible outside the window are used to make natural steroids popular on the Chinese market. Some of the lamb and beef is served in the dining room. The green-lipped mussels and fish on the menu come from nearby waters.

The olive oil comes from the orchard. Guests who turn up in May or June can help with the olive harvest—but first, they'll have to drag themselves from the view and the New Zealand wine that's always close at hand.

Planning a Trip

Temperatures are generally moderate, rarely dropping below 40°F, even in the cool months of June through August. In the warm months of November to March, temps rarely rise above 70°F.

Kaikoura is located about 110 miles north of Christchurch on New Zealand's South Island. Getting there requires a vehicle. Roads are generally good.

Room rates at Hapuku Lodge + Tree Houses include a multicourse dinner and breakfast. Facilities include a pool, spa, and bicycles.

FACING PAGE, TOP: The Farm at Hapuku Lodge + Tree Houses.
BOTTOM: Deer at Hapuku Lodge + Tree Houses.
THIS PAGE, TOP: Hot tub in the Secret Garden at Hapuku Lodge + Tree Houses.
BOTTOM: Hiking through the Fern Garden at Hapuku Lodge + Tree Houses.

JAPAN

A World Apart

GREAT FOR	COST	WEBSITE
ACTIVE COUPLES, FAMILIES WITH CHILDREN 10 OR OLDER	$$$	EN.TREEFUL.NET

Visitors often think of Japan as a scene from *Lost in Translation*, a neon universe of sleek high-rise hotels and elaborate sushi restaurants. The islands of Okinawa tell a different story.

Nearly 1,000 miles southwest of Tokyo, Okinawa lies in a subtropical zone warm enough for sugarcane and pineapple. It's not just the weather that sets it apart. In medieval times, Okinawa was the seat of the Ryukyu Kingdom, which dominated seagoing trade in the region. The dramatic Shuri Castle, severely damaged in World War II and again by a 2019 fire, is undergoing reconstruction.

Its history and nature have led to a distinctive architecture. While other parts of Japan lean toward natural wood and minimalist styling, Okinawa's structures feature muddy red tile roofs and courtyard walls of white limestone walls. Fukugi trees proliferate, acting as a natural windbreak against storms.

Okinawa even has its own liquor, *awamori,* a potent whiskeylike beverage distilled from rice and stored in traditional clay pots.

It's also home to Yanbaru National Park, at 33,000 acres one of the largest subtropical rainforests in Asia.

On Yanbaru's edge sits **Treeful Treehouse Sustainable Resort.** A pet goat greets you at the gate. Inside, you find a haven of mangroves, ferns, and pines running along a stream. Above are four treehouses—not just houses amid trees but houses circling sturdy trunks, as if they've grown around them.

Treeful Treehouse Sustainable Resort is the manifestation of a childhood dream inspired by a book. When Satoru Kikugawa grew up, he began searching for land with the right arboreal life to support a treehouse. When a real estate agent found land harboring a massive *akagi,* or bishop wood, tree on Okinawa, he took it as a sign. Success didn't come easily. After 7 years of trial and error, YouTube tutorials, and help from a team, Kikugawa and his daughter opened Treeful Treehouse Sustainable Resort.

Today, Treeful Treehouse Sustainable Resort features four sets of accommodations plus a main gathering spot called the Party Treehouse, where you can order sake, beer, or a surprising selection of wines. The three original treehouses are two-part sets combining an air-conditioned aero house near the ground, with a skylight and floor-to-ceiling windows, and a lofty treehouse. Each of the treehouses is unique: One features tatami mats in a teahouse style,

Exterior of Treeful Treehouse Sustainable Resort.

another a glass pavilion above a stream, a third a traditional design. The newest, the Bamboo Treehouse, is a two-level glassy cylinder cantilevered over a ridge. All accommodations offer running water and toilets.

From their perches, guests can smell the loam and leaves and, come evening, a DYI grilled dinner of fresh vegetables and pork or beef. Back on Earth, they can visit the sauna or spa or head into the woods in search of rare woodpeckers and the flightless Okinawa rail. Don't plan to move quickly; this is a place for quiet and contemplation.

Planning a Trip

The best time to visit Okinawa is October through April, when highs hover around 70°F.

Treeful Treehouse Sustainable Resort is located near Yanbaru National Park. The closest airport is in Naha. The road to the resort is rugged, and using a local taxi arranged by the resort is recommended.

A light breakfast is included. Dinner must be booked in advance.

***TOP:* Exterior, Treeful Treehouse Sustainable Resort room.**
***MIDDLE:* Guestroom.**
***BOTTOM:* Goat at Treeful Treehouse Sustainable Resort.**

GREAT BRITAIN

In a Forest Medieval

GREAT FOR	COST	WEBSITE
COUPLES, FAMILIES	$$	TREEDWELLERS.CO.UK

The medieval villages and rolling hills of the Cotswolds are the stuff of *Downton Abbey, Bridget Jones's Diary,* and *Harry Potter.* Towns of Bibury and Castle Combe vie for bragging rights as England's prettiest, with their stone facades and gabled roofs. Miss Marple might well have lived here, though Agatha Christie never would confirm.

This region northwest of London is also home to Wychwood Forest, 120 square miles covered with ancient oak, beech, and ash; farmlands; and fruited brambles dating to medieval times. The forest wraps Cornbury Park, a private estate and former royal hunting lodge visited by none other than Queen Elizabeth I. And within Cornbury's 1,700 acres sits **TreeDwellers,** an enclave of seven treehouses amid pines and sycamore, ferns, and fruited brambles.

At first glance, this might be a set for *Alice's Adventures in Wonderland.* Two treehouses are angular wood-paneled cottages; the other five are clad in aluminum and curved like caterpillars. Each is set in its own glen, with clear wooded interiors that echo the forest outside. These forest cocoons are designed for serene, self-contained holidays, with wood-burning stoves and underfloor heating, king beds set with hypoallergenic sheets, fully-equipped kitchens, and bathtubs with woodland views.

Guests looking for adventure can follow public walking trails, shop for cheese and pickles at farm shops, or consult with the on-site concierge about horse-riding, fishing, and deer hunting. But such energetic pursuits run counter to the TreeDwellers' core ethic: to slow down, contemplate the bluebells blooming beneath the trees, and let the mind go free. Your private deck becomes an amphitheater for the chorus of trilling frogs, tweeting thrushes, and screeching barn owls. You can't hear that in the local pub.

Planning a Trip

TreeDwellers is located in Oxfordshire, about a half-hour from Oxford and less than 2 hours from London. Picturesque villages, including Upper Slaughter, Bourton-on-the-Water, and Moreton-in-Marsh, are a short drive away. Several pubs are within walking distance of TreeDwellers.

The region hosts numerous festivals in the spring and summer. Winter is often rainy and cold, with highs in the 40s Fahrenheit.

Two treehouses can accommodate four people; the others are set up for two. One unit is accessible for those with mobility issues.

Aerial view of TreeDwellers cabin.

CHAPTER 2

IN A BUBBLE: SKY-WATCHING DOMES & NATURE YURTS

An aerial view of Premium Bubble at Finn Lough (p. 40).

Only in the darkness can you see the stars.
— Martin Luther King Jr., Civil rights activist

Remember to look up at the stars and not down at your feet. Try to make sense of what you see and wonder about what makes the universe exist. Be curious. And however difficult life may seem, there is always something you can do and succeed at. It matters that you don't just give up.
— Stephen Hawking, Physicist

For my part, I know nothing with any certainty, but the sight of the stars makes me dream.
— Vincent van Gogh, Impressionist painter

Tiny bubbles
In the wine
Make me happy
Make me feel fine
— Leon Pober, Lyricist

UTAH, USA

Hoodoo, Voodoo & a Step into the Space Age

GREAT FOR	COST	WEBSITE
COUPLES, FRIENDS, FAMILIES	$$	CLEARSKYRESORTS.COM

A giant sat here and dribbled wet sand from his massive hand.

That's what you think when you see the pink towers from Bryce Canyon's 8,000-foot-high plateau. Miles of stone spires stretch out before you, carved from sandstone, mudstone, limestone, and other sedimentary rocks that once sat beneath ancient lakes. There's no plan to the crenulations: turrets here, steeples there, obelisks across the sloping amphitheater.

Officially, these strange rocks are called hoodoos, likely after a Southern Paiute word for something that evokes fear, though possibly after voodoo. Either way, the idea that one of those awkwardly balanced rocks could tumble is downright scary. But they don't, of course, which is part of the wonder.

Another bit of wizardry: On a crystal-clear 70°F summer day, the level walkway around the amphitheater and the trails below are surprisingly peaceful. Aside from the one influencer who invariably blocks the best viewpoints, you can walk right up to the split-rail safety fence and gaze over the glowing spires for as long as you wish. It's not that you're alone: Bryce sees some 2.5 million visitors each year, about half the number of Grand Canyon or Zion National Park. But there's far less frenzy than at parks closer to major highways. And when you drive deep into the park on the tarmac road aside the juniper forest, you scarcely see another car.

Bryce sits at the pinnacle of the Grand Staircase, a 100-mile-long series of rock layers rising from the depths of the Grand Canyon. The land is marked by cliffs and plateaus, hills, and valleys dotted with scrub. Just a few miles from Bryce, you turn into a rock-rimmed valley set with 60 geodesic domes.

Each offers a view to the dramatic landscape. The smallest measures more than 400 square feet and comes with indoor seating and an outdoor firepit. The largest sleeps eight in two bedrooms plus a loft. All have modern bathrooms with showers. Drapes allow you to block the sun.

Domes and the main gathering area have a space-age vibe, but some take it to the whimsical max, with a dance-floor that twinkles with the bass and a disco ball. In my "Supernova"-themed dome, I can put my feet on the Eames-style chair upholstered in coral-colored vinyl or stretch out on the mustard-colored vinyl sofa. Other dome themes—Big Dipper, Milky Way, Andromeda—feature less glitz and more Earth tones.

***TOP:* Bryce Canyon National Park in Utah.**
***MIDDLE:* The domes at Clear Sky Resort Bryce Canyon.**
***BOTTOM:* Nova bar at Clear Sky Resort Bryce Canyon.**

Back near reception, at the Space Age Bar, you can sip on a tequila sunrise while taking in the desert sunset. Opt for one of the futuristic tables set on Astroturf—no point in wasting water on grass—and listen to the folk singer who lives just down Highway 12. The Rings of Saturn vegan eggplant lasagna and Stargazer Burger of wild boar, Wagyu beef, elk, and bison hit the spot. Most folks have just enough room left for a s'more.

Planning a Trip

Clear Sky Resort Bryce Canyon sits about 20 minutes east of Bryce National Park. Unlike its sister, Clear Sky at Grand Canyon, Clear Sky Resort Bryce Canyon is open year-round. Domes are climate-controlled. Hikes, horse rides, and star-gazing with a high-power scope are offered.

Dome at Clear Sky Resort Bryce Canyon.

TOP LEFT: *Sitting area in Klarhet bubble tent.*
TOP RIGHT: *Klarhet bubble tent.*
BOTTOM LEFT: *An aerial view of Klarhet.*
BOTTOM RIGHT: *Klarhet bubble tent at night.*

Stretch Your Muscles, Clear Your Mind

GREAT FOR	COST	WEBSITE
COUPLES, SMALL FAMILIES	$$$	LIVEKLARHET.COM

When Klarhet founders Nicole, a nurse, and Kirk Leand, a Web developer, moved from Minneapolis to the village of Lutsen in 2020, they were looking for a new start. The stillbirth of one of their twins had left them devastated. "The only place we felt solid and safe was here," Nicole said, in these hills north of Lake Superior. They named their resort for the solace they found here; in Swedish and Norwegian, **Klarhet** means "clarity."

They had renovated an in-town apartment as an Airbnb rental and had a taste for hosting. They also developed a keen interest in food purity and became all too aware, thanks to COVID, how vulnerable far-flung communities like Lutsen could be in a crisis.

Inspired by a project they'd seen online, they ordered four 20-foot-high domes with little idea of what to do with them. Friends helped. They built four concrete slabs with floor heat powered by solar batteries and compost, set facing south so light would boost the power. Interiors were designed for ultimate functionality, with big bathrooms and kitchenettes, but minimal distraction from the nature outside.

The four domes sit in their own little patch of birch, spruce, and poplar. Nearby, the food forest begins. Herbs, vegetables, and mushrooms grow in layers on a mounded path winding through the 25 acres, amid birds and pear, apple, and cherry trees whose bounty is used at Goldie's, their farm-to-table eatery. One of the 40-odd goats occasionally slips through its enclosure and grabs a snack. The chickens do a slightly better job of staying near their roost. A farm tour and goat cuddle are part of the experience.

Minnesota's grand outdoors are even more famous. Explorers can kayak on Lake Superior, take the gondola ride to the top of Moose Mountain, and hike to the 120-foot High Falls of the Pigeon River, the state's tallest. Nearby, the Grand Portage marina serves as the launch point for the ferry to Isle Royale, one of the nation's least-visited national parks. A visit takes a full summer day, minimum.

Whether they head to the lake or simply curl up by their dome fire, most guests come here for one reason: They want to sweep out the cobwebs. Even on misty days, they may find what they're seeking: clarity.

Planning a Trip

Lutsen sits just north of Lake Superior, a 90-minute drive from Duluth or a 4-hour drive from Minneapolis, Minnesota. Two-night minimum required.

NORTHERN IRELAND

Cocooned in an Irish Wood

GREAT FOR	COST	WEBSITE
COUPLES, ADULT FRIENDS, FAMILIES WITH CHILDREN OVER 16	$$	FINNLOUGH.COM

Candles flicker as we float—seemingly weightless, despite the ginger ice cream at lunch—on our backs in the warm salt pool. The lights brighten to let you know it's time to wrap up in your thick terry robe and step along the forest path to the next station along Finn Lough's spa trail. The warm pine sauna is scented with rosemary and birch, a fragrant reminder of the trees edging the lake just outside the window. For the bold, there's the chance to plunge into the lake; for the cold-averse, a hot tub and fireplace by a tree-view window are just down the path.

Ireland was once a land of the forest. Today, woodlands are rare. **Finn Lough** has long inhabited this thicket just 30 minutes from the seaside town of Donegal. A drive through meadows thick with sheep brings you to the shore of Lough Erne. Here, in 1980, Bobby and Rosie Beare started this resort as a family-friendly space along the water's edge. In 2013, siblings Michael and Gillian Beare took it over with a new vision: an adult escape surrounded by nature that could restore the serenity so often missing from harried lives. The name conveys the concept; in Irish, *Finn Lough* means "calm lake."

A bike ride or stroll through the 50 acres and down a wooded trail takes you to Finn Lough's most striking feature: 15 adults-only bubble domes set within an ancient copse. Guests enter their private garden and step inside a pair of conjoined bubbles, one for the four-poster bed and another for the curved bathtub. Inside the cocoon, you're surrounded by oak, silver birch, hazel, ash, rowan, and alder adorned with the bearded lichen and moss that grow only in the purest air. As the day wanes, you may want to settle in for a soak—a glass of bubbly in hand, of course—and watch as a doe slips by. When night thickens, you can search for stars—if the Irish weather cooperates. Come morning, your bedmate creeps to the door, fetching the hamper for breakfast in bed.

Planning a Trip

Finn Lough is a 30-minute drive from the airport at Donegal and a 3-hour drive from Dublin. Bubble lodgings are available in a single bubble with bedroom and en suite bath or a premium bubble featuring two domes. New are river cabins edging a stream with an indoor sunken tub. Lodgings are also available in Sky Suites above the House Bar and in a couple of the original cabins. Finn Lough is closed Tuesdays and Wednesdays.

Dining is available at the House Bar, where a film is shown nightly, and at the farm-to-table Lasair restaurant. The town of Belleek, home to the namesake pottery and glassware, sits a few miles away. The visitor center and museum are open Monday through Saturday.

Weather is surprisingly consistent year-round, with highs ranging from about 50°F to 65°F.

TOP LEFT: *Bubble tent at Finn Lough.*
TOP RIGHT: *Bathtub in the Premium Bubble at Finn Lough.*
BOTTOM: *Forest Bubble at Finn Lough.*

Aerial view of Sun City Camp.

A Lunar Night in the Ancient Desert of Wadi Rum

GREAT FOR	COST	WEBSITE
COUPLES, FAMILIES	$$	SUNCITYCAMP.COM

You climb into the rear of an open desert pickup and roar into the desert valley stretching between rocky cliffs that serve as Mother Nature's fortifications. The drive to camp takes nearly 45 minutes through the ancient ocean bed of Wadi Rum. There's a reason the otherworldly setting reminds visitors of *Lawrence of Arabia* and *The Martian:* Both were filmed here.

A stop at a slim gorge allows time to view petroglyphs of camels, ibex, humans, and symbols. People have lived here for thousands and thousands of years, documenting nomadic and agrarian life that has stretched across millennia.

Then, it's back in the truck for the ride to your home for the night: **Sun City Camp's** village of geodesic domes and bedouin tents in the crook of a sandstone tower. Domes feature wide desert views, with draperies for privacy when you want it. The bathroom—complete with shower and plush robes—is tucked out of public view. It feels like you're on the moon.

But there's no time to relax now: Your desert driver is beckoning you back to the truck.

You fly along the reddening sand, chasing the dwindling light. Your driver delivers you to the foot of a ledge, and you scramble up for the day's last clear views. The long dusky plain sprawls out before you, rimmed in sandstone cliffs. The glowing sun slips behind a crag and then into twilight. It's a moment for silence.

Back at camp, you head to a giant dining dome set with tables and (your back thanks you) proper chairs. From the generous buffet, you fill your plate with hummus and tabouli, fresh tomatoes, chicken and lamb cooked for hours underground, rice, and olives and pickled peppers. Across this arid land, water is the beverage of choice.

The night is as clear and dark as you've ever seen, and you're tempted to grab your telescope to bring the heavens closer. Instead, you snuggle beneath the covers and search for the Great Bear. Before you know it, you're asleep, leaving the Twins and the Hunter on their own.

Planning a Trip

The Wadi Rum visitor center is about an hour's drive from the airport in Aqaba and a 90-minute drive from Petra. Temperatures are mildest in the spring and fall. Stargazing is best in the long, cold winter months and during the Perseid meteor shower in August, but there's plenty to see year-round.

Rooms at Sun City include bubbles and bedouin tents; rates include breakfast and dinner. Camel rides, desert tours, and hot-air balloon rides are separate fees.

ARGENTINA

At the Glacier's Edge

GREAT FOR	COST	WEBSITE
COUPLES, FAMILIES	$$$$	CALAFATE.PRISTINECAMPS.COM

Decades ago, the Patagonian hills around El Calafate were vast sheep farms that operated as self-contained villages. The early 20th century did away with the baronial states, and outposts like El Calafate sprang up.

If not for its unique location, this place would still be a crossroads. But the lakefront town of El Calafate—named for the omnipresent bushes that, come summer, burst with sweet berries—affords the closest access to the mountain-climbing mecca of El Chalten. This is also a jumping-off point for the Perito Moreno Glacier. Covering almost 100 square miles, Perito Moreno is one of the planet's largest freshwater reserves.

Most visitors stay in town, an hour from the glacier's edge. The geodesic domes at **Pristine El Calafate Luxury Camp** on Lake Argentina offer a far better vantage point. As early rays summit the snowy Andes and dance on the glacier below, guests here witness it all—from their king beds.

Patagonia's dramatic landscapes, literally outside the windows, draw guests outside. Will they go on e-bikes, ride horses, or walk? Horseback riding usually wins out; this is gaucho country, after all, with 3,000 rolling acres of grassland and forest. The wind blows your hat back onto your shoulders, and you imagine you're driving cattle across the pampas—though the coziness of the eucalyptus-lined dome beats a basic herding shack.

The afternoon is reserved for the main attraction: a visit to the glacier by 4×4 and boat. The face sits only 1,000 feet from a series of wooden walkways, allowing intimate views. The icy blue spikes form a bulwark reaching 200 feet above the water and another 365 feet below. Ten miles of cracked shards reach to the peaks behind; another 10 miles of ice lie beyond what you can see. The face jags left, runs another 1,000 feet or so, and then jags right. The center is higher by 60 feet or so, a mass of wicked spears and splinters. Sturdy private boats for 10 take visitors along 1,200 feet of waterfalls, a fraction of what's here. Pop, crack, crash, splash: You feel Earth at work.

Back at camp, visitors can float in private hot tubs and take another look at the glacier that brought you here, as the Milky Way emerges from the silky darkness.

Planning a Trip

The El Calafate airport sits about 90 minutes from the camp along a bumpy dirt road; transportation is included. Low temperatures from June to August hover around freezing. From November to March, temperatures range from lows of 45°F to around 65°F. Rain is minimal year-round.

Pristine El Calafate Luxury Camp's six domes are set on individual wooden decks and set apart for privacy. Each includes an en suite bathroom, indoor and outdoor sitting area, and heat. It is 100% solar-powered. Meals served in the central dining area feature local ingredients, often including lamb. Glacier visits are included in the rates.

Interior of a dome at Pristine El Calafate Luxury Camp.

ALBERTA, CANADA

In the Land of the Métis

GREAT FOR	COST	WEBSITE
COUPLES, FAMILIES	$$	METISCROSSING.COM

North Saskatchewan River runs from Canada's Columbia Icefield some 800 miles to the east before it melds with the waterway's southern arm and then flows on to the Hudson Bay. In the 1700s, when European fur trappers came here for beaver, rabbit, and mink, the river was both wayfinder and highway. But the most important guides were the Indigenous people who lived here.

The traders and local people married. Over time, their descendants developed a distinctive culture known as the Métis.

You get a bit of this history when you check in at **Métis Crossing,** a thoughtfully rustic riverside resort designed to share Métis culture with the rest of the world. In addition to the 40-room wood lodge, opened in 2021, eight sky-gazing domes debuted here in 2023. These cozy heated igloos have a kitchenette, bathroom, and giant window open to the sky.

While the sun still shines, you want to visit the historic homesteads of the farmers who lived on these 500-plus acres, watch traditional dances, and check out the traditional two-wheeled river carts used to haul farm goods a century ago. After that, most head off on a wildlife tour to see the Percheron horses, elk, and rare white bison.

Come dusk, you'll sit around a campfire with a Métis storyteller and learn how the sky serves as a map, calendar, and portal to the spirit world. As the sky darkens, guests settle beneath the handmade patchwork quilt covering their dome beds.

They're awakened by rays dancing overhead—electrically charged particles sneezed by the sun that have collided with atoms and molecules in Earth's atmosphere, creating the Northern Lights. Lines of magnetic force cause them to wave and shimmer, washing the land in green and turquoise and pink. Too soon, the light show settles, revealing the indigo blanket overhead that, as visitors have learned, is lit through pinpricks pierced by a hummingbird in ancient times. This is how the stars came to be, say the Métis, and who are you to argue?

Planning a Trip

Métis Crossing is open year-round, offering season-specific activities and multiday workshops on traditional crafts, such as making moccasins and the colorful blanket-coats known as capotes. In winter, temperatures can drop to –20°F. The best time to see the Northern Lights is September to April.

The closest airport is Edmonton, Alberta, about 90 minutes to the west.

TOP LEFT & RIGHT: Indigenous people share traditional customs at Métis Crossing. MIDDLE: Northern Lights over Métis Crossing. BOTTOM: Reindeer at Métis Crossing.

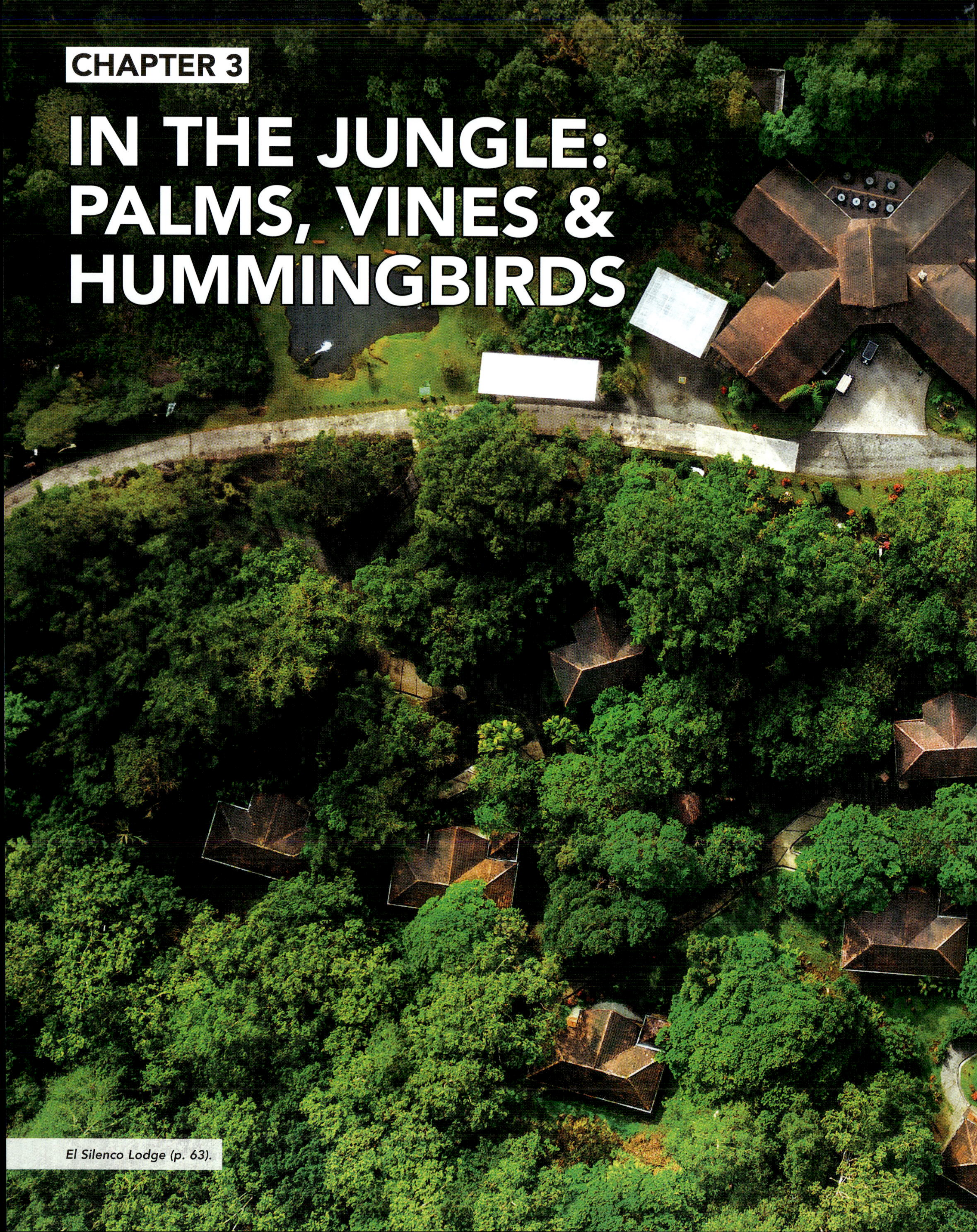

CHAPTER 3

IN THE JUNGLE: PALMS, VINES & HUMMINGBIRDS

El Silenco Lodge (p. 63).

> *The jungle speaks to me because I know how to listen.*
> *— Rudyard Kipling*
>
> *The jungle is dark but full of diamonds.*
> *— Arthur Miller*
>
> *Magic is the science of the jungle.*
> *— Carl Jung*

CAMBODIA

Just Get Wild

GREAT FOR	COST	WEBSITE
COUPLES, FAMILIES WITH OLDER CHILDREN	$$$$$	SHINTAMANI.COM

Up 110 feet—that's 98 steps—to the top of the tower. Strap in, snap the helmet—and I'm flying on a zip line 75 feet above the mahogany trees, bamboo, and palms to the lower tower, then across the river to the Landing Zone Bar.

It's a fitting welcome to **Shinta Mani Wild,** 850 untamed acres along a river at the southern edge of Cambodia's vast Cardamon National Park. I could have gone for automotive transportation to the headquarters tent, but really, why not get right into the spirit of this place?

I am now "Bong," the salutation for an honored person. My adventure butler—escort, guide, interpreter, wardrobe advisor, motorbike driver, spa booker, laundry organizer—arranges the schedule. But first, I walk along the stone-covered path, across the wooden bridge, and through the trees to the expansive tent set on a wooden deck by the river that is my Shinta Mani home.

Outdoors, beneath the fans, I find a sloped bathtub, spacious sitting area decked with joyful prints, and a dining table. Inside, in air-conditioning, are sinks, shower, platform bed, and library/sitting area, all with a vintage flair that hints at Cambodia's colonial past. Coffee and spirits sit at the ready; a cold box is stocked with ice and fresh garnishes.

Back at headquarters, dinner is served on the wide deck overlooking the waterfall. Butterflies—black, speckled, yellow, cream with orange-tipped wings—flit beneath the tree canopy. The ambitious eight-course chef's dinner is delicate and complex. A cheese puff with garlic aioli and salted egg yolk is followed by a poached prawn in coconut broth, soup with raw and pickled beetroot, burnt orange sorbet, local fish garnished with wildflowers, duck breast with cauliflower and apple foam, and chocolate mousse with raspberry sorbet. How will I ever eat breakfast?

In the morning, I hop on the back of my butler's motorbike and head out on patrol with the Wildlife Alliance. Each day, a motorbike squad of a half dozen members—alliance rangers, environmental police, and rifle-bearing military escorts—heads into the protected park lands in search of poachers and illegal loggers. The alliance zooms off-road on muddy paths, past a herd of water buffalo, beyond coconut palm farms and mango orchards, over a crumbling wooden bridge, and into a mountain forest. Previous forays have rescued trapped sun bears used in traditional Chinese medicine, civet cats whose excrement is valued by Vietnamese coffee growers, and wild boars. This day, we follow the tractor track left by illegal loggers, who have escaped before we arrive.

Shinta Mani Wild Tents.

Bathroom, Shinta Mani Wild.

Conservation is the soul of Shinta Mani Wild. Hotelier Bill Bensley and a Cambodian business partner bought the 850-acre tract of jungle to save it from mining and development interests. What Bensley most wants his guests to understand is that the rainforest is worth protecting. "That rainforest creates all of the rain for the rice bowl of Laos, Cambodia, Vietnam, and Thailand," he says. "If we cut it down, we're going to have a lot of hungry people."

Planning a Trip

Shinta Mani Wild is a 3-hour drive from the international airport at Phnom Penh. Transfers, activities, and meals are included. It is open year-round, though the best time to visit is the dry season of November to April.

Wild is part of the Shinta Mani Collection, with hotels near Angkor Wat and in Mustang, Nepal. A trio of camps in the Republic of Congo is underway.

FACING PAGE, TOP LEFT: *Guestroom, Shinta Mani Wild tent.*
TOP RIGHT: *Dining table, Shinta Mani Wild tent.*
BOTTOM: *Terrace of guestroom, Shinta Mani Wild tent.*

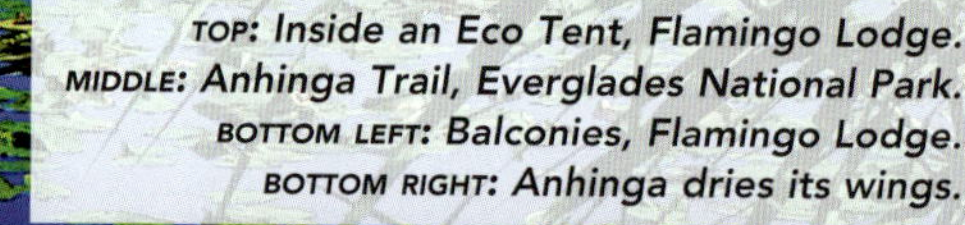

TOP: Inside an Eco Tent, Flamingo Lodge.
MIDDLE: Anhinga Trail, Everglades National Park.
BOTTOM LEFT: Balconies, Flamingo Lodge.
BOTTOM RIGHT: Anhinga dries its wings.

FLORIDA, USA

In the River of Grass

GREAT FOR	COST	WEBSITE
FAMILIES, COUPLES, FRIENDS	$$	FLAMINGOEVERGLADES.COM

The odd pine pokes through the broad sawgrass prairie like an unruly cowlick. A few miles down the two-lane road, pines and palms clump into what passes for a Florida Everglades forest—islands in the slough.

Why all the fuss? you wonder as you gaze across the brownish prairie that never seems to end. And then, the place begins to take shape. Cypress and pines cluster along the edge of the tarmac. A snowy egret flashes across the sky. Mangroves thicken and then part to reveal a hidden pond.

In truth, the Florida Everglades is a bit shy, its subtle beauty veiled by a tawny veneer and armored by sharp-edged grasses, snakes, mosquitos, and muck. What matters most here is not what you see but how this unique wetlands works as a slow-moving sheet of water to support wildlife, habitats, and drinking water. The national park protects 1.5 million acres of this "River of Grass," as author Marjory Stoneman Douglas dubbed it in 1947. Restoration projects long in the works aim to restore much of its original 3 million acres.

To really appreciate this strange and unique ecosystem, you need to get in a kayak, stroll through a hardwood hammock, and stare at the stars scattered like sequins across the velvet sky over Florida Bay. You need to drive 38 miles into the heart of the Everglades and stay a night or two.

Until recently, that hasn't been so easy. After hurricanes decimated the former Flamingo Lodge in 2005, overnighting in Flamingo meant camping or piloting a rented houseboat. In 2019, the park added 20 glamping tents set above the grass on wooden platforms with electricity and comfortable mattresses—but with toilets down the planked path.

As of 2024, visitors can stay in a new **Flamingo Lodge** featuring 24 air-conditioned suites overlooking Florida Bay, with a restaurant next door. Each is appointed with a sitting room with pull-out couch, small kitchen, separate bedroom, and a generously sized bathroom with tub. The lodge and restaurant are built on concrete stilts to mitigate encroaching sea rise.

From the snug balcony, you can watch the sun cast its orangey glow across the bay. A boat ride brings sightings of tri-colored heron and a spoonbill, species nearly lost to the 1880s' fashion craze for plumage.

The wisdom of the late Marjory Stoneman Douglas, penned in 1947, comes to mind: "There are no other Everglades in the world. They are, they have always been, one of the unique regions of the earth; remote, never wholly known. Nothing anywhere else is like them."

Planning a Trip

The 1.5 million square miles of Everglades stretch across lower Florida from Homestead, south of Miami, west to Everglades City. Winter is the best time to go, when temps are mildest and mosquitos largely absent.

ARGENTINA

The Power of Iguazu

GREAT FOR	COST	WEBSITE
COUPLES, FAMILIES WITH OLDER CHILDREN	$$$$	AWASI.COM

If you want to measure your own small presence against the magnitude of nature, Iguazu Falls is the place to come. With 175 cascades and flows averaging more than 400,000 gallons per second, this torrent dwarfs other world-class waterfalls. "My poor Niagara," lamented Eleanor Roosevelt when she visited here in the 1940s. The "thundering smoke" of Africa's Victoria Falls is higher, but it can't compare with Iguazu's breadth or intensity.

Like those two other waterfalls, Iguazu straddles an international border. To fully appreciate its power, you need to see it from above and below, and from both countries. From Argentina, the view is intimate, overlooking opaque streams and picturesque pools surrounded by bromeliads and palms. Brazil provides the more impressive view, as cascade after deluge after avalanche stretch across a horseshoe-shaped precipice more than 2½ miles wide. The roar is thunderous, and the refreshing spray welcome on a humid day.

What isn't welcome are the crowds. Iguazu draws more than 1.5 million tourists per year who jam onto buses, walkways, and the train to the Argentine boardwalk. Most visitors ignore the surrounding rainforest and its human history.

Guests at Awasi's **Iguazu Lodge** have a jump on the throngs, thanks to a special arrangement with the site and private guides allowing them to see the falls early. By the time crowds thicken, guests are back at one of Awasi's 14 air-conditioned wooden villas on stilts set amid kapok trees and passionfruit vines, each with a private pool.

The rest of the day is open for visiting the ruins of 17th-century Jesuit citadels where priests sought to convert the Indigenous Guarani people, kayaking, or going to a local village in the company of a Guarani elder.

Or perhaps you just want sit on your deck and watch the wildlife. A monkey is unlikely this close to the main lodge, but maybe you'll see a toucan.

Planning a Trip

Iguazu Falls can be reached via nearby airports on the Brazilian and Argentine sides. If all you want to do is see the falls, staying at a hotel inside the national park on either side is most convenient. In any case, be prepared for steps.

Awasi Iguazu is located in Argentina. Private transportation from the local airport in either country is included, along with all meals, drinks, and excursions. A minimum 3-night stay is required.

Awasi lodges at Chile's Atacama Desert and Torres del Paine National Park are also highly rated.

TOP LEFT: Iguazu Falls, Argentinian side. TOP RIGHT: Road to Awasi Iguazu. MIDDLE: Kayaking at Awasi Iguazu. BOTTOM: Restaurant, Asasi Iguazu.

ECUADOR

Cosmos in the Clouds

GREAT FOR	COST	WEBSITE
FAMILIES, COUPLES	$$$$	MASHPILODGE.COM

The open-air gondola slips across the canopy cable, a constant babble of waterfalls chattering from the forest floor below. From *The Dragonfly*, you can peer down on the magnolia, balsa, and palm trees vying for sunlight, their trunks wrapped in vines and dripping with crimson blooms. Hikers climb down the tower halfway across the 1¼-mile route for a trek to one of the waterfalls. Less ambitious souls take in the view from the gondola as they slide slowly into the mists that give the cloud forest its name.

Three hours north of Quito, **Mashpi Lodge** is a stylish outpost that combines comfort, research, and access to the 2,500-acre Mashpi Reserve. What started as a conservation effort to protect former logging lands has become a celebrated adventure lodge with attentive service, gourmet menus—fresh pastries, crisp salads, tender grilled octopus, and braised beef rib—and expert-led explorations into the rainforest.

Visits start with a gentle 20-minute hike to the Life Center. There, a wide veranda offers views of the gardened hillside, where weasel-like tayra and agouti creep cautiously from the forest to snag a bite of banana laid out by a guide. Inside, scientists cultivate caterpillars that, with time, metamorphose into the giant owl-eyed butterflies that flit through the center's net-covered pavilion.

Mornings, afternoons, and evenings offer a choice of hikes, canopy tours, bird-watching, and nature walks. There's something for everyone: fit honeymooners, retiree couples, families with curious children and grandparents in tow. A stroll around the lodge grounds reveals an endangered giant snail nestled into a bed of walking iris and a millipede that, you learn, moves far more slowly than the centipede with half the number of legs. On a night walk in a stream, a sharp-eyed guide spots frogs smaller than your fingertip with voices the size of an opera star's.

A 15-minute ride up a bumpy dirt road brings you to the Hummingbird Garden, thick with bananas, heliconia, flowering ginger, and palms. Hummingbird feeders filled with sugary water draw plump long-beaked birds with shiny purple bodies and tiny green hummingbirds that soar swiftly past with an audible whir. A long-tailed male with an iridescent blue head hovers above a feeder. Five flitting birds perch on a man's hand, dipping their beaks in turn into a single sugar-water dispenser. Their incessant need for calories to sustain constant motion leaves them with little time for rest.

TOP: *Mashpi Lodge.*
BOTTOM LEFT: *Slender opossum mouse near Mashpi Lodge.*
BOTTOM RIGHT: *Sky Bike at Mashpi Lodge.*

Thankfully, you've got plenty of time to lounge. From the outdoor deck cantilevered over the mountainside and the two-story windows inside the air-conditioned lodge, you take in the view. Spare, deft architecture erases the barriers between indoors and out. You become part of the jungle, of the loamy earth and surging vines and 400 species in this complex cosmos. You've always been part of it, you realize; it took coming here to reconnect.

Torrenteer frog at Mashpi Lodge.

Planning a Trip

Mashpi Lodge sits about 60 miles northwest of Quito. Don't be fooled by the short distance; the drive takes about 3 hours. You can arrive on your own or opt for a package that includes transportation, lodging, and dining at Casa Gangotena Boutique Hotel in the heart of Quito's historic district. Lodge stays include guided activities and gourmet meals. The hotels are owned by Metropolitan Touring, one of Ecuador's oldest and best-known tourism companies.

FACING PAGE, TOP: Wayra guestroom at Mashpi Lodge.
BOTTOM LEFT: Yaku Suite bathroom.
BOTTOM RIGHT: A tayra on the grounds of Mashpi Lodge.

TOP: Aerial view, El Silencio Lodge and Spa.
MIDDLE: Bar at El Silencio Lodge.
BOTTOM: Rock climbing at El Silencio Lodge.

Sounds of Silence

GREAT FOR	COST	WEBSITE
ACTIVE COUPLES, FAMILIES	$$$	ELSILENCIOLODGE.COM

Twenty years ago, most of these 500 acres were farmland. Today, visitors sit in a manicured garden edging a stream in a subtropical cloud forest dripping with bromeliads. The transformation is a testament to nature's resilience, with the bonus of farm-flattened paths where even a stiff-kneed urbanite can wander easily and soak in the birdsong.

The 90-minute drive from San José's international airport to **El Silencio** is a bit more rugged than my husband and I expect, with winding potholed roads that rise to more than a mile above sea level before plunging down a seemingly endless series of switchback curves.

But by the time we settle onto the lodge deck with a Tico julep, the journey is erased from memory. The babble of water on rocks lulls me into tranquility, and it's all I can do to make it to my wood-trimmed villa. Tomorrow will be soon enough for archery and horse riding.

For now, dinner wins out. The menu presents difficult decisions: grilled octopus to start, followed by suckling pig with grilled peach? Or home-made gnocchi in sauce crafted from the squash from the garden just up the hill? An Argentinian pinot noir will pair nicely with either. Sated, we head back to our villa. The private hot tub on the deck is shielded from view by a bamboo screen beneath a canopy that's straight out of a magazine spread.

Come morning, a clay-colored thrush belts out a song loud enough to rival a rooster. Jose, the resident naturalist who leads the early-morning bird walk, explains that the thrush has to compensate for its plain plumage with a beautiful voice. Attracting a mate isn't easy, even for the national bird.

Other avian residents are showier. Hummingbirds flit in a hibiscus; near the horse stables is a euphonia, a bird with a jaunty blue cap. Novice bird-watchers find the birds easier to hear than to see; it takes Jose's trained eye to spot the plump red-breasted trogon high in a tree.

The big prize is the quetzal, a regal bird with a crimson breast, sweeping tail, and green-and-blue wings. Chances of seeing it near the lodge are nil, but the nearby trio of waterfalls offers better odds. You hike along a stream, up a hill, down to the rocks, and up to a viewing platform. From here, you see the triple cascade of Promise waterfall. I wonder what vows have been uttered here. No sight today of a quetzal, but it was worth the walk all the same.

Planning a Trip

The best time to visit Costa Rica is the dry months of December to April. You'll want a sweater for evenings at El Silencio.

The nearby village of Bajos del Toro offers several casual restaurants. The area is home to many of Costa Rica's best waterfalls, including Catarata del Toro. Area activities include hikes, tubing and rafting, and a child-friendly dino park. Arenal Volcano is a 2-hour drive over uneven roads.

COSTA RICA

Arenal on the Horizon

GREAT FOR	COST	WEBSITE
COUPLES, FAMILIES, MULTIGEN GROUPS	$$$–$$$$	NAYARARESORTS.COM

I'm resting my head against the edge of my private thermal pool, curtained from the world by 8-foot heliconia. Stirred by the early morning light, the birds are beginning to trill and whistle. A hummingbird zips past, in search of the first of his 2,000 daily sips of nectar. In the high canopy above, I spot a pair of toucans perching close together, one angular yellow beak preening the black feathers of the other.

When they fly away, I'm faced with a decision. Should I walk up the hill for an iced latte and bagel topped with smoked trout, enjoyed beneath the smoldering face of Arenal Volcano? Or stroll down the terraced garden path in search of red-back tanagers, caracals, and sloths? Or simply slip back beneath the gauzy canopy of the four-poster bed of Costa Rica's **Nayara Tented Camp?**

For decades, Costa Rica has been a top stop for nature and adventure enthusiasts. Rope bridges and zip lines lead through orchid-filled tree canopies that are home to butterflies and dozens of hummingbird species. The constant moisture of a mile-high cloud forest nurtures vines and towering tree ferns, capuchin monkeys, and green parrots. Whitewater rafting, ATV tours, horse riding, bungee jumping, and even waterfall rappelling are widely offered.

Not everyone wants to work that hard for their jungle fix. And even those who do may also want a frothy organic pisco sour and a volcanic mud scrub on the side—which they can get at Nayara, home to three sister resorts.

The tented camp evokes an African safari mixed with a touch of Bali. A hammock is stretched across the deck; the outdoor shower is cloaked by bamboo. The peaked tent top of our private villa is stretched between staunch metal poles. The walls are canvas, though they cover a hard, sturdy frame to ensure that this tent isn't going anywhere. A desk, cushioned settee, and window seat sit above a polished wood floor. A wide vanity with double sinks, capacious double wardrobe, closed toilet closet, and indoor shower surround the curved tub that anchors the airy bath.

It wasn't always so lush. A half dozen years ago, the jungle that surrounds Nayara was open farmland. Owner Leo Ghitis created a village for workers where they could purchase their homes at favorable prices. He reforested the 4,500 acres with thousands of trees—palms, papaya, sloth-friendly cecropia—and dressed the hillside with ornamental gingers, birds of paradise, and a profusion of orchids. Nature did the rest, filling tree limbs with basketlike bromeliads and sun-searching vines.

Sloth at Nayara Tented Camp.

Today, the rainforest eases along the mountainside. The spectacular views of Arenal Volcano from the pool deck disappear as I walk downward along terraced pools, cascades and barefoot bars, and a hanging bridge to dinner. If we overdo it, an electric cart will return us to our tent.

Planning a Trip

The dry season runs December to April; other months bring more rain, but smaller crowds. Roads around the country have been improved, but once you veer from the main highways, you still find rough, rutted roads. Nayara's three resorts are located in the Arenal area 3 to 4 hours northwest of the airport in San Jose. Allow more driving time than you might expect.

TOP LEFT: La Terrza Restaurant at Nayara Tented Camp.
MIDDLE LEFT: Sukha Spa, Nayara Tented Camp.
BOTTOM LEFT: Casa Paloma, Nayara Tented Camp.
TOP RIGHT: Bedroom, Nayara Tented Camp.
BOTTOM RIGHT: Las Lapas pool bar, Nayara Tented Camp.

BRAZIL

The Amazon, Sans Mosquitos

GREAT FOR	COST	WEBSITE
COUPLES, FAMILIES	$$$$	ANAVILHANASLODGE.COM

You're idling on your paddleboard, just gazing across the black stream, when a pink dolphin swims close to check you out. You get a good look at the long toothy snout it uses for fishing. These giants are playful, you've been told, and you can only hope this 7-foot-long guy doesn't decide to take off with your paddle. Apparently, it happens from time to time.

The freshwater dolphins are the marine stars here on the Rio Negro. Guests watch them from the floating bar as they sip an icy Brahma beer on an 85°F day. When they putter up a stream edging the thick rainforest for bird-watching, a pair of dolphins leaps and twists just off the bow.

Back at **Anavilhanas Jungle Lodge,** you settle into the hammock in your air-conditioned cottage in the rainforest. Such comfort didn't exist when owner Guto Costa Filho came here just out of college. In those years, getting deep into the Amazon basin was an expedition involving weeks of hard travel on local boats. As he grew older, the software engineer and his wife, Fabi, a banker, grew increasingly concerned about deforestation and decided to do something about it. They gave up their jobs and embarked on a quest to help people better understand the Amazon without having to rough it.

In 2007, they opened Anavilhanas Jungle Lodge on the Rio Negro, a 3-hour drive north of busy Manaus, where travelers can immerse themselves in the wonder of the world's largest rainforest. Here, visitors can look for spider monkeys and such birds as the orange Guinan cock-of-the-rock, paddle through streams dyed black by tannins, and fish for the giant Tambaqui. They don't have to worry about mosquitos; the pests can't breed in the acidic black river.

The Amazon rainforest absorbs about 25% of the planet's carbon dioxide, but land clearing for large-scale cattle and soybean farming is causing absorption rates to drop dramatically. Clearing also diminishes habitats for endangered species, including jaguars, giant otters, harpy eagles, and those playful river dolphins. Indigenous people, too, are threatened.

Reading about the consequences doesn't compare with personal experience. As Filho understands so well, being here is a privilege.

Planning a Trip

Brazil is home to about 60% of the Amazon rainforest. The rest spills into Peru, Colombia, and other nearby countries. Temperatures are mildest from December to June.

Anavilhanas Jungle Lodge offers pick up from Manaus by car or float plane. Rates include activities and dining. Twenty-four spacious bungalows sit on 740 acres just outside Anavilhanas National Park. The lodge minimizes impact with its own photovoltaic plant, composting and growing much of its food. Architecture is designed to mesh with the forest. Staff come from local villages, where the lodge supports schools, libraries, and education.

TOP LEFT: Floating bar at Anavilhanas Jungle Lodge.
TOP RIGHT: Aerial view to Negro River.
MIDDLE: Bungalow, Anavilhanas Jungle Lodge.
BOTTOM: Villa Bacurau, Anavilhanas Jungle Lodge.

Hummingbird Haven

GREAT FOR	COST	WEBSITE
COUPLES, SMALL FAMILIES	$$	TABLEROCKBELIZE.COM

The trills and whistles in the mahogany and palm trees create a concerto. But it's a whisper compared with Montezuma's oropendola, a yellow-tailed bird that lives in basketlike nests hanging from ceiba trees. Oscar, the bartender at **Table Rock Jungle Lodge,** pulls out his cellphone to show a video of a male dipping his body so far off the branch, you're convinced he'll fall. The bird rights himself, belting out a mournful squawk that feels almost prehistoric.

In this jungle lodge with only 10 rooms, Oscar and fellow workers have time to visit with each guest. When I say I'm going to walk on the farm leading to the lodge gate, he gets a bag of food scraps from the kitchen. "The donkeys will expect you to come with a treat," he says, handing me enough for a visit to the bunnies too. No, he assures me, the rabbits don't end up on the menu; local children take them home as pets.

With 105 acres, Table Rock is as much farm as jungle lodge. Stately royal palms line the rock lane past the vegetable garden, through the orange grove, around the donkey enclosure and rabbit hutch and chicken coop, past the solar panels that provide all electricity here, and around to a small parking lot. Abraham minds the beans, tomatoes, peppers, and corn that will be part of dinner. A woodshop births all the furniture here.

A concrete walkway provides easy access through the groomed garden of red sisters, iris, and striped broadleaves. Blooming orchids cling to trunks. Poisonwood trees are marked with red ribbons so guests know to stay clear. At a thatched house, you find the concierge, and then a deck that serves as the gathering spot, restaurant, and bar. Beyond lies the path to the infinity pool cantilevered over the forest and the path leading to the slow-moving Macal River below.

The water moves slowly enough for kayaking. That seems like too much work, and instead I grab a life vest and a tube and plop into the muddy river. It's a leisurely float, leaving plenty of time to take in the afternoon light shimmering across the jungled shore and try to catch sight of the singing birds.

My cabana is readied, with pink hibiscus blossoms sprinkled across the canopied bed. Rainfall tinkles on the roof, playing a song that seems muted at home. Here, it awakens birds and calls guests to cocktail hour. I'm on my way.

Planning a Trip

The best time to visit is during the dry season, December to May, when temperatures drop below 70°F. Table Rock is a 90-minute drive from the international airport in Belize City. Roads are smoothly paved; the hotel arranges transportation and excursions to nearby sites if you don't want to rent a car.

Cabanas are cooled by fans. Thirteen suites with air-conditioning are planned for 70 adjacent acres.

TOP LEFT: Both Table Rock and Blancaneaux (p. 73) are within easy reach of Xunantunich, an ancient Mayan temple. TOP RIGHT: Guestroom at Table Rock Jungle Lodge. BOTTOM: Pool at Table Rock Jungle Lodge.

Pretty as a Movie Set

GREAT FOR	COST	WEBSITE
COUPLES, FAMILIES	$$$	THEFAMILYCOPPOLAHIDEAWAYS.COM

The 2-hour drive from Belize City to Mountain Pine Ridge winds through a country far more varied than when the British governed Belize. Towns where every grocery has a Chinese name give way to dairy farms owned by Mennonites who came from Mexico in the 1950s. The occasional Hindu temple appears on a rise.

Wetlands become broadleaf jungles. Then, the road climbs sharply upward into the **Mountain Pine Ridge Forest Reserve.** Near the crest, at 1,500 feet, sits the country's best-known nature lodge: **Blancaneaux,** owned by film director Francis Ford Coppola.

These 78 acres are pretty enough for a movie set. Twenty villas with wrap-around decks and tall Maya-style thatched ceilings are set amid flower ginger, frangipani, palms, and pines. Stone walkways lead through the grass lawn. The Privassion River rolls through the narrow valley and over a waterfall.

But aside from the clever shell phone—the cabana-to-reception connection located in a giant conch shell on the desk—everything else here is as close to 100% natural as Coppola and his team can make it. Electricity is powered by a hydro turbine. Water collected by cisterns is used for landscaping and in the garden, where vegetables grow on wide terraces near the vegetarian restaurant.

Blancaneaux opened in 1993, just over a decade after Belize became independent. Eleanor Coppola, filmmaker and the late wife of Mr. Francis, as the staff calls him, decorated the free-standing cabanas with hand-made textiles from nearby Guatemala. The bok choy, lettuce, kale, and eggplant came later, along with the stables that are home to 22 horses.

Horse rides through the trees take guests to Big Rock Falls, where they can plunge into a natural pool, or into Noj Kaax Meen Elijio Panti National Park, home to elusive tapir, jaguars, and ocelots. The choice of ways to spend time seems endless: archeology tours to Maya ruins, easy forest walks, rugged bike rides, cooking classes, child-oriented bug hunts, and, of course, lazy afternoons by the pool.

The greatest adventure may well be a visit to the sacred cave known as ATM, short for Actun Tunichil Muknal. After a 40-minute trek through the jungle, you pull on your life vest, helmet, and headlamp and plunge into a glassy underground stream, then thread your way through water and crevices. Stalactites drip from the ceiling. Fish swim in the clear water around you. Pottery, skeletons (likely from human sacrifices), and artifacts pay witness to the ATM's 2,000-year-old past as a Maya ritual site. The rocks are slippery, some of the rock scrambles are challenging, and guests emerge dirty but wowed.

Pool cabana, Blancaneaux Lodge.

Back at the lodge, you're ready for Jaguar Juice made from local Craboo liqueur, aged rum, and fresh pineapple juice. A yellow-billed toucan flits into a tree just outside your window, and your day is complete.

Planning a Trip

The drive from Belize City's international airport takes about 2 hours along well-paved roads; Blancaneaux can arrange transportation. Resort cabanas range from a two-bedroom enclave with a private pool to comfortable, private studio villas with a wrap-around deck. New luxury cabanas feature private plunge pools. The hilly terrain may pose challenges for those with mobility issues.

Toucan at Blancaneaux Lodge.

FACING PAGE, TOP: Entrance to Blancaneaux Lodge.
MIDDLE: Francis Ford Coppola villa at Blancaneaux Lodge.
BOTTOM: Riverfront Cabana, Blancaneaux Lodge.

TOP: Canoeing on the Rio Grande.
MIDDLE LEFT: Aerial view of Copal Tree Lodge.
MIDDLE RIGHT: Rum Bar at Copal Tree Lodge.
BOTTOM: Snorkeling near Placencia.

From Tree Canopy to the Caribbean Sea

GREAT FOR	COST	WEBSITE
COUPLES, FAMILIES, ANGLERS	$$$	COPALTREELODGE.COM

A dozen fin-toting swimmers clamber onto the canopied motorboat for the 9-mile putter down Belize's saltwater Rio Grande. A roar sounds from the palms and Ficus lining the banks, bringing a flash of hope that you'll get a rare glimpse of jaguar. The bellow turns out to be the fierce call of a bare-throated tiger heron, a bluish wading bird standing more than 2 feet tall, with a stripe down its belly, but no paws or spots.

You laugh, chagrined, and then turn your attention back to the guide leading your "Snorkeling with the Chef" foray as you edge toward the Caribbean Sea. The next few hours will be spent exploring coral reefs and searching for the lobster that you hope to eat for lunch.

The 16,000 acres of **Copal Tree Lodge** stretch from treetops high above a hill to the river 365 steep steps below, a walk that will leave your thighs quivering. Thankfully, a pair of motorized trams—one to the river, a second up to the hilltop—provide relief.

When it first opened in 2018, Copal Tree catered to fly-fishers aiming for permit and tarpon. Over the years, owner Todd Robinson added sugarcane fields and a distillery that produces four Copalli rums and operations that transform lodge-grown beans into coffee and cocoa into chocolates. Guests can sign up for rum tastings, yoga sessions, farm tours, and bean-to-bar chocolate-crafting classes, where you witness the process from tree to irresistible rum-filled squares. Thirsty? Elmer at the bar explains how to whip up a frothy Ginger Buck from rum, lime, and ginger syrup.

Anglers still come here to try their luck. Each evening, guests gather around the bar, sipping mojitos and watermelon smashes and trading exaggerated tales of the fish that (of course) got away. They move to the second floor of the airy Caribbean-style lodge and out onto the wide deck for farm-grown lamb or jerk-spiced shrimp. Before the sun fades, you can see hilltops in the distance and the ocean beyond.

Overnight guests stay in spacious villas with air-conditioning, a giant steam shower, and a screened porch cocooned in the jungle without bugs.

A spiral concrete walkway from the lodge to hilltop Canopy Suites leads through angel-wing begonia, spicy wild peppers, and Ficus trees, where you might just spot a troop of black howler monkeys. Don't worry if you've had a rum drink or two; you can always opt for the tram instead.

Planning a Trip

Copal Tree Lodge provides transfers to nearby Punta Gorda, home to an airstrip serviced by Tropic Air's fleet of Cessna Caravans. The flight to the international airport in Belize City takes about an hour.

COLOMBIA

A Forest Refuge

GREAT FOR	COST	WEBSITE
COUPLES, FAMILIES, ACTIVE TRAVELERS	$$	BIOHABITATHOTEL.COM

To the south, over the forested hills, lie the town of Armenia and the wide green valley beyond. To the east, the snow-dusted Andes and Nevado del Tolima volcano. And west, the sky is painted in orange as the sun slips behind the Pacific arm of the Andes at the end of the day.

That's the view Julian Escobar and Jorge Gonzales saw in the hills behind their hometown of Armenia, Colombia, as school boys. When they were grown, Escobar, an architect, and Gonzales, an engineer, joined forces to create a construction firm. When the land they had played on was earmarked for a condo project, they decided to buy it instead. Here, they created a hotel immersed in the tropical rainforest.

In 2018, **Bio Habitat Hotel** opened with just 12 suites. Today, that number has grown to 28; a total of 32 are planned. Half overlook the coffee farms and rolling hills of Quindio, Colombia's smallest state, with long views to the Andes. The others are nested in the palms, papaya, and mango trees of the forest.

Bio Habitat Hotel is near and far. A swift 15-minute drive takes you to the 18th-century heart of Armenia and its 300,000 residents. But the mindset is a universe away from the nonstop hustle of Bogota, Medellin, and Cali. The hotel's owners intend it as a refuge, symbiotic with the land, where visitors can soak in the pool, immerse themselves in the ancient forest, and look for the 150 bird species so vivid, they must have fallen into a paintbox.

Air-conditioned suites—called habitats—bring nature to floor-to-ceiling windows. What few walls guests see are hewn from local wood and stone. High ceilings promote airflow; roofs are covered with foliage that protects the structures from the rainfall that, in the wettest months, can top 10 inches. Solar provides much of the electricity; on-property treatment pools convert gray water for irrigation.

The landscape may resemble other jungled places, but it's unique. Stubby palmlike plants called *frailejones,* or "big monks," grow in this netherworld between tree line and snow line. Wax palms, the world's tallest palms, shoot up as high as 200 feet.

Two-thirds of the hotel's 40 acres are still covered with native plants, including trumpet and cedar trees. Lemon, papaya, and mango added to the grounds supply the bar and kitchen.

The hotel is conveniently located for horseback rides into the protected Cocora Valley, treks into the high mountain land above the tree line, and forays to look for howler monkeys in the tropical Barbas River canyon. Those with Disney-loving children may want to visit the nearby village of Salento, the real-world *Encanto.*

Grand Master Suite, Bio Habitat Hotel.

Guestroom, Bio Habitat Hotel.

Then, it's back to the hotel for a dip in the pool and a margarita. Two nights each week, cocktails come with a live music session popular with locals and guests. The sun dips behind the peaks, echoing the school-boy forays that led to Bio Habitat Hotel's creation.

Planning a Trip

Bio Habitat Hotel sits at about 7,800 feet. The average temperature is around 70°F year-round. The driest months are December through February and July through August. The closest airports are Matecaña International Airport, about 30 miles from Armenia, and the local airport in Armenia.

FACING PAGE, TOP LEFT: *Outdoor dining at Bio Habitat Hotel.*
TOP RIGHT: *Wooden swing at Bio Habitat Hotel.*
BOTTOM LEFT: *Horseback riding near Bio Habitat Hotel.*
BOTTOM RIGHT: *Massage treatment at Bio Habitat Hotel.*

THAILAND

Romance on the River Kwai

GREAT FOR	COST	WEBSITE
COUPLES, FAMILIES WITH OLDER CHILDREN	$$	THEFLOATHOUSERIVERKWAI.COM

The Kwai River streams like life itself, constantly moving through jungled hills from mountains and eventually to the sea. From the deck of your floating villa, it feels like a metaphor Buddha might have embraced: Jump in or watch it pass you by.

You could slip into the murky water from where you sit. But it seems more reassuring to go for an official "river jump" from another resort a few miles upstream under the watchful eye of the driver of a narrow, long-tailed boat typical of Thailand.

Secured in a life jacket, I jump in and go with bobbing coconuts and the flow, through a narrow gorge of reddish rock face and fluttering bamboo. A cloudless sky glows overhead. The occasional bird and butterfly flit past.

I glide in harmony with nature . . . until I try to go against the current. Getting to the rope at the exit point requires determination and skill. My boatman ties up and helps me onto the floating deck that leads along the boardwalk, past the spa and near the restaurant of FloatHouse River Kwai.

For Westerners, this river became a familiar name following the 1957 film *Bridge on the River Kwai*. Though the storyline is fiction, its World War II foundations are fact. In the 1940s, the Japanese conscripted Asians and Allied prisoners of war to build the Burma Railway, stretching more than 250 miles through the jungle from Burma (now Myanmar) to Thailand. An estimated 16,000 POWs and more than 90,000 Asian civilians died in the effort. The story is powerfully recalled at the Thailand-Burma Railway Centre in Kanchanaburi, about 50 miles away.

From the decks of the **FloatHouse** villas, that painful past seems eons away. Set in a river bend, the 20 air-conditioned villas rest cantilevered over the water on solid posts; only the decks actually float on pontoons. Teak floor, peaked thatched roof, and bamboo screens surrounding the indoor-outdoor shower connect you with the breeze. The bright canvas deck chairs and pillows on the canopied bed recall the bright hues of a Thai temple weaving. The river gurgles beneath your feet. Those looking for romance have found their place.

Planning a Trip

The best time to visit Thailand is during the dry season, from November to April. Summers are hot, sticky, and sporadically wet. The same company owns two nearby resorts, the rustic Jungle Rafts and the land-based River Kwai Resotel, which has a pool.

FloatHouse is a 3-hour drive from Bangkok—if you don't get stuck in the endless traffic. Better to take the train to Kanchanaburi and then get a local taxi to the pier for boat transportation to FloatHouse.

The FloatHouse River Kwai.

CHAPTER 4

ON AN ISLAND: CLOSE, BUT FAR

Soneva Kiri (p. 104).

Every island holds the potential for an adventure, a journey into the wild heart of nature.
— Joseph Conrad
To explore an island is to embark on a voyage of discovery—of the land, and often of oneself.
— Amelia Earhart
Escape to an island, where time slows, and the pressures of the world dissolve into the horizon.
— Jules Verne

PANAMA

Dancing with Boobies, Flying with Fish

GREAT FOR	COST	WEBSITE
COUPLES, FAMILIES	$$$$	ISLASSECAS.COM

Boobies with vivid blue feet stomp and then sway and spread their wings in a mating ritual half-way between a waltz and a wedding reception chicken dance. Male frigate birds puff out lipstick-red chin pouches in a bid to attract the ladies. Both species are signatures of the Galápagos islands. But there's another, less crowded place to see them: the privately owned archipelago of Islas Secas, 20 miles off the Pacific Coast of Panama.

In summer months, those feathered males are the center of attention. Come July, migrating humpback whales send guests dashing for binoculars. In winter, whale sharks swim through the turquoise water, creating a chance for scuba swims with the world's largest fish.

Year-round, the small, remote **Islas Secas** resort offers birding, underwater explorations, and fishing. Turn off the air-conditioning in your villa to hear the morning wake-up song from tanagers, parakeets, kingfishers, and even boobies with Louboutin-red feet. Snorkel at nearby reefs to see angelfish and parrot fish. Take a scuba certification class and dive with sharks and rays. Visit Coiba National Park, a former penal colony turned UNESCO World Heritage site. Cast a line into the gulf for dorado, tuna, grouper, and mahimahi.

Fishing, birding, sailing, paddle boarding, croquet, picnic, yoga, sunset cruises, and diving in the Gulf of Chiriqui are included activities for guests. Catch-and-release trips to Isla Montuosa, one of the world's most prolific marlin grounds, can be arranged.

Tented casitas for two and multi-bedroom family villas make up the total of eight accommodations, all located on the largest of the 14 islands. Thatched peaked roofs and wide terraces are designed to encourage air flow. Wooden shutters shade windows for that afternoon nap. All lodgings are tucked into the landscape for privacy. A short walk leads to the spa, pool, beach, and restaurant, where culinary offerings center on local ingredients. (Will it be ceviche for lunch or the Caribbean lobster roll?)

But canopied beds, bamboo construction, and wagyu burgers are frills. The real reason to come is the pristine bounty Islas Secas helps preserve in partnership with government and private agencies. Commercial fishing has been limited since 2023, and tracking programs already show an increase in local populations of humpbacks, whale sharks, and sea turtles.

Guests can help monitor magnificent frigate-bird nests, whale flukes, and corals. Or they can simply walk through the rainforest, smell the earth, and swim through the crystal sea.

TOP LEFT: Beach, Islas Secas. BOTTOM LEFT: Jetskiing at Islas Secas. TOP RIGHT: Fishing tour at Islas Secas. MIDDLE RIGHT: Boat tour with Islas Secas. BOTTOM RIGHT: Movie night at Islas Secas.

Aerial view of Islas Secas.

Planning a Trip

Temperatures are a constant 75°F to 80°F year-round. High season is mid-December to April, when humidity is lowest. August and September are prime time for whale migration.

Islas Secas offers transportation via Twin Otter plane or boat from the airport at David, Panama, for a fee. Rates include activities, meals, and some spa treatments. A minimum 3-night stay is required.

FACING PAGE, TOP: *Tented Casita, Islas Secas.*
BOTTOM LEFT: *Beach bar and restaurant, Islas Secas.*
BOTTOM RIGHT: *Terraza restaurant, Islas Secas.*

NEW YORK, USA

In the Hudson River

GREAT FOR	COST	WEBSITE
FAMILIES WITH OLDER CHILDREN, COUPLES, FRIENDS; STAIRS REQUIRED	$$	SAUGERTIESLIGHTHOUSE.COM

Who hasn't dreamed of staying in a lighthouse? And then the reality of remote location; dampness; long, curved staircases; and inconvenient bathrooms sets in. **Saugerties Lighthouse** on the Hudson is one of the few places where your lighthouse fantasies can be realized—in comfort.

A half-mile boardwalk leads through cottonwoods, maples, and vines. From the small bridge over the wetlands, you see a snapping turtle and a sunfish swim past; a wren flutters by. A few yards farther, and the island and its square brick house come into view. Over the roofline, you see the glass coppola of the beacon.

When the lighthouse first opened in the 1830s, the Erie Canal linking the Hudson River and Lake Erie had recently opened, smoothing the way for cargo transports to New York that had once been unthinkable. Many stopped at Saugerties, 100 miles north of the city, but avoiding shallows near the harbor required sharp eyes. A tower lit with whale-oil lamps and parabolic reflectors was built to illuminate the entry.

In 1848, a fire broke out, destroying the lighthouse. A second beacon was installed on the site but soon became obsolete. Advanced technology powered the current lighthouse, which went into operation in 1869. Daniel Crowley was the keeper in those days, but failing eyesight put him out of a job. His daughter Katie took over, somewhat to the surprise of the sailors she and her sister had to rescue.

This history is memorialized in the small lighthouse museum, along with the Fresnel lens brought from France in the 1850s to increase the beam. Most striking, perhaps, are images of the dilapidated building from the 1980s, after automation replaced human keepers. Volunteers stepped up to save it from demolition. After almost 15 years and $1 million, the lighthouse reopened in 1990. Today, it looks much as it did in the early 1900s.

Visitors can relive those days as overnight B&B guests, with sole use of two heated bedrooms, a small sitting room with a Victrola, and a shared bathroom. When they climb the tower for sunset, the river will look a bit different, with 100-foot cargo barges instead of schooners and steamships. But they can still imagine the stormy nights when young Katie Crowley and her younger sister rowed out to the rescue. Good thing they were there.

Planning a Trip

Saugerties Lighthouse is rented overnight year-round on Thursdays through Sundays, one couple or family per rental. Linens and breakfast for up to four people are included. Fridays and Saturdays book up months in advance.

Walkway to Saugerties Lighthouse.

On the Great Barrier Reef

GREAT FOR	COST	WEBSITE
COUPLES, FAMILIES WITH CHILDREN 10 & OVER	$$$$	LIZARDISLAND.COM.AU

From 5,000 feet, the sea looks like a finger painting in lavender and azure and indigo, with an occasional dot of turquoise plopped on for fun. The green and brown of the 2,500-acre island fills the view as the Cessna Caravan prepares to land.

A short ride on an electric buggy ends at the **Lizard Island Resort** lodge deck overlooking Watson's Bay and the Coral Sea beyond. From there, it's a short stroll to the 40 beach house–style rooms set in low-slung villas facing the water. The walkway linking them to the Marlin Bar is easy on bare feet, which is just the right footwear for a visit to the northernmost resort on the Great Barrier Reef.

Though Captain Cook stopped here back in 1770, this national park island remained untouched until the 1970s. The Australian Museum's Lizard Island Research Station came first, in 1973. When then-Prince Charles decided to visit a few years later, the first four villas were built. Over time, the lodge, watersports center, remaining villas, and gourmet restaurant were added. Most recent is a three-story, three-bedroom house on the beach.

Staff naturalists are on hand to explain the climate change, bleaching, storm erosion, and invasive species that threaten the Great Barrier Reef. Despite the decline, snorkelers can still see branching and leafy corals, green and hawksbill turtles, and shimmering blue damselfish. Creatures get big here: The reef hosts 3-foot-long potato cod and iridescent purple-lipped giant clams more than 4 feet wide and 100 years old.

For big-game anglers, these waters are the mother lode for 1,000-pound-plus black marlin, running September to December, along with tuna and wahoo. Such birds as rainbow bee-eaters and willie wagtails—considered a sign of good luck—flit in the brush. Lizard lovers find dozens of species, including 3-foot-long yellow-spotted monitors lounging on rocks.

But the best reason to stay on Lizard Island is access. Lodge guests virtually have the place to themselves. Day-trippers and anglers may stop by—it is a national park—but most of the 24 beaches, the research station, birding tours, naturalists, kayaks, and sea scooters are for resort guests only. So is the Salt Water Restaurant, with such dishes as Skull Island prawns in honey and sumac and roast duck breast with pickled melon. Perhaps try the McLaren Vale Grenache blanc?

Planning a Trip

Lizard Island guests arrive via a 1-hour flight from Sydney. Weather is best May to October; humpback and minkes migrate through around June. Meals are included in the rate.

***TOP LEFT:** Scuba diving tour at Lizard Island. **TOP RIGHT:** Mermaid Cove beach. **MIDDLE:** The Pavilion, Lizard Island. **BOTTOM:** The House guestroom, Lizard Island.*

INDONESIA

Swimming with So Many Marvelous Fishies

GREAT FOR	COST	WEBSITE
MARINE-LOVING COUPLES, FRIENDS, FAMILIES WITH CHILDREN WHO SWIM	$$$	MISOOL.INFO

A hawksbill turtle paddles beneath you, above the pipe and fan coral growing 10 feet below. A massive swirl of silvery fish—are they big-eyed scad or fusiliers?—swims all around. You become one of them: a fish in the sea, without a care. (Until a tuna or dolphin decides to eat you.)

As a human, that's not really an issue. Still, the sense of otherworldliness lingers as you free-style back to the dock and flip yourself into a hammock.

For snorkelers and divers, the Raja Ampat region of Indonesia is the ultimate prize. Here, at the meeting point of the Indian and Pacific Oceans, forceful currents and underwater geology create an unmatched marine biodiversity. Some 1,400 fish species live here, along with 75% of the world's coral that, so far, seems to be resistant to warming. Rare blue-ringed octopus, brilliantly hued mandarin fish, and epaulette sharks that use their fins to "walk" on the ocean floor make these 24,000 underwater acres home.

Its remote location west of New Guinea helps preserve the area. Lodgings are few and generally rudimentary, which is why **Misool Resort** is fully booked years in advance.

There's nothing posh about these 12 villas made of reclaimed hardwood, but everything needed for comfort is here: fans, air-conditioning, shaded decks with hammocks, en suite bathrooms. Eight of the cottages are set on stilts over the sea; four sit on the sand. The restaurant centers on ingredients grown locally and line-caught fish. Afternoon tea, fresh juices, and cocktails are readily available.

Misool is the dreamchild of a European couple who dived in the area and wanted to help preserve it. After 3 years of construction, they opened Misool in 2008. The land beneath it and the surrounding 300,000-acre marine reserve are leased from local landowners. Harvesting fish from the protected waters is prohibited.

Underwater species are the main attraction here, but there's action on land as well. Raja Ampat is home to cockatoos, hornbills, sea eagles, kingfishers, and parrots. Birds-of-paradise are especially hard to spot. But you never know; in paradise, anything can happen.

Planning a Trip

Year-round, highs hover around 88°F; the water is calmest between October and April.

Best to plan ahead; Misool is often fully reserved years in advance.

Flights arrive at Sorong Airport. From there, Misool's covered motorboat provides the 5-hour transportation. Meals, self-guided snorkeling on the house reef, and use of kayaks and stand-up paddle boards are included. The minimum stay is 7 nights.

TOP LEFT: Villa Utara, Misool Resort.
TOP RIGHT: SUP at Misool Resort.
MIDDLE: Aerial view of Misool.
BOTTOM: Beachfront suites at Misool.

CANADA

Barren Beauty at the Edge of Earth

GREAT FOR	COST	WEBSITE
COUPLES, FAMILIES WITH CHILDREN 8 OR OLDER	$$$$	FOGOISLANDINN.CA

As a visitor to this 90-square-mile island, it would be easy enough to stay behind the panoramic windows with other guests who can afford the hefty tariff at **Fogo Island Inn.** That's why every guest is linked up with a local guide, just a regular resident living on this rocky outpost who can show you around.

Yours is Mary, a retired teacher whose accent holds traces of her Irish roots, even though it's been hundreds of years since her forebears came to this island off an island in Iceberg Alley. She drives past the Old Post Office, built in the early 1900s, and points out shops offering locally made items, such as the quilt on your hotel bed. There's a restaurant or two if you decide you want to try local fare beyond the inn's three-course dinner. And here are her favorite hiking trails.

When you ask how things have changed here, she explains that little did in those first few hundred years, when the island had no phone or electricity. Most folks lived on their catch of cod salted for preservation that they bartered for goods. That is, until the big refrigerated fishing boats came in from Europe in the 1960s, and the residents in the 11 villages nearly gave in to a government resettlement plan. A documentary filmmaker went around the island and connected them, and the residents realized that most everyone wanted to stay. And they did.

The 29-room inn is a nonprofit economic generator that fuels community projects and local businesses, such as the furniture maker that crafts tables and beds and the ladies who sewed your quilt. That's thanks to Fogo Island native Zita Cobb, who made a fortune in Silicon Valley and then returned and created the nonprofit that built the inn.

Now you, too, are under Fogo's spell. Perhaps you want to try your hand at a pottery wheel. Pick berries to make jam. Face the chilly Labrador current that sweeps icebergs from Greenland to these shores as you fish for snow crab and cod. Look for puffins and razorbills and harlequin ducks and migrating whales and reindeer. Bike and hike and take in the scents of mosses and lichen seasoned with salt.

At last, you sit and lounge before the fire in this stilt-borne perch above the granite shore. As the fog rolls in, you silently thank the islanders for sharing the barren beauty that now feels strangely like home.

Planning a Trip

Fogo Island Inn is open April 1 to October 31. The closest airport is Gander. Rates include all meals and some activities.

TOP: Guestroom at Fogo Island Inn.
MIDDLE: Fishermen at Fogo Island.
BOTTOM LEFT: Aerial view of Fogo Island Inn.
BOTTOM RIGHT: Glaciers near Fogo Island.

Birthplace of Bond. James Bond.

GREAT FOR	COST	WEBSITE
FAMILIES, COUPLES	$$$$	GOLDENEYE.COM

James Bond's recent exploits have taken him to Shanghai, Istanbul, and the Faroe Islands. Fans of the original film, *Dr. No*, will know that 007 got his start in Jamaica, at author Ian Fleming's breezy waterfront home, **GoldenEye.**

Neither Fleming, himself an agent during World War II, nor Bond is in residence anymore. But the 13 spy novels written here remain part of GoldenEye's creative legacy, along with musical hits written here by Sting and Bono. In the 1960s, painter Lucian Freud; photographer Cecil Beaton; and actors including Katharine Hepburn, Laurence Olivier, Alec Guinness, and Elizabeth Taylor gathered for parties that rotated between GoldenEye; playwright Noel Coward's house, Firefly; and Bolt, a 50-acre estate owned by an heiress named Blanche Blackwell.

Firefly is now a museum; Bolt is available for vacation rentals. GoldenEye's 52 acres are now a 49-room resort including villas on the beach, casual cottages on the edge of a lagoon, and the three-bedroom house where Fleming penned his novels. All have an island vibe, with high wooden ceilings, plantation shutters and fans to keep the breeze moving. Some are air-conditioned; others feature outdoor showers beneath the banyan trees.

Above the water and below, guests are immersed in nature. Cottages nest in a tropical garden of agave and hibiscus, mahogany and flame-orange poinciana, and coconut palms that host orchids with blossoms in bright crimson and ghost white. Guests can follow Kate Moss's example and add to the collection through GoldenEye's "plant a tree" program.

Shutters open to the Oracabessa Bay Fish Sanctuary, founded in 2010 to increase marine diversity by planting corals and reintroducing turtle species. The program is working: In just 4 short years, the government reported a 150% increase in fish biomass in the region. Snorkelers and divers now swim among a profusion of hawksbill turtles, bright green stoplight parrotfish, sergeant major fish adorned with regimental stripes, and blue tang fish that inspired Dory in *Finding Nemo*. Those who swim out to the edge of the Cayman Trough find the rainbow hues of elephant ear and rope sponges, green moray eels, and pink king crab.

Today, GoldenEye is owned by Island Records mogul Chris Blackwell (yes, Blanche's son; see above). While he may not be hanging around, you can be sure he has instructed the bartender on how to make a proper martini—shaken, not stirred.

Guest hut on the beach at GoldenEye.

Planning a Trip

Most visitors fly into Ocho Rios, a 2½-hour drive from GoldenEye on Jamaica's north coast. Highs remain a steady 77°F to 86°F throughout the year. The rainy season runs May to June and September to November.

GoldenEye is part of Blackwell's Island Outpost group of hotels, which includes The Caves in Negril and Strawberry Hill in the Blue Mountains.

THIS PAGE, TOP: *Beach at GoldenEye.*
MIDDLE: *Chef with fresh fish at GoldenEye.*
BOTTOM: *Villa at GoldenEye.*
FACING PAGE, TOP: *Lounge, Fleming Villa at GoldenEye.*
BOTTOM: *Outdoor bathtub at GoldenEye.*

IAN FLEMING
LUCKILY
I HAD
AN ISLAND
HIDEAWAY
THE TRAVELBOOK
Dr. NO

Aerial view of Mamula Island.

An Island in History

GREAT FOR	COST	WEBSITE
COUPLES, FAMILIES WITH CHILDREN 12 & OVER	$$$$	MAMULAISLAND.COM

TV shows like *Games of Thrones* and *My Lady Jane* have rekindled childhood dreams of sleeping in a castle, secured by battlements and a massive wood gate—but no damp dungeon, thank you very much. Let's have a fortress with modern bathrooms, an ocean view, and a Negroni at the bar.

From the town of Mirista, a 3-minute boat ride across the Bay of Kotor ends at cozy **Mamula Island.** Though it measures less than a quarter of a square mile, the restored fortress shelters a trio of dining options, a beach and pool, speakeasy-style bar, spa, and 22 suites and 10 rooms. Historic chambers sit beneath vaulted ceilings adorned with fragments of original frescoes. Newly added suites with tall windows and balconies have been carefully designed to look as if they've been there all along. All rooms have ocean views.

The Austro-Hungarians built this stronghold in the mid–19th century to protect the harbor against enemy ships. During World War II, the Italian fascist government under Benito Mussolini used it as an internment camp known for its brutal practices, a sad past recognized in the hotel's Historical and Memorial Gallery.

Like other historic forts in the region, Mamula fell into disrepair, and from 1970, it sat empty. In 2016, the government approved a 49-year lease to an Egyptian billionaire. After 7 years of careful reconstruction and additions, Mamula Island opened in 2023 as a luxury hotel.

The deck atop the crenelated walls feels like the center of the world, surrounded by the deep clear sea and the forested hills beyond. From Mamula, guests can hop in a kayak to swim in the luminous Blue Cave, take off on a water bike, or go fishing with the hotel staff. On the mainland, you stroll along cobbled streets of coastal villages, stopping under a canopy for a bowl of clams or grilled octopus just plucked from the sea.

A 2½-hour drive—or a short helicopter ride—takes guests to Durmitor National Park. Thick pine forest grows on mile-high peaks that plunge to a dramatic landscape of lakes and canyons carved by glaciers eons ago. Among them is Europe's deepest chasm, the Tara River Gorge, that plunges a mile downward. You head for a hiking path through the black pine forest and marvel at a golden eagle soaring overhead. Who needs the city?

Planning a Trip

Mamula Island is convenient to airports in Tivat and Podogorica in Montenegro and Dubrovnik in Croatia. Boat service is offered from Tivat. Alternatively, guests can take a taxi to Mirista and a boat from there. The hotel restaurant is open to nonresidents, but reservations are required.

THAILAND

Under the Coconuts, Chocolate on the Side

GREAT FOR	COST	WEBSITE
COUPLES, FAMILIES	$$$$	SONEVA.COM

A wooden boardwalk leads to the platform near the water's edge. A triangular bamboo pod awaits, with seats for four and a teak table set for an artful nibble. From above, a host enables the motorized lift, and slowly, slowly, you rise above orchids and palms and vines and await your canapes in the canopy overlooking the Gulf of Thailand. You've slipped into a *White Lotus* fantasy, minus the murder.

The host has arrived by zip line with a snack of dragon fruit and grapes on skewers and fish mousse on cucumber topped with roe. You could have opted for a heartier meal, but then how would you manage the smoked Tomme from the cheese room and homemade macarons from the chocolate room?

Though **Soneva Kiri** is home to only 33 canvas-topped air-conditioned villas, the dining options are expansive: authentic Thai on a deck in the mangroves, Japanese-Peruvian fusion at sunset over a bay, lunch under the palms at the beach, barbecue in the organic garden, a plant-based repast featuring mushrooms grown in the mushroom cave—even room service delivered by your Barefoot Guardian, as your personal concierge/butler is officially dubbed, and served in your private outdoor bathtub.

Still, there's more than food to this 102-acre retreat. While other Thai resorts have become bustling tourist centers, Soneva Kiri remains serene, thanks to its remote location on Koh Kood island.

No shoes, no news is the suggestion here, reinforced by the lack of news channels piped to the villa TV. Guests are here, smell the frangipani, send the kids to the children's labs, and indulge at the spa. Each villa comes with a golf cart recharged at night by the staff. Thick trees separate the villas. Kingfishers, barbets, and cuckoos sing for their mates.

Excursions outside the resort take guests to a hornbill reintroduction project near one of the island's best-known waterfalls. A steep climb leads down to a series of pools where you can wade, cool off, and watch small fish swim past. Other forays take guests to night snorkeling with bioluminescent plankton and cooking classes with a local chef.

Come dark, when guests return to the resort, the frogs win the evening. One barks like a dog; another honks like a Canadian goose. It's a fitting refrain for *The Frog Kingdom*, the evening's nighttime cartoon at the lakefront outdoor cinema before more-adult films play. Here, nature rules.

Planning a Trip

The best time to visit Thailand is during the dry season, November to April. Soneva Kiri includes transportation from Bangkok via its private Cessna Grand Caravans.

TOP: Aerial view of Soneva Kiri.
MIDDLE: Dining in the Treepod at Soneva Kiri.
BOTTOM: Beach at Soneva Kiri.

TOP LEFT: Tour of Granda City from Jicaro Island Lodge.
TOP MIDDLE: Hiking at Ometepe.
TOP RIGHT: Dinner on the floating deck at Jicaro Island Lodge.
BOTTOM: Guestroom, Jicaro Island Lodge.

In History's Shadow

GREAT FOR	COST	WEBSITE
COUPLES, FAMILIES WITH CHILDREN OVER 12; SOME STEPS REQUIRED	$$$	JICAROISLAND.COM

Some 20,000 years ago, Mombacho volcano spewed rock and ash into Lake Nicaragua, Central America's largest body of inland water. The debris scattered across the 3,100-square-mile lake and created 365 islets. One of those is **Jicaro Island.**

Black boulders lining the 9-acre island's paths recall its volcanic origins. Today, the once-sharp rock edges have been softened by giant ferns, leafy ginger spiked with red blooms, and yellow iris planted amid the stepping-stones. Gurgling fountains sing in harmony with birds in the Panama trees.

Here, guests do more than observe nature—they live within it. The restaurant sits on a shaded deck above a cenote, where guests breakfast on eggs fresh off a nest and mangoes just off the tree. A chunky black bird with a black-and-white striped beak perches on a branch; a young boy rows past in a red fishing scow.

Everything here is made from reclaimed wood, fashioned from trees felled in a storm on Nicaragua's Atlantic Coast. Guests stay in one of nine wooden treehouses ringing the island's outer edge, hidden from neighbors by tall palms and basket-woven wooden screens.

Inside, mahogany steps lead from a cozy living area to sink and shower, then up to the sleeping loft, with a king bed cloaked by netting. A fan spins quietly overhead. Thoughtful architecture allows plenty of air and light, with panels that slide open to decks and the outdoors, making you feel like you, too, are a bird living in the Panama tree.

Guests lounge in poolside chaises, dip in the lake, fish with a local family, or search for some of the 700 bird species at one of the local reserves. Volcanoes Ometepe and Mombacho are close at hand. Just 30 minutes away lies Granada, one of Central America's most stately colonial-era cities. Historic churches, markets, and breezy cafes welcome visitors with a smile.

My last night at Jicaro brought a candlelit surprise: dinner by the pool at a table for two. The memory will last long after the guava-glazed ribs are gone.

Planning a Trip

Granada is an hour south of the airport in Managua. A 20-minute ride in a motorized wooden boat brings you to Jicaro. The best time to visit is November to May. Rooms are not air-conditioned.

Nicaragua's authoritarian ruler, Daniel Ortega, has forcefully quashed opposition. The U.S. government warns against visiting because of the country's "arbitrary enforcement of laws, the risk of wrongful detention, and limited healthcare availability." Despite warnings about crime, Nicaragua's homicide rate is among the lowest in Latin America.

DOMINICA

Polynesia in the Caribbean

GREAT FOR	COST	WEBSITE
NATURE-ORIENTED COUPLES & FAMILIES	$$–$$$	DISCOVERDOMINICA.COM

Most Caribbean islands are rimmed with white-sand beaches. Dominica feels more like Polynesia. Rainforest, lava flats, hot sulfur springs, and abundant marine life create a nature haven unlike any place else in the Caribbean—and the reason why filmmakers chose it for *Pirates of the Caribbean*.

Around the island, dive and snorkel sites bring views of green turtles, lesser electric rays, and the beautiful but invasive lionfish. The coral at Champagne Reef isn't as colorful as nearby shoals, but it has something few others do: bubbles released from volcanic vents beneath the ocean floor.

Just off shore is the world's first designated sperm-whale reserve, home to 200 year-round residents. Some marine species come out at night, and it's only with the help of a guide's lamp that you catch sight of a basket star as it unfurls from its daytime ball-like position into a fluttering fan.

Daytime is for hiking. Dominica's best-known trek is the ambitious 8-mile walk across the fuming Valley of Desolation to the Boiling Lake, a cauldron heated by fumaroles. Easier routes lead to waterfalls and thermal springs.

It makes sense that the island's best-loved resorts blend in with the rainforest.

When Dominica-born Sam Raphael opened **Jungle Bay Dominica** in 1995, he was mindful of ecology and local people. Nineteen acres on a south-shore cliff are filled with mangoes, pineapples, pomegranates, avocados, and herbs that regularly wind up on the menus at dinner and in the spa. The resort partners with the Kalinago people, believed to be the last remaining tribe of pre-Columbian Carib Indians, and when the timing is right, guests can witness a full-moon ceremony. A Kalinago village resort is in the works.

On the north coast, **Secret Bay**—with different owners—offers a more exclusive experience, with 27 villas on 40 acres high above a trio of small beaches. Each villa features its own plunge pool and gourmet kitchen and comes with a dedicated attendant who will cook up your breakfast or dinner on request. But you may not want to pass up the art-filled Bwa Denn restaurant, home to a microbrewery and a four-course dinner created to each guest's specific taste.

Planning a Trip

Dominica is located about 600 miles southeast of the Dominican Republic. (The two are not related.) The best time to visit is the dry season, December to April.

Jungle Bay Dominica ($$; junglebaydominica.com) offers rooms by the night and multiday packages including meals and activities.

Secret Bay ($$$; secretbay.dm) requires minimum stays.

TOP LEFT: *Reading nook, Villa Suite, Jungle Bay Dominica.*
TOP RIGHT: *Aerial view of Secret Bay.*
BOTTOM: *Zing Zing Restaurant and Gommier Spa at Secret Bay.*

Glassy Seas & a Gentle Breeze

GREAT FOR	COST	WEBSITE
COUPLES, ADULTS WITH CHILDREN OVER 16	$$$$	TRADE-WINDS.COM

The gang on Gilligan's Island should have been so lucky. Tucked amid palms and passionfruit vines, **Mandala Eco Resort** on 3-acre Fetoko Island offers the barefoot freedom of an off-grid island—plus conveniences. A proper bathroom and private shower, open to the breeze. Electricity for charging cameras. Cell service, if you really must. A motorized boat for getaways.

Guests are the first in the world to see the sunrise each morning, thanks to Fetoko's location just over the International Date Line. Those cone-shaped islands visible from the bed? They're volcanic mountains higher than the Himalayas in the 37,000-foot-deep Tonga Trench.

During a weeklong stay, guests spend most of their time by, on, and in the crystal blue water of the Vava'u archipelago. The trade winds that brought explorers Captain Cook and Abel Tasman to this region are a constant presence, meaning that guests can sail the Hobie Cat at will. Snorkeling and diving excursions go to caves and coral gardens rich with rays, butterflyfish, and turtles. The island is on the migration route for humpback whales, and guests can often see them between July and October

When guests decide to go to town, they hop aboard an e-kart and head off to the weekly market. Tapa cloth made from mulberry bark and painted with Earth-toned dyes is the prize here. A turtle design or a pure geometric? Tough call.

Back at Fetoko, fresh mango juice and fish sandwiches are offered at the alfresco restaurant, supported by curved columns that make you feel like Jonah in the whale. Like everything else here, this gathering place was built by hand by a sailor couple whose 42-foot sloop brought them here in 2004. One project led to the next, and in 2013, they opened to guests.

The structures reflect their yachting know-how. Bungalows were designed with high ceilings to draw hot air skyward and stay reasonably cool without air-conditioning. Electricity is provided by solar power; water comes from cisterns and desalination. Waste is handled through a composting septic system.

The houses blend with leaves and trees. For this moment, you're Ginger and Mary Ann, the Professor, and the Howells. Come on, Lovey. Let's have another cocktail.

Planning a Trip

From the U.S., guests fly via Fiji Air to Nadi, Fiji, and then on to Vava'u, Tonga. The resort will arrange a taxi and boat transfer from there. Stays are 1 week, from Saturday to Saturday. All meals and most activities are included.

TOP LEFT: Diving near Mandala Bay. TOP RIGHT: Guestroom at Mandala Resort. BOTTOM: Aerial view of Mandala Resort.

CHAPTER 5

IN THE DESERT: DUNES, CLIFFS & TAWNY SAND

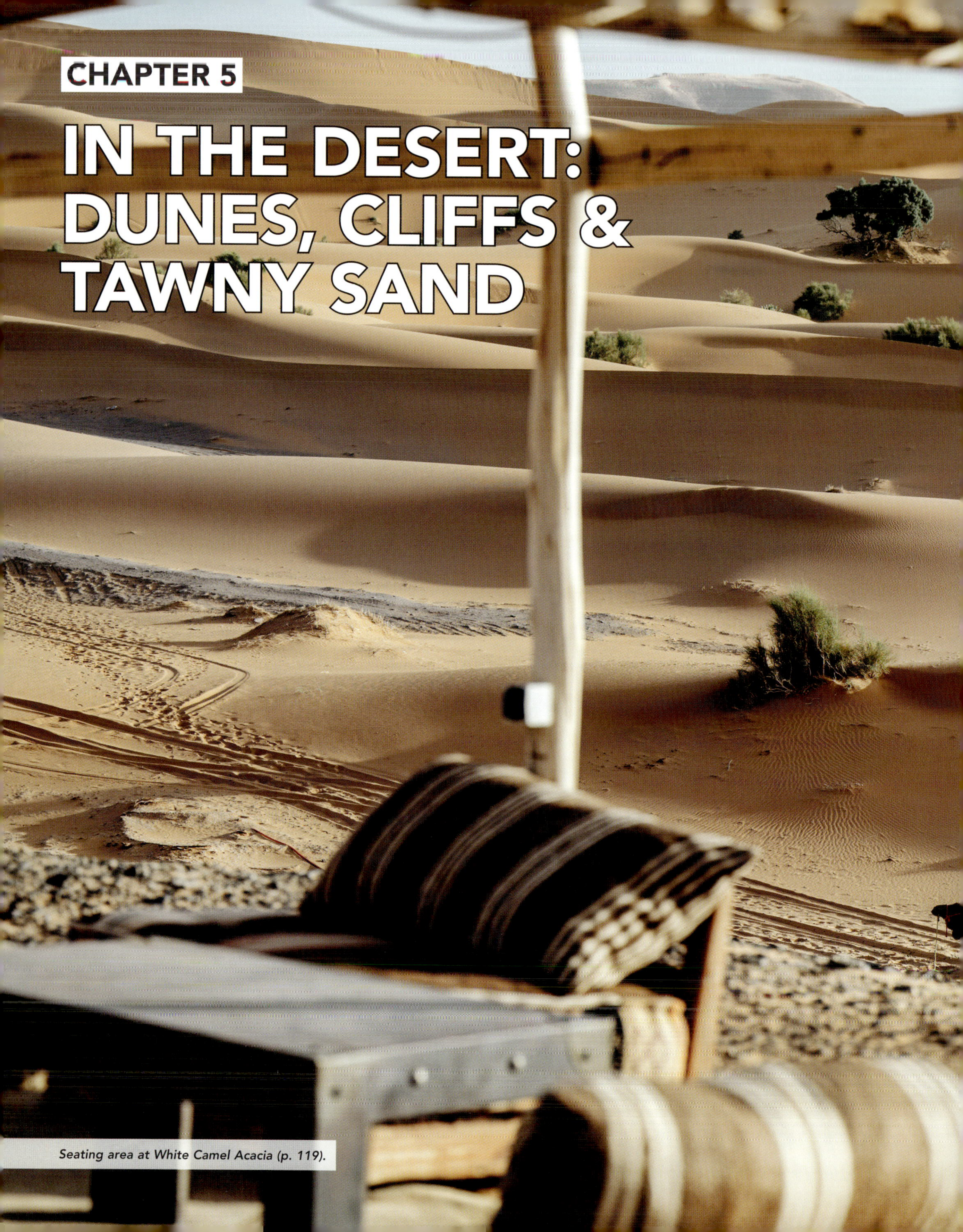

Seating area at White Camel Acacia (p. 119).

"The desert is a place of silence, light and space with beauty in its arid landscape, and wildflowers tucked into its crevices. Spend enough time here and the desert will weave a spell upon you.
— Victoria Geelan
What draws us into the desert is the search for something intimate in the remote.
— Edward Abbey"

TOP: Stargazing at the salt flats in Death Valley.
MIDDLE: Aerial view of The Oasis at Death Valley.
BOTTOM: Pool at The Oasis at Death Valley.

CALIFORNIA, USA

Lushness in an Arid Land

GREAT FOR	COST	WEBSITE
COUPLES, FAMILIES	$$$	OASISATDEATHVALLEY.COM

The very name brings a shudder. Death Valley is so very, very hot—in fact, the hottest place on Earth, with a record 134°F. At an average of 2 inches of rain per year, it rates as the driest place in the U.S., which explains such landmark names as Deadman's Pass, Coffin Mountain, and Funeral Peak. From the goldpanners of 1849 to more recent times, too many people have died in this forbidding bowl of rock and sand.

And yet a stark beauty unfolds in vast views that seem to shift with every step. Rocks turn to dunes painted by minerals in pink, blue, and green. The nonstop switchbacks and rock faces of Titus Canyon make you glad you checked the tires before you started the drive. The salt flats of Badwater Basin look like an icefield—home to a snail that lives nowhere else.

This place isn't really dead at all. Jackrabbits and big-horn sheep roam the 5,200 square miles of Death Valley National Park; in the spring, the hills are covered in wildflowers. At The Oasis at Death Valley, an incongruous patch of green is crowned by a stucco tower atop a stone lodge that's no mirage.

Since 1927, **The Oasis at Death Valley** has welcomed such Hollywood elites as Marlon Brando, Clark Gable, and Carole Lombard. Like any Hollywood star, it's had a facelift or two. The latest, a $250-million renovation completed in 2018, restored the 66-room lodge to historical accuracy (except for the modern bathrooms, thank goodness). Twenty-two one-bedroom casitas were added to the grounds.

With date palms, bougainvillea, and a spring-fed pool, this really does look like a film set, complete with a spa. A mile down the road, course collectors can golf at the nation's lowest ground, 214 feet below sea level.

After you've had a hot day of hiking, the pool calls. As the sky above the peaks turns rosy and the desert night begins to chill, you curl up by the stone fireplace and draw the blanket closer. The desert can be hospitable after all.

Planning a Trip

Death Valley is a 2-hour drive from the closest major airport, in Las Vegas. From June to August, temperatures can soar to more than 100°F. Even in cooler months, this arid place can be deadly; visitors are urged to keep ample water supplies with them at all times.

Along with the inn, guests can stay at the 276-room Ranch at The Oasis, run by Xanterra, and 17-room Shoshone Village (shoshonevillage.com), run by the Indigenous Timbisha Shoshone, who lived here 1,000 years before white settlers arrived.

EGYPT

In Luxor's Ancient Desert

GREAT FOR	COST	WEBSITE
COUPLES, FAMILIES	$$$	MOUDIRA.COM

From the hot-air balloon, the rocky cliffs surrounding the Valley of the Kings and royal tombs appear serene and majestic. By the time you land, however, the dusty roadways and ancient sites dotting the rugged desert of Luxor are jammed with eager tourists.

Who can blame them? Each monument is more jaw-dropping than the last, a testament to Egypt's 5,000 years of accomplishment in this parched and raw land. Stony sentinels stand nearly 100 feet high, proclaiming the glories of king gods whose reigns flourished while Rome was yet a village. Startling yellows and reds adorn the walls of cavelike tombs where the ruler's name is written hundreds of times so that his spirit may reenter this world after his death and he can rule again. History is revealed through painstakingly carved hieroglyphs covering wall after column after wall.

But after hours of touring on a warm day, your spirit has gone so dry that you can't even brave the bazaar. A 30-minute drive past motorcycle carts, modest villages, and the occasional camel brings you to an oasis. Step through the arched doorway of **Al Moudira,** and the rocks and dust disappear. You've entered a garden palace from the past, with intricately carved lintels, Arabesque wooden screens, and tiled fountains. The hand-painted walls, domed bathroom, and carved headboard in the suite are straight out of an Agatha Christie novel.

In truth, this "oasis" is fewer than 25 years old. Hotel founder Zeina Aboukheir created these courtyards, gardens, pools, lounges, spa, and 52 guest rooms from the ground up, opening it as a hotel in 2001. Though she sold the hotel a couple of years ago, she has stayed on to ensure that its timeless style lives on. Recent additions—the farm garden below the pool, five garden villas, and several artisan studios—look as historic as the rest.

It's windy out, and our plan for a dip in the pool literally blows away. There's an alternative: a velvet seat in the 1930s vintage Shahrazade bar, Manhattan in hand.

Planning a Trip

Temperatures are mildest from October to March, with highs around 80°F. Flights land at nearby Luxor International Airport. The hotel can arrange transportation, guides, hot-air ballooning, and other area activities, including tours by vintage Mercedes.

TOP LEFT: *Karnak Temple in Luxor.* TOP MIDDLE: *Living room, Al Moudira.* TOP RIGHT: *Guestroom, Al Moudira.* BOTTOM: *Lobby, Al Moudira.*

Atop the Great Dunes

GREAT FOR	COST	WEBSITE
COUPLES, FAMILIES	$$$	WHITECAMELACACIA.COM

Sunrise in the Merzouga Desert calls for a camera. Over a nearby dune comes a surprise: a still lake rimmed by tawny dunes. When the first shimmer of gold appears above the horizon, there's no one else around—a feat in this popular tourist zone.

There are so many surprises here: The lake in the desert. The solitude. The ancient fossils scattered across a hillside for anyone to pick up. Our now-turbaned guide, so transformed from his city jeans that we fail to recognize him.

And perhaps most of all, the **White Camel Acacia** desert camp with just four glass-fronted guest tents set around the dining tent, without another camp in view.

Lacsen, our guide, grew up here and knows how to navigate the unmarked Chebbi Erg, with dunes rising as high as 500 feet. Stops along the way reveal fruit and small pink blossoms growing in what seems to be barren land. A few drops of water illuminate a stone embedded with ancient mollusks. A flag outside a simple lean-to acts as the "open" sign, and a nomadic woman and her children come forth with dates and tea—poured from as high as the arm can reach, to gracefully aerate the scalding liquid.

Back in the air-conditioned SUV, we head off to examine engineered wells and the community garden it irrigates. No visit can be complete without a sunset camel ride on this sea of dunes.

At White Camel Acacia, the sand has been lit with candles. Fellow campers sip gin while a group of local musicians plays cymbals and a stringed instrument. The chicken tagine and roasted stuffed peppers are ready for the table. It's time to eat, but my husband is shimmying to the Tuareg tunes. No more gin for him.

Planning a Trip

The Merzouga Desert lies west of Marrakech near the Algerian border on the edge of the Sahara. Spring and fall are the best time to visit, with highs around 80°F.

The four air-conditioned tents at White Camel Acacia feature king beds, a sitting area, and en suite bathroom. The same company runs the larger Desert Luxury Camp in the same region, White Camel Agafay near Marrakech, and We Are Morocco Travel.

The closest airport is at Errachidia, about 2 hours away. Most travelers come from Marrakech through the Atlas Mountains, with an overnight stop along the way.

TOP LEFT: Guestroom, White Camel Acacia.
TOP RIGHT: Camel rides, White Camel Acacia.
BOTTOM LEFT: Enjoying the views of the dunes at White Camel Acacia.
BOTTOM RIGHT: Camels in the desert near White Camel Acacia.

ARIZONA, USA

Orchard, Canyon, Creek & Zen

GREAT FOR	COST	WEBSITE
COUPLES, FAMILIES	$$	ENJOYORCHARDCANYON.COM

Cathedral Rock's jagged spires reach almost 5,000 feet above sea level, making it hard to believe that this entire area was once beneath the ocean surface. But it's not the geology or history of these red, red rocks that take the breath away—it's their sheer beauty. No wonder the Hopi, Apache, and Yavapai held sacred ceremonies here, or that many people find Sedona a deeply spiritual place.

Cathedral, Courthouse Butte, and neighboring Bell Rock have been seared into our collective psyche through thousands of films and commercials. The sandstone formations are colored by iron oxide, or rust, in the dusty soil. Some contain hematite or other compounds that combine into a maroon tone. At sunset, when the light strikes just so, they seem to glow from within. Winding hikes offer dozens of vantage points, each with Insta-worthy views. Red-tailed hawks often glide overhead, while great horned owls rest in the shade.

But popularity has a price: Each year, about 3 million visitors come to this town of 10,000, creating traffic that can sap serenity. On the outskirts of town, the grounds and simple cabins of **Orchard Canyon** on Oak Creek help restore a sense of Zen.

From Flagstaff, Route 89A runs through the Coconino National Forest, along a fault line that long ago split into half-mile-deep Oak Canyon. The 16-mile drive through a series of switchbacks and along Oak Creek is considered one of the most beautiful byways in America. The discreet sign for Orchard Canyon on Oak Creek is easily missed.

A short drive leads to 17 historic cabins—some from the 1930s—beneath oaks above bubbling Oak Creek. The 10 acres are home to organic gardens and some 350 apple trees. It's also a sanctuary for guests who cherish the simplicity of relaxing on their porch and lounging without the temptations of TV or phone. The rustic cabins have updated bathrooms and big plush beds; some have fireplaces and air-conditioning. The family who runs it calls those on the creek Honeymoon Cabins, because so many return guests claim to have started their families there.

Breakfast and dinner are included in the room rates and served in the timbered dining room. Be prepared for a feast of fresh-from-the-earth salads; flat-iron steak, salmon, or pasta; and dessert including—of course—an apple cake.

Orchard Canyon on Oak Creek lies just up the road from Slide Rock State Park. Its 43 acres were acquired as a homestead in the early 1900s and transformed into an apple orchard. Like Orchard Canyon on Oak Creek, the park sits a few miles north of downtown Sedona.

Planning a Trip

Sedona is a 2-hour drive north of Phoenix and 1 hour south of Flagstaff. Temperatures are often above 90°F from June through September, but moderate other times of year.

TOP: Guestroom, Orchard Canyon on Oak Creek.
MIDDLE: Cabin, Orchard Canyon on Oak Creek.
BOTTOM: Steam Boat Rock, Sedona.

TOP LEFT: *Hot-air balloons in Cappadocia.*
TOP RIGHT: *Aerial view of Argos.*
MIDDLE: *Guestroom at Argos in Cappadocia.*
BOTTOM: *Seki Lounge, Argos.*

On the Edge of a Fairy Land

GREAT FOR	COST	WEBSITE
COUPLES, FAMILIES	$$$$	ARGOSINCAPPADOCIA.COM

Hot-air balloons sail through Cappadocia's sunrise, painting a familiar image. The land beneath is more of a mystery.

From the sky, the land is stubbled with rocky spires shaped like mushrooms and dusty hills that look like camel humps. Ravines seem to crawl along the land like caterpillars. Amid the landscapes are roads, church steeples, and vineyards—marks of the people who have lived in Türkiye's Cappadocia region since biblical times.

Back on Earth, you learn how life and the land have intertwined. For thousands of years, caves offered protection from conflict, marauders, and religious persecution. Inside the volcanic mounds, people dug houses and hostels, monasteries, and warrenlike towns with ventilated rooms for sleeping, dining, and storage. Chapel interiors are carved with arches and painted with frescoes rivaling the murals of Istanbul's spectacular Hagia Sophia.

Many of the rock formations are pocked with niches for pigeons, whose utility is memorialized near the town of Uchisar in dramatic rock folds called Pigeon Valley. In ancient times, the birds served as food, their excrement as fertilizer, their eggs to make paints. And, as transportation—as legend has it, the beautiful daughter of a wealthy landowner became a pigeon to escape her father's wrath and join her beloved.

Overlooking this valley is one of the region's 800 cave hotels, **Argos in Cappadocia.** Carved into the hillside are 71 cozy rooms with curved walls, stone-lined vaulted ceilings, and fireplaces—and some even have private underground pools. Throughout the hotel, bright hand-woven rugs add a decidedly Anatolian touch. If the concept of sleeping in a cave seems cloying, Argos also offers regular rooms overlooking the valley.

Whatever the room, it will come with a view. At night, when the valley is lit with 1,000 lights, you look out from your window and think of the determined people who adapted so brilliantly to life in this rugged land. Take courage.

Planning a Trip

Two airports serve Cappadocia; the most convenient to attractions is at Nevsehir. Roads are smooth, making car rental a reasonable option. To avoid crowds, it's best to visit in the spring and fall. Winter temperatures drop near freezing.

Argos is staggered on multiple levels; if mobility is an issue, consult with the hotel before you book. Its highly rated restaurant, Nahita Cappadocia, features Anatolian dishes crafted from ingredients sourced within 40 miles and spiced with currants, apricots, yogurt, and cumin. It is open to the public; you'll need to book in advance.

Dinosaurs & Nomads

GREAT FOR	COST	WEBSITE
CULTURALLY CURIOUS COUPLES & FAMILIES	$$$	THREECAMELLODGE.COM

It takes only an hour for the pile of sticks and cloth to become the nomadic equivalent of a comfortable suburban home. First comes the 4-foot-high, accordion-style crosshatch of wood—like folding child-safety gates—set in a circle 20 feet across. The ends are lashed to a low wooden door. Next, a notched wooden wheel is raised aloft with two 7-foot poles, set in the center of the circle. Dozens of spokes are set into the "wheel" notches and then lashed to the trellis, creating the skeleton of an igloolike hut. But there's no ice here; instead, the "bones" are covered with a thick layer of felt and topped with canvas.

At **Three Camel Lodge** in the Gobi Desert, spacious *gers* are already in place and furnished with thick rugs, camel-hair blankets, a wood-burning fireplace, and stone-lined en suite bathroom. For those who want to learn more about Mongolia's nomadic lifestyle, Three Camel will arrange a *ger*-building lesson—along with visits to nomadic families, cooking classes, archery, horse riding across the steppe, and plodding across the dunes on a two-humped camel. Or they can just ask the staff; all are Mongolian.

The 40 *gers*—or yurts, as they're called in the west—sit at the edge of the Gobi, centered around a stone lodge. Meals crafted from the garden and local ingredients are served in a separate *ger*.

Thanks to arid conditions and a history of windstorms, the Gobi is dinosaur central. The first nests of dinosaur eggs were discovered here in the 1920s, and still today, a gentle brush in the sand can reveal a Protoceratops skull. Dinosaur discoveries continue; in 2025, scientists uncovered a new herb-eating species named Duonychus tsogtbaatari, distinguished by its large, two-clawed hands.

Three Camel's parent, **Nomadic Expeditions,** was founded to promote Mongolia's thousand-year history of adaptation. The fierce Genghis Khan, China, and Russia have all held control; in 1990, its people voted for democracy.

Throughout time, Mongolia has been deeply Buddhist. About 30% of its people are still nomadic herders, moving livestock seasonally from grasslands to the foothills. They are a welcoming people, cheerfully setting aside embroidery and child-minding to offer you a snack of hardened sour cream or fermented mare's milk. Guests are expected to try all that is offered. No matter how unfamiliar those "treats" taste, the welcome lingers as a heartwarming memory.

Planning a Trip

Three Camel Lodge is open from May to November, when highs are around 68°F. It provides pickups from the airport at Dalanzadgad, about an hour away. Minimum packages are 2 nights and include all meals and activities. The annual Naadam Festival is July 11–13 and takes place throughout Mongolia.

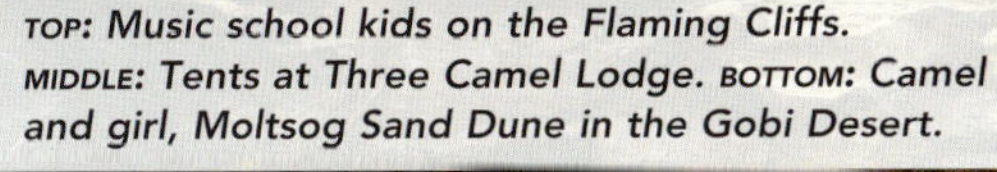

TOP: Music school kids on the Flaming Cliffs. MIDDLE: Tents at Three Camel Lodge. BOTTOM: Camel and girl, Moltsog Sand Dune in the Gobi Desert.

TEXAS, USA

A Cave Beneath the Stars

GREAT FOR	COST	WEBSITE
COUPLES	$–$$$	SUMMITBIGBEND.COM

Scarcely a tumbleweed appears on the 2-hour drive from artsy Marfa to Big Bend, where the Rio Grande turns sharply southward to form the boundary between Texas and Mexico. The closest airport lies almost 200 miles away, which is why the skies here are considered some of America's darkest. The arid land seems to stretch forever, from the biggest state park in the big state of Texas to a national park bigger than Rhode Island.

Between Big Bend Ranch State Park and Big Bend National Park sits Terlingua, population 138 at last count. Lodgings are in short supply here, which is why the two cave rooms at **The Summit at Big Bend** must be booked well in advance. Snagging one of the glampsite's star-gazing domes is a bit easier, but the idea of staying in a cave feels more extreme and exotic, especially when it comes with a king bed, private bathroom, heat, and air-conditioning. The glass-fronted opening offers panoramic views of stars across the expanse of the Chihuahuan Desert.

You expect desolation. Instead, there's a layered drama of fast-flowing water, deep canyons flanked by limestone walls, and elevation shifts of 6,000 feet to the top of the Chisos Mountains. The area is considered one of the world's most biodiverse, which translates into dozens of cacti, hundreds of colorful birds, and the piglike javelina.

Once night falls, stars glimmer brightly across the 10,000 acres of the Big Bend International Dark Sky Reserve. Weather willing, there's plenty to see with the naked eye: the shyer sisters of the Pleiades and the brilliant planets of Mars, Mercury, and Saturn. The Milky Way takes on a luminous glow invisible even in most small towns.

For sharper views, the nearby MacDonald Observatory hosts outdoor Star Parties with high-powered telescopes manned by astronomers who explain the starry night. For an amateur, that's a bonus.

Planning a Trip

Temperatures are mildest November to March.

The closest major airport is in El Paso. The drive takes about 5 hours. For contemporary-art buffs, Marfa and the Donald Judd Foundation sites located there are a must. Marfa is also home to a mysterious phenomenon of irregular floating orbs known as the Marfa Lights.

***TOP LEFT:** Rafting through Santa Elena Canyon in Big Bend National Park.*
***TOP RIGHT:** Cave guestroom, The Summit at Big Bend.*
***BOTTOM LEFT:** Cows in Big Bend National Park.*
***BOTTOM RIGHT:** Stargazing dome, The Summit at Big Bend.*

Sailing the Nile

GREAT FOR	COST	WEBSITE
COUPLES	$$	DAHABIYANILESAILING.COM

The intricate reliefs of Kom Ombo honor its patrons, the crocodile-headed god Sobek, and the falcon-headed Horus—amazing that the temple is still standing after 2,500 years. But then, you're traveling in much the same way as Cleopatra: aboard a dahabiya.

The Nile is home to a fleet of tourist-friendly vessels, from tech-savvy river ships to bare-bones feluccas. Traditional wooden sailing ships called dahabiyas are the happy compromise, offering tea and meals on the breezy upper deck with spacious en suite cabins below. When the winds fail, a motorized tugboat provides power.

More luxurious ships pass on voyage from Aswan to Luxor. But find a boatload of strangers-turned-friends having a better time, and there's a *very good price* on a camel waiting at the next bazaar.

Open-backed trucks transport your group to the weekly camel market. Sudanese traders showcase dozens of dromedaries secured by tying a front leg to the shoulder. On command, the camels hop in a circle, showing their strength and prowess. You're the only tourists in sight.

On the island of Bisaw, local women invite you to bake just as they have for centuries, in ceramic ovens heated by live fire. The roof serves as a dining room, with honey and yogurt for the fresh bread. Below are simple wooden boats that soon will take you fishing on the Nile.

By the time you return to the 10-cabin dahabiya, the crew has transformed a wooden lean-to at the Nile's edge into a dinner club with carpet and a table set for 12. After you've consumed grilled sausages and chicken, a trio of local musicians strikes up Nubian tunes. Before long, you're twirling with fellow passengers and the friendly staff in a makeshift dance party.

The fortresslike Edfu Temple is on the itinerary, along with the restored murals of Esna. Between, guests lounge aboard the shady boat, taking in the dusty mountains and desert behind the palm-lined shore of Africa's longest river as it flows from south to north. Egyptian geese and sacred ibis soar overhead. The fiery sun slips between the hills, bringing peace to the ancient Nile.

Planning a Trip

Dahabiya Nile Sailing is locally owned and provides moderately priced, culturally oriented sailings for 3 and 4 days. Sailings include guided tours, family-style meals, and en suite cabins.

For greater luxury, check out dahabiya companies Nour el Nil and Set Nefru.

TOP: Visiting a market on a tour with Dahabiya Nile Sailing.
MIDDLE: Edfu temple in Aswan, Egypt.
BOTTOM LEFT: Dahabiya Nile sailboat.
BOTTOM RIGHT: Woman making bread on a tour with Dahabiya Nile Sailing.

CHAPTER 6

ON SAFARI: WATCHING FOR WILDLIFE

Sunset at Green Safaris Chisa Busanga Camp (p. 136).

> *If there were one more thing I could do, it would be to go on safari once again.*
> *— Karen Blixen (pen name Isak Dinesen)*
>
> *The love of all living creatures is the most noble attribute of man.*
> *— Charles Darwin*

BOTSWANA

Up on the Boardwalk

GREAT FOR	COST	WEBSITE
COUPLES, FAMILIES WITH CHILDREN 6 & OLDER	$$$$$	XIGERA.COM

The 900-mile-long Okavango River creeps around islands and arid plains, ending in a slow-moving water garden of marsh and hammocks. Our guide poles the narrow wooden mokoro through the lily pads, occasionally startling a greenish kingfisher or one of the awkward-looking secretary birds with stiltlike legs. The odd fish swims by.

On a patch of land, rough gray canvas stretches across a bulk of fan-shaped ears, domed head, shoulders—the natural upholstery of a storybook giant ambling through grass as tall as a termite mound. Another, another, another eases down from the dusty brown plain, until seven elephants stand at the water's edge, less than a touchdown away.

Then, it's back to **Xigera Safari Lodge,** 12 air-conditioned tents set on boardwalks above the slow-moving waters of the Moremi Game Reserve inside the lush Delta landscape.

This ever-changing landscape is shaped by rainfall from Angola that flows through the Kalahari Desert, dragging sand through the contours of waterways and land. While the 1,900-square-mile reserve was once primarily marsh, years of cyclical drought have resulted in an increase of dry land. Two lion prides now live on Xigera's 17 square miles. Leopards, elephants, zebras, giraffes, and buffalo move around and sometimes through the camp. Hippos chill in the water.

When the camp was opened in 2020, sustainability was top of mind. Solar creates electricity; scraps are composted and distributed to local farms, from which the camp buys its produce. Fallen trees have been crafted into tables. All artwork—from decorative copper panels to branchlike ceramic lamps—in the lodge and 2,000-square-foot tents is designed and crafted by African artisans.

The songs of kingfishers, monkeys, and baboons punctuate the morning. To hear deeper voices, guests stay overnight in Xigera's three-story baobab-shaped treehouse. From the top, they can hear hippo grunts, lion roars, and the occasional elephant trumpet. If sleeping on the roof feels a bit *too* natural, they can move to the enclosed air-conditioned bedroom or radio the staff for a quick return to the lodge.

Planning a Trip

The best time to visit the Okavango Delta is June to September, during the dry season. Shoulder months of April and May are wetter, but temperate. October and November are hottest, with highs in the 90s and above Fahrenheit.

Xigera is reached only via air from Maun about 60 miles away. Rates include game drives, electric boat and mokoro rides, walking safaris, gourmet dining, and other wildlife activities. Facilities include a spa and pool.

Wildlife in front of Xigera Safari Lodge.

AFRICA: WHEN & WHERE TO GO

The buzz is all about the Great Wildebeest Migration, when wildebeests, zebras, and other wildlife move through Kenya and Tanzania following water availability, generally July to September. The sight of hundreds or thousands of beasts crossing a river is an amazing sight worth experiencing. But it can also resemble a circus, with dozens of vehicles crowded for views.

That's why many operators recommend going in June or October, when you might still catch a crossing or two, but without the crowds. Or you can simply go another time of year and have other types of spectacular animal encounters with far less company.

Here's some of what you might expect to see:

- Kenya and Tanzania have wide, open plains that are home to great herds of freely roaming animals.
- South Africa's landscape is more varied, including private fenced reserves and national parks that often result in close encounters. Kruger National Park is likely to provide viewings of the Big Five in a short period of time.
- Botswana's wetlands offer unique viewing experiences of elephants, hippos, and other water-oriented creatures, plus mokoro safaris.
- Zambia features a wide network of national parks, which leads to high wildlife density of the Big Five: lions, cape buffalo, leopards, rhinos, and elephants.
- Zimbabwe is known for great herds of elephants.
- Rwanda and Uganda offer the best opportunities to see mountain gorillas. Rwanda is more expensive but offers viewing areas closer to a major airport. Uganda is less expensive, but getting to gorilla areas takes more time. Both also have chimpanzee reserves.
- The Republic of Congo is emerging as an eco-destination due to its lowland gorillas.

Each location has its own hot, cold, and wet seasons, notes Deborah Calmeyer, CEO and founder of Roar Africa. She recommends avoiding East Africa in April and November, which is its rainy season, and Botswana in the heat of October. Cape Town, South Africa, is rainy in July and August and crowded in December.

Jay Hanson, a safari expert with African Travel Resources, recommends thinking first about why you want to go to Africa and then narrowing to the locations that offer that experience. "If I say to someone, the best way to have a safari in East Africa is sleeping under canvas, the power is solar, and the days are quite long in the vehicle, they might say, 'Oh no, I want a pool. I want air-conditioning. Those days sound really long.' Then actually, South Africa and Kruger might be a better fit."

TOP LEFT: Lamp at Xigera Safari Lodge.
TOP RIGHT: Library at Xigera Safari Lodge.
MIDDLE RIGHT: Floodplains of the Okavango in Xigera's glass-bottomed mokoros.
BOTTOM: Lounge at Xigera Safari Lodge.

ZAMBIA

In the Nest

GREAT FOR	COST	WEBSITE
COUPLES	$$$$	GREENSAFARIS.COM

A herd of elephant ambles across the plain. Your eyes have scarcely drooped for an afternoon snooze before dozens of wildebeest come into view. And where there are wildebeests, lions often follow. At **Green Safaris Chisa Busanga Camp,** there's so much to see without even leaving the nest.

There are, quite literally, four nests set 12 feet off the ground, created from bamboo and thatch to resemble a weaver bird's nest at human scale. Each comes with a king-size bed, sitting area, deck, and en suite bathroom. Nests are lined with canvas, so the elements don't seep in between the twigs and branches.

The design is a response to annual flooding in the Kafue National Park. As Green Safaris founder Vincent Kouwenhoven and architect Bert Meerstadt surveyed this land, they sought a solution to the plains' chameleon character as a wetland during the rainy months and grassland during the dry.

The Busanga Plains lie in the northern part of Kafue National Park, one of Africa's lesser-known parks, despite being one of its oldest and largest. At 8,600 square miles, Kafue is bigger than Wales but gets only 25,000 visitors per year. Much of the park is covered by woodlands, a prime habitat for elephants, cape buffalo, and antelope.

Unlike the rest of Kafue, the Busanga Plains are nearly treeless, with only clumps of fig and sausage trees like those that surround Chisa's nests. Vast herds of red lechwe, puku, and other antelope graze on the plains, luring lions. Elsewhere, most cats avoid water, but here, they have adapted to hide in shallow channels, lying in wait before they ambush their prey, often hunting in packs. While gruesome, the hunt is necessary for the cats' survival—and a likely sight in these plains.

Hunts are best seen on vehicle safaris, where Chisa guests may also encounter climbing cats—lions, cheetah and leopards — along with elephants and buffalo. On walks, they may see rare wattle throated cranes, monitor lizards, and even hippos.

The company uses quiet electric safari vehicles throughout its 9 properties and has introduced e-boats as well. All camps and vehicles are powered by solar.

Between forays, guests cool off in the plunge pool, dine in the bush, and hang out in their nests, keeping a birds' eye open for Cape buffalo and whatever may come their way.

Planning a Trip

Chisa and other Busanga Plains camps are open May to November One of Chisa's nests features a lift for those with mobility issues.

The company also operates the riverside Ila Safari Lodge, a family- and solo-friendly tented camp in central Kafue National Park, open March through January.

Nest room, Green Safaris Chisa Busanga Camp.

CANADA

Polar Bears on the Tundra

GREAT FOR	COST	WEBSITE
SOLOS, COUPLES, FAMILIES WITH CHILDREN 8 & OLDER	$$$$$	FRONTIERSNORTH.COM

A pair of half-grown cubs follow their shaggy white mother across the fresh snow. All three look well-rounded, a sign that a seal may have recently met its end. They're lucky; polar bears depend on sea ice as a platform for snagging seals that come up to breathe. With the Arctic ice melting so quickly, seals have become harder to catch. Even in good times, females often go 8 months without eating.

These bears are surprisingly close to the electric Tundra Buggy, a warm bus set high on thick tires that easily navigate the rocky roads built by the military decades ago. Off-roading is not permitted; the fragile ground would be damaged or destroyed. Cameras click madly as the bears pass by.

Polar bears head to the Hudson Bay region near Churchill, Manitoba, each October as the sea ice begins to form. When they first arrive, tree leaves still shimmer with orange and red. Before long, the snow starts, splashing the landscape with white.

Views, of course, are never guaranteed. According to Polar Bears International, the Hudson Bay bear population dropped by almost 30% between 2016 and 2021, the most recent survey. But most guests visiting between mid-October and mid-November do experience multiple sightings—and at closer range than in Scandinavian bear country, with its strict distance requirements.

The bears set the pace. Some are curious and come right up to buggies and the lodge. Others choose to stay a little bit farther away. Young males can be seen sparring, practicing for the ursine version of Tyson vs. Holyfield in winter, when mating rights are the prize.

After a full day of bear safari, it's back to the **Tundra Buggy Lodge** for a filling three-course meal, scientific talks, and a chance to see the Northern Lights. Whether the aurora borealis appears is up to Mother Nature. But here in the middle of the tundra, there's at least a good chance.

Planning a Trip

Polar bear safaris from Churchill, Manitoba, operate in October and November.

Frontiers North has been operating the Tundra Buggy Lodge and viewing safaris since the 1980s. Multiday trips combine air travel from Winnipeg; a day of activities, such as museum visits and dog sledding, in Churchill; 2 nights in Winnipeg; full-day safaris; and 2 nights at the newly refurbished lodge. Day tours from Churchill are also offered and book up quickly.

The lodge is a series of connected trainlike cars with a glass-top lounge, diner, outdoor observation deck, and bunk-style sleeping quarters. It holds 22 guests.

Polar bears near Tundra Buggy Lodge.

KENYA

On Slow Safari

GREAT FOR	COST	WEBSITE
COUPLES, FAMILIES	$$$$	SERIAN.COM

Hundreds of zebras skitter anxiously on the riverbank, hesitating to plunge into the water. Finally, one goes, and then the next, and then a dozen all at once. Numbers bring safety, and those at the back of the herd—often babies and weaker animals—are vulnerable to crocodiles and swift water that can drag them downstream. A foal struggles, crying for its mother. Nature is unforgiving.

Africa's annual wildlife movement is often called the Great Wildebeest Migration because it involves as many as 1 million wildebeests. But zebras and antelope are part of the flow as well, following the rainfall and the grass it nourishes. And so, increasingly, are humans. Dozens of safari trucks can crowd around a crossing, creating a spectacle of their own.

For long-time camp owner Alex Walker, that human spectacle is just one more argument for slow safaris that let nature unfold around you. "If you have more time to spend, then you don't need to rush to where everybody else is going. The guides are all on the radios, talking to each other. When they're all going one way, you can go another way." His guides also encourage pre-dawn starts so guests are in position before a river crossing even begins. By the time guests from other camps are starting out, his have moved on to watch giraffes gracefully strolling across the skyline and baboons grooming and walking with the resident photographer.

This is big-cat country. More than 50 lions live in the region, along with leopards and cheetahs. Maasai giraffes have irregular blotches that look more like a child's drawing than the geometric patterns of other species.

The slow approach applies at all 11 **Serian** camps across the Masai Mara and Serengeti. At each, guests are assigned a private vehicle and guide. Camps are small, with fewer than a half dozen tents. Permanent camps, such as Ngare Serian, feature comfortable canopied beds on wooden decks; mobile camps are tented and tuned to nature. All feature en suite bathrooms, but no air-conditioning or Wi-Fi.

Ngare Serian is set close to the Mara River, where guests can see hippos in the water and smaller wildlife crossings. Serian's 1,500 acres allow for night drives and fishing. A short stroll away is The Nest, a treehouse where you can sleep under the stars.

Whatever the camp, Walker encourages guests to forget capturing every Instagram moment and let nature unfold. "I think our biggest challenge is that people are cash-rich and time-poor," says Walker. "The real luxury is slowing down and taking time, and not trying to do everything."

Planning a Trip

July and August are prime time for the migration. Walker recommends coming on the edges, from mid-June to November, or at other times of year, when wildlife is plentiful and crowds are few.

TOP LEFT: Viewing lions on safari with Ngare Serian.
TOP RIGHT: Guide at Ngare Serian.
MIDDLE: Fireplace in guestroom at Ngare Serian.
BOTTOM: Interior of bedroom at Ngare Serian.

TOP LEFT: Hiking near Mandu Mandu Gorge.
TOP RIGHT: Paddleboarding at Ningaloo Reef.
MIDDLE LEFT: Stargazing at Ningaloo Reef.
BOTTOM LEFT: Whale shark in Ningaloo Reef.
BOTTOM RIGHT: Tent suite at Sal Salis.

Ningaloo Reef

GREAT FOR	COST	WEBSITE
COUPLES, FAMILIES WITH CHILDREN 10 & OLDER	$$$$	SALSALIS.COM.AU

Go! Go! Go!

The alert has been sounded. A plane has spotted a whale shark on the rise, and it's time to move.

We slip from the boat platform and swim quickly to our guide, whose fluorescent pink arm is raised high above the water as our marker. The dozen in our group line up shoulder to shoulder as quickly as the waves allow, a formation that enables views without impeding the path.

And suddenly, the giant spotted fish appears, swimming alongside our human shark. My friend and I kick furiously as we try to keep pace with the world's largest fish. Though we're the required 10 feet from his fin, we can clearly see three massive gills pulsing as the 18-foot male glides through the sea. He's a juvenile; adults can grow to 60 feet and live more than 100 years.

Though the whale shark seems unhurried, he outpaces us soon enough, and we paddle back to the 75-foot Blue Strike that serves as our platform for this 5-hour foray along Australia's west coast in the Indian Ocean.

A rare rainstorm gathers by the time we're back on shore, and we barely make it to our tent at **Sal Salis** before the sky opens and a deluge pummels the brushy dunes of normally arid Cape Range National Park, near Exmouth. From the porch, we watch the surf breaking over the Ningaloo, the world's longest fringing reef set incongruously against a desert.

Inside the park's no-fishing sanctuary, the only lodging is Sal Salis. The camp and 16 tents have everything we want—comfortable mattresses, bedside lamps powered by solar—without superfluous frills. Each tent offers views of the Ningaloo Reef edging the beach, where a short snorkel brings black-and-white cardinal fish, yellow-and-blue striped sweetlips, and butterfly fish in a multitude of yellow patterns.

Communal dinners served with Australian wines encourage new friendships.

"You're just arriving?" says a guest who's departing tomorrow. "I envy you. You won't want to leave." And so it is.

Planning a Trip

Rates at Sal Salis include all meals, hikes, and shore snorkeling. Whale-shark excursions are extra and provided by licensed local companies. Several motel-style lodgings are located in the small town of Exmouth, about 45 minutes from Ningaloo Reef.

Whale-shark swims are offered April through August; May and June are prime months. Reservations book early. From July to October, you can book snorkeling trips with humpback whales, though these are advised only for the strongest swimmers.

CALIFORNIA, USA

Africa in the U.S.

GREAT FOR	COST	WEBSITE
COUPLES, FAMILIES	$$	SAFARIWEST.COM

When the zebras appear on the rocky hill, a little boy asks if they're the *Cat in the Hat*'s horses. He's got something there: Why else would a herd of wildebeests or antelope be strolling along a California wood if this isn't a book or a film set?

Hollywood did inspire **Safari West,** a 400-acre wildlife preserve near Santa Rosa. As a child, Peter Lang became familiar with lions and chimpanzees while hanging out on sets with his father, Otto Lang, who directed wild-animal shows, including *Daktari* and *Sea Hunt*. When his personal collection of exotic animals outgrew his home, Lang bought a former cattle ranch and moved the herd.

In his mission to create a breeding program for endangered species in his collection, he reached out to local zoological programs. At the San Francisco Zoo, he met the lead curator, who became his wife. Together, they created the preserve as it is today: a learning, breeding, and conservation center where children and adults can go on a game drive in a converted military ambulance to learn how oryx horns help regulate their body temperature, check out giraffes, and get as close as to the white rhinos as safety allows.

When the game drive ends, most guests head out the gate. We check in to our overnight safari tent, feeling remarkably like we've been transported to Africa. We and other overnight guests have much of the park to ourselves. From our deck, we watch a pair of crowned cranes with hairdos like Doc Brown's in *Back to the Future* strut about the yard while giraffes munch on leaves from a sack hanging high on a pole. After a grilled dinner of ribs, chicken, and mac-n-cheese, our flashlight shows the way back to our tent. We turn on the electric blanket on the plush bed, zip the flaps, and close the bathroom door against the chill. Bellows and grunts of heaven-knows-what creatures waft through the night.

Morning comes with chirps and trills. We've got time before the day guests arrive to check out the enclosures for the cheetah, rested porcupine, and bearded De Brazza's monkey that looks amazing like the wizard Gandolf. The aviary is filled with painted birds—scarlet ibis, Abyssinian hornbills, and mandarin ducks among them. Not quite Africa, but closer.

Planning a Trip

Safari West is about 20 minutes north of Santa Rosa, in the heart of Sonoma's Wine Country.

***TOP LEFT:* Red ruffed lemur at Safari West.**
***TOP RIGHT:* Viewing zebras at Safari West.**
***MIDDLE:* King tent at Safari West.**
***BOTTOM LEFT:* Rhinos at Safari West.**
***BOTTOM RIGHT:* Cape buffalo at Safari West.**

A Precious Hour

GREAT FOR	COST
FIT ADULTS	$$$$$

Our small group tries to keep the proscribed distance of 20 feet, but the primate family of 15 ignores the theoretical boundary. One female brushes against my leg on her way to new perch. When another suddenly moves out of the thick green bush, there's no time to scramble out of the way. Our ranger tells us to stand still until she passes and then beckons us out of the way lest she reverse course.

Even without that simple brush against my leg, the encounter with the gorillas is far closer than my husband and I expect. So is their total disregard for our presence. Humans might share 98.4% of their DNA with these linebacker-size ape, but by most appearances, they couldn't care less.

The No. 2 male, Kalembezi, munches away on figgy fruits thrown down from the trees by the younger, lighter juveniles. Just up the slope, a female emerges through the green, a baby clinging to her back. Another with baby aboard shimmies down the trunk of the sturdy Ficus. And finally, the silverback lumbers through the jungle and into view.

The opportunity to spend an hour in the wild with one of the world's estimated 1,000 mountain gorillas draws tens of thousands travelers to Uganda and Rwanda each year. About 30 troops have been habituated through gradual contact with rangers and scientists, a practice that ensures safety for all and minimum disruption to the gorillas.

Still, finding a troop can take hours of uphill trekking. Sightings are not guaranteed.

Once you find a family, the visit will be limited to a single hour. If your guide doesn't remind you, the family silverback will. When his internal iWatch goes off, he may simply move his troop to another part of the forest. Occasionally, a silverback will stand up and beat his chest—a clear way of saying time is up.

Planning a Trip

Mountain-gorilla viewing is easiest in the African nations of Uganda and Rwanda. The gorilla-viewing experience is similar in both countries. Permits should be booked well in advance. All treks involve small groups with rangers. Weatherwise, the best times to visit are June to September and December to February.

***TOP:* Mountain gorillas in Rwanda.**
***MIDDLE:* Volcanoes Safaris Virguna Lodge.**
***BOTTOM:* Intore dancers at Volcanoes Safaris Virguna Lodge.**

For travelers short on time, Rwanda is the convenient but expensive choice. Permits cost $1,500 per person per day. Top resorts include **One&Only Gorilla's Nest** (oneandonlyresorts.com), **Singita Kwitonda Lodge** (singita.com), and **Virunga Lodge** (volcanoessafaris.com).

Uganda is less expensive but requires more effort. Permits cost $800 per person. Top resorts here include **Mount Gahinga Lodge** (volcanoessafaris.com) and **A&K Sanctuary Gorilla Forest Lodge** (abercrombiekent.com/sanctuary). **Mahogany Springs Lodge** (mahoganysprings.com) offers a moderately priced upscale experience.

SAFARIS ON A BUDGET

For most people, a safari is a once-in-a-lifetime experience. That doesn't mean you need to spend Earth. A budget-conscious group safari can cost less than $200 per person per day, double occupancy, with overland travel, basic accommodations, and local food; some activities will cost extra.

Group safaris also involve a set itinerary on specified dates. Group size matters: Small groups are more nimble, and you may get better views. But you can also end up with a cranky person or two. Mid-priced options include **Backroads** (backroads.com), **Geographic Expeditions** (geoex.com), **Natural Habitat** (nathab.com), and **Overseas Adventure Travel** (oattravel.com). Even deeper savings can be found with such companies as **Exodus** (exodustravels.com), **G Adventures** (gadventures.com), **Intrepid** (intrepidtravel.com), or Colette Tours (gocollette.com).

Many companies specializing in group tours will put together individual itineraries as well. After researching mid-priced lodges, I asked an outfitter (now closed) to create a trip with a private guide and lodging at mid-priced hotel group **Serena Hotels,** with one tented camp as a splurge. We ended up with a great wildlife experience with comfortable lodgings at a price we could afford.

FACING PAGE, TOP LEFT: Golden monkey at Volcanoes Safaris Virguna Lodge.
TOP RIGHT: Deluxe room, Volcanoes Safaris Virguna Lodge.
BOTTOM LEFT: Nest bar, One&Only Gorilla's Nest.
BOTTOM RIGHT: Guestroom at One&Only Gorilla's Nest.
THIS PAGE: Adolescent gorilla.

TANZANIA

The Beautiful Edge

GREAT FOR	COST	WEBSITE
COUPLES, FAMILIES WITH CHILDREN 8 & OLDER	$$$$	NOMAD-TANZANIA.COM

We're waiting at the guard gate when it opens, making us the first vehicle of the day in Ngorongoro Crater. Our early start pays off; just minutes into our drive, we catch sight of a rare black rhino, one of Africa's most critically endangered species. Even though it's too far for a detailed view, we're fortunate to have spotted it at all.

Less shy species are easier to see. A herd of zebras blocks the road, forming a decorative "fence" of striped behinds. Spritely gazelles spring about the open land; long-faced wildebeests wander, looking (to my eye) ever forlorn. Elands look up to watch us, as if they didn't see some 2,000 visitors each day. Elephants flap their ears to cool themselves. Flamingos seem to wallpaper the lake like some Florida cartoon.

By the time the park's most popular viewing spots have become surrounded by safari vehicles, our private guide has moved us to a rocky area rarely visited. It seems anticlimactic—until we spot a male lion still feasting on his kill. We have him all to ourselves.

Circumventing the crowds requires staying close to the access gate. **Nomad Entamanu Ngorongoro Safari Camp** provides that proximity on a private road, plus a private guide. There's no wrangling with other guests about wake-up times.

Originally, Entamanu Ngorongoro Safari Camp featured tents, but given the camp's windy location on the rim, the canvas was often noisy. Today, all 10 cottages are crafted from wood and designed to blend with the surrounding grasses while providing views across the crater bowl. The main lodge serves as meeting place and cocktail lounge, with a dining room for meals crafted from local ingredients. Guests then retreat to cozy bungalows with curved wooden roofs and en suite bathrooms, all warmed by gas fires.

From the camp's rim location, guests can walk into the grasses of the Serengeti Plains and a local Maasai village. On the crater side, a stroll along the rim leads to a plateau ideal for a sundowner, champagne in hand.

Planning a Trip

All Big Five game animals—Cape buffalo, rhino, leopard, lion, and elephant—live in Tanzania's Ngorongoro Crater; giraffes live outside. The crater has its own microclimate and is often cool; because of its unique situation, it is not subject to the wildebeest migration. Every time of year brings something different, but June to October is generally considered high season.

A visit is usually part of a safari loop through Kenya and Tanzania. Nomad and other companies can arrange safaris linking multiple destinations.

TOP: Flamingoes, wildebeests, and zebras, Ngorogoro Crater.
MIDDLE: Guestroom, Entamanu Ngorongoro.
BOTTOM LEFT: Maasai warrior surrounded by his community in the Ngorongoro Highlands.
BOTTOM RIGHT: Guestroom, Entamanu Ngorongoro.

INDIA

Roaming with Tigers

GREAT FOR	COST	WEBSITES
COUPLES, FAMILIES	$$+	TREEHOUSEHIDEAWAY.COM, KINGSLODGE.IN, OBEROIHOTELS.COM

The regal Bengal tiger is an apex predator, and by the way it strolls undaunted through the forest, it knows it. Orange-and-black stripes ripple over sinewy muscles visible even from a safari vehicle. Sloth bears and deer need beware.

Preservation efforts launched in 1973 reportedly doubled India's Bengal tiger population between 2006 and 2023. More than 3,000 tigers—more than 70% of all the world's wild tigers—now live in 53 preserves across the country.

Wildlife-viewing experiences here are more tightly controlled than in other parts of the world, making them more affordable, but also less customized. In Africa, guests often stay in private reserves or camps located within vast protected parks, with safaris led by private guides. In India, safari drives inside reserves are run by the government at set, inexpensive fees. Guests book lodgings separately. Most lodgings and private safaris operate only in buffer zones, not in the parks themselves.

Many reserves are unfenced, meaning that wildlife is free to roam across the invisible borders. At Bandhavgarh National Park, porcupines, civet cats, elephants, and even tigers sometimes wander onto the grounds of **Tree House Hideaway,** a collection of six houses on stilts set on 21 acres in the park's buffer zone. Rustic exteriors give way to spacious, air-conditioned bungalows, with en suite facilities, canopied beds, and open decks. Animals are shy and generally slip away when they hear humans about.

More conventional lodgings are located nearby at **Kings Lodge,** also in the buffer zone. From the verandas of the 18 cottages, guests can take in the thick forest between Jeep and walking safaris with lodge naturalists and bike rides on the grounds.

Odds of a tiger sighting are even greater at Ranthambore National Park. But it also gets far more visitors, thanks to its location convenient to Jaipur and Delhi. The remedy: a stay at **Oberoi Vanyavilas Wildlife Resort,** where 25 air-conditioned tents are inspired by the royal opulence of a bygone era.

Planning a Trip

India is home to 58 tiger reserves. An entry permit to each park is required and includes a half-day game drive; prices vary by park but generally cost less than $50. Permits should be reserved well in advance. Only a handful has lodging within the core reserve. Lodgings in the buffer zones sometimes offer a wider range of activities.

The dry season of March to June is best for viewings, but temperatures are often higher than 100°F.

TOP: *Tigers in Bandhavgarh National Park.*
MIDDLE: *Statue of Lord Vishnu in Bandhavgarh National Park.*
BOTTOM LEFT: *Guestroom, Tree House Hideaway.*
BOTTOM RIGHT: *Tree House Hideaway.*

TOP: Firepit at &Beyond Phinda Forest Lodge.
MIDDLE: Library at &Beyond Phinda Forest Lodge.
BOTTOM: Game reserve walk at &Beyond Phinda Forest Lodge.

Lions, Hippos & Whales

GREAT FOR	COST	WEBSITE
COUPLES, FAMILIES	$$$$	ANDBEYOND.COM

The sardines start running between May and July in a sometimes-fatal urge to reproduce. Literally billions group together in shoals that can measure 4 miles long and 1 mile wide, as they migrate northward along the KwaZulu-Natal coast of eastern Africa. So much food brings a frenzy of predators: sharks, humpback whales, penguins, mackerel. If the timing is right, you can see the run one day and the Big Five Game the next, at Phinda Private Game Reserve.

Missed the run? Whales, dolphins, and turtles are always in residence, which means you can pair a morning marine safari with an afternoon game drive, thanks to Phinda's proximity to the sea. Buffalo, lions, leopards, elephants, and rhinos are part of the resident population on Phinda's 73,800 acres.

Unlike some other countries, where national parks dominate wildlife viewing, South Africa is a patchwork of public and private reserves, often abutting one another. One of the largest and most diverse is Phinda, home to seven distinct ecosystems, including wetlands, savannah, mountains, and woodlands. That variety translates into animals that aren't always seen in a single preserve, including hippos, giraffes, rhinos, zebras, spotted hyenas, and African wild dogs.

Most unique is its dry sand forest, which was once under the sea. Now, it is home to the elusive suni antelope, shimmering red-and-green trogon, 1,500-year-old Lebombo wattle trees, and shrubby sand apple. To minimize impact on this fragile land, preserve owner **&Beyond** created 16 glass suites that float on stilts above the forest floor. The central lodge and the suites feature floor to ceiling glass walls designed to make guests feel like they're sleeping inside the trees, but with the comforts of air-conditioning, modern bathrooms, pools, and a wine cellar rich in South African varietals.

The **Forest Lodge** is one of six &Beyond lodges within Phinda. While each setting is distinctive, all offer game drives with Zulu trackers and experienced rangers, bush walks, e-bikes, and interactions with the local communities.

Guests can also help monitor a reintroduced pangolin (a scaly anteater), collar an elephant for monitoring, or dehorn a rhino, devaluing it for poachers. Such experiences underscore how difficult protecting this environment can be.

Planning a Trip

The sardine run typically occurs between May and July. While prime game viewing is during the dry season of May to September, marine and animal experiences are offered at Phinda year-round.

Important: Children under 6 are not permitted on standard game drives at some lodges.

SCOTLAND

In the Far Isles

GREAT FOR	COST	WEBSITE
COUPLES, FAMILIES	$$$$$	GLENAPPCASTLE.COM

A minke whale leaps alongside the 42-foot launch, as if it were the official escort to Scotland's Hebridean Islands. With the aid of binoculars, sea otters come into view. But it's the birds that are the most frequent visitors: Oystercatchers, golden eagles, black guillemot, and fulmars are on the list. One of them, **Glenapp Castle's** own sea eagle, Ripley, rides atop the weather-proofed vessel, spreading her 7-foot wings as she soars on the hunt for her dinner.

Around you are miles of water dotted with rocky mounds, grass-covered cliffs, and pinnacles off Scotland's Atlantic Coast. About 500 isles are part of the Hebrides, though only about 100 are populated. The best known is Skye, home to the Old Man of Storr, a 180-foot-tall volcanic plug said to be a giant's thumb. On Mull, Finnegan's Cave feels like a natural cathedral, with basalt pillars and deep resonant acoustics. Other islands are home to 3-billion-year-old rocks, waterfalls, mountains, and grassland, prime hiking territory.

The archipelago's relative remoteness has given rise to unusually rich wildlife. Hardy black-fleeced Hebridean sheep roam the hills and moors, sometimes sprouting multiple Medusa-like horns. Gray seals, minke whales, and a variety of dolphins swim the sea.

Glenapp Castle's Hebridean Sea Safaris are oriented toward wildlife, hiking, and natural beauty. But each program is crafted to match visitors' passions. And if that includes 5,000-year-old rock circles, castle ruins, whiskey distilleries, and pubs rocking with the Gaelic music that was born here, so be it.

Itineraries start and end at 19th-century Glenapp Castle, fashioned with all the fantasy elements of battlements, turrets, and towers, and 17 suites lavishly furnished with antiques. During their safari, guests sleep in a glamping tent, set up Scottish-style with tartan blankets and candlelight. The private chef who is part of the safari team leans on local ingredients, such as lobster, halibut, and lamb, for picnic lunches and hot dinners.

Back at Glenapp, visitors can opt for country estate–style activities on the 110-acre grounds, including falconry, hiking, fishing, and field sports. Area nature reserves are home to deer, osprey, geese, and the coralroot orchid—not what you expect in a place where the high rarely goes above 50°F. Star-gazing excursions visit nearby Galloway Forest, recognized as a Dark Sky Park. While there's no golf course at Glenapp, Turnberry is only 30 minutes away. Because, aye, it's Scotland.

Planning a Trip

Glenapp Castle is about 90 minutes from Glasgow. The warmest months are May to October, when highs are 60°F and above. Rain is common, no matter what the month.

TOP LEFT: Viewing puffins on boat trip. TOP RIGHT: Glenapp Castle. MIDDLE: Tents at Sea Safari camp. BOTTOM LEFT: Learning about owls at Glenapp Castle. BOTTOM RIGHT: Hairy coos on Hebridean Sea Safari.

TOP LEFT: Leopard at Yala National Forest.
TOP RIGHT: Monkey at Yala National Forest.
BOTTOM LEFT: Guestroom, Leopard Trails Yala Camp.
BOTTOM RIGHT: Warthog at Leopard Trails Yala Camp.

Tracking Leopards

GREAT FOR	COST	WEBSITE
COUPLES, FAMILIES	$$	LEOPARDTRAILS.COM

A leopard feeds on a carcass on the ground—something you'd likely never see in Africa, where leopards protect their kill by hauling it into the trees. But in Sri Lanka, the leopard is the apex predator, with little to fear.

In Sri Lanka's wildlife preserves, leopards are accustomed to safari vehicles, which makes spotting them easier than in Africa. On the island's southeast coast, the open plains of **Yala National Park,** the country's most popular wildlife preserve, give them fewer places to hide. **Wilpattu National Park** in the northwest is more wooded, but larger, and with far fewer visitors.

Experts debate which park has the higher density of the endangered leopard, a unique subspecies that is stockier, bigger, and a deeper golden color than most leopards elsewhere. And while leopards generally are nocturnal, the Sri Lankan subspecies is more active during the day—a bonus for visitors who want to add them to their wildlife list.

So, which to visit—Yala or Wilpattu? Leopard Trails has camps at both, and a third mobile camp inside Kumana National Park. Founded on a passion for guiding, Leopard Trails has become a full-service hospitality company, with lodgings featuring comfortable beds, air-conditioned tents, and pools. Camps are no longer allowed within the parks, so all camps sit in adjacent buffer zones.

The Yala camp features eight tents, most with private plunge pools. Twice-daily game drives and boat safaris take guests in search of cats and such species as sloth bears, misnamed by an 18th-century zoologist who mistakenly thought that the fruit-and-bug-eating bears were related to sloths. Shaggy and a bit unkempt, they have a white collar that looks like a misguided fashion statement. Four species of mongooses also live here, including Indian gray cousins of the fictious Rikki-Tikki-Tavi. Among the 100 bird species are peacocks that belt out the daily wake-up call.

With one-tenth of the visitors, Wilpattu National Park offers a more secluded experience. It, too, has Asian elephants and sloth bears, along with wild boars, deer, two types of mongooses, hornbills and kingfishers, and monarch butterflies. After a heavy rain, Atukorale's dwarf toads, hourglass tree frogs, and Sri Lanka wood frogs strike up a match-making symphony. The purple-faced leaf monkey lives here, notable for its debonair white beard. As its name suggests, this primate eats leaves—though, alas, it is not really purple.

Planning a Trip

Along with wildlife, Sri Lanka offers beaches, ancient Buddhist and Hindu temples, tea plantations, and whale-watching. The country has four monsoon seasons that occur at varying times in different parts of the country. The best time for seeing leopards is the dry season, from May to September. (August is prime time.)

KENYA

Between Savanna & Sky

GREAT FOR	COST	WEBSITE
COUPLES, FAMILIES, MULTIPLE GENERATIONS	$$$$	ANGAMA.COM

From this perch some 1,000 feet above the valley of the Maasai Mara, it's easy for visitors to imagine they're experiencing a real-life *Out of Africa* moment—because they are. Lying on a checked blanket with bubbly in hand, guests watch cloud shadows dance on the tawny valley from the very spot where Meryl Streep and Robert Redford shared their own intimate repast.

Some 20 million years ago, the tectonic plates of Africa pulled apart and created the Oloololo Escarpment and the Great Rift Valley. **Angama Mara** sits atop the cliff, providing sweeping views of the wide plains. From lodge and tent decks cantilevered over the forest, elephants, buffalo, and giraffes are visible with the naked eye. With binoculars, guests can see antelopes, such as eland and impalas, and Thomson's gazelles springing through the savanna, not to mention screaming olive baboons.

Each of the 15 spacious tents is set on the cliff, offering views of balloons at sunrise through glass doors, an arrangement that allows the creak of canvas and smell of rain without the full force of gusting winds. With 1,000 square feet of space, there's plenty of room for bed, sitting area, bathroom, and tub with a view. The "butler's lobby" provides a place for jackets, boots, and morning-coffee delivery without disturbing guests.

A 10-minute drive in a safari vehicle brings guests into the valley, where stealthier creatures await. A lioness and her cubs lie in the tall grasses. Warthogs wiggle their bums. Jewel-toned Mara Rock lizards sun on the stones. Mischievous black-faced vervet monkeys traverse the savanna. Great herds of cape buffalo graze along the plain. Elephants amble by. Grunts and roars and trumpets punctuate the air, along with the whistles of blue-and-orange superb starlings and the raucous calls of the striped bateleur eagle. Between July and October, great herds of wildebeests and Grant's zebras plunge down the banks in river crossings as they migrate from Kenya to Tanzania, just 20 miles from Angama Mara.

The name *Angama* means "suspended in mid-air," which fits the camp's cliffside location. The goal, says Kate Boyd, daughter of founders Steve and Nicky Fitzgerald, is to provide a 3-D experience unavailable from photos or films. All the staff are Kenyan; about 70% are Maasai, including women who teach beading in the lodge studio and the garden butler who serves lunch in the vegetable garden.

Prefer to take meals on safari, in the library, by the pool, or in a lantern-lit forest? All can be arranged. Just ask.

***TOP:** Maasai men looking over Angama Mara.*
***MIDDLE:** Wildebeest migration at Angama Mara. **BOTTOM:** Maasai women do beadwork at Angama Mara.*

ANGAMA
MARA

Angama Mara at sunset.

Planning a Trip

Flights from Nairobi to the Angama airstrip take about 45 minutes; the drive to the camp takes about 6 hours. The wildlife migration takes place between July and October. Year-round residents include lions, buffalo, elephants, leopards, rhinos, giraffes, and some antelope species.

In addition to the mountainside lodge, Angama offers an intimate camp inside the Mara reserve and a 10-suite lodge in Amboseli National Park, with views of Mount Kilimanjaro. Tents include Wi-Fi.

AFRICA: MIX & MATCH LUXURY SAFARIS

If you're looking for well-run camps but don't necessarily want to stay with one brand, use a specialist travel advisor (see above) or a highly rated outfitter offering customized itineraries, such as **Go2Africa** (go2africa.com), **Infinite Safari Adventures** (infinitesafariadventures.com), **Roar Africa** (roarafrica.com), **Micato Safaris** (micato.com), **Thomson Safaris** (thomsonsafaris.com), and **Vaya Adventures** (vayaadventures.com).

I've also worked with **African Travel Resource** (africantravelresource.com), a highly knowledgeable online agency with offices in the United Kingdom and Africa that arranges custom tours at a wide variety of price points. All of its advisors have lived in Africa.

If you're in for a no-holds-barred splurge, consider a top company like **A&K** (abercrombiekent.com), **Singita** (singita.com), **Asilia** (asiliaafrica.com), or **&Beyond** (andbeyond.com). These companies will arrange all-inclusive experiences with internal transportation at camps they own and operate. **Serian** (serian.com) has several camps in Kenya and Tanzania; **Nomad** (nomad-tanzania.com) has several camps in Tanzania.

FACING PAGE, TOP LEFT: Guide at Angama Mara. TOP RIGHT: Lounge at Angama Mara. MIDDLE: Dancers at Angama Mara. BOTTOM: Safari in Maasai Mara.

CHAPTER 7

ON WORKING LAND: FARMS, VINEYARDS & RANCHES

> *The soil is the great connector of our lives, the source and destination of all.*
> *— Wendell Berry*
>
> *We are the children of our landscape. It dictates behavior and even thought in the measure to which we are responsive to it.*
> *— Lawrence George Durrell*

Horseback riding near Rumiñahui Volcano with Hacienda el Porvenir (p. 175).

BUTLER

OREGON, USA

Two for the Road

GREAT FOR	COST	WEBSITE
COUPLES; CHILDREN NOT ALLOWED	$$	ABBEYROADFARM.COM

Amid the hype of points ratings and appellations, it's easy to forget that wine comes from the earth. **Abbey Road Farm** is a good place to remember.

Morning starts as it does on farms everywhere: with the call of a rooster. A red tractor chugs through a field of vines. A flock of starlings soars overhead. A farmhand rolls up in a truck that looks like it might have come from the year the Beatles were born.

Donkeys and a trio of cows add farm charm to the 82 acres. But the reason most people come to Abbey Road, and the Willamette Valley, is wine, and the 700-plus vineyards that produce it.

It's a friendly corner of the world, more casual than California's Napa and Sonoma to the south. "Where Farm, Industry and Town Unite for Pleasant Living," proclaims the WPA-style poster plastered to the side of an old grain elevator in nearby Carlton, population 2,200. Tasting rooms, field-to-table restaurants, and an ice-cream shop line the main street.

Hazelnuts are grown here, too, but the king is the grape. Pinot Noir is the most famous varietal, but it's not the only fruit on the vines. At the tasting room on the Abbey Road Farm, guests sip chardonnay, Tempranillo, and cabernet franc from the Abbey Road and Wilkins Family labels as they nosh on a charcuterie board of local cheeses and meats.

Across the vegetable garden sits a trio of grain silos fused to create Abbey Road's B&B. The covered deck opens into the seating area and a self-serve bar fit for a stylish boutique hotel. To the right and left are two suites each—one on the ground floor, the other up a curved staircase—overlooking a rose garden outside our window and green hills beyond. In the rooms: a big iron bed, wood trimmed chairs, wooden floors, and curved walls.

Come morning, the rooster beckons guests to breakfast on the porch of the main house. Fried chicken and waffles with maple-cherry syrup are topped with shaved parmesan. Granola with house-made whipped yogurt and blueberries is drizzled with chocolate mint yuzu.

Maybe it's a good thing we can only stay 1 night. Or not.

Planning a Trip

Willamette Valley lies an hour south of Portland. Temperatures are generally mild; cooler months from November to March typically bring rain. Any time of year, you'll likely want a jacket.

Abbey Road Farm features a tasting room open to the public. Overnight stays come with a sumptuous breakfast.

***TOP:* Enjoying wine from Abbey Road Farm vineyards. *MIDDLE:* Entrance to Abbey Road Farm silos. *BOTTOM:* B&B suite at Abbey Road Farm.**

MONTANA, USA

A Dude Ranch for Every Age

GREAT FOR	COST	WEBSITE
ACTIVE COUPLES, FAMILIES OF ALL AGES	$$$	LONEMOUNTAINRANCH.COM

The town of **Big Sky** is a modern place, created to serve hikers, skiers, and gallerygoers in the 1970s by late broadcaster Chet Huntley. Fifty years later, it's home to sushi restaurants, resorts, and a sleek hospital that serves the 2,000 full-timers and the visitors who come to play in the curve of the Rockies, summer and winter.

Just minutes up the hill lies a far different world, where winter sleigh rides deliver guests to an evening of huckleberry cobbler and storytelling, and summer barrel racing is a weekly event.

For its first dozen years, Lone Mountain Ranch was a working cattle ranch. In 1927, spruce-and-juniper forest and proximity to **Yellowstone National Park** caught the attention of Chicago paper-mill tycoon J. Fred Butler, and since the late 1920s, Lone Mountain Ranch has been a ranch-away-from-home for guests of one sort of another who come to ride or hike through fields filled with glacier lilies and old-growth forests of lodgepole pines and Douglas firs. It's impossible to know where The ranch's own 148 acres end and the surrounding **Gallatin National Forest** begins. It doesn't really matter. It's all nature's playground, filled with waterfalls (nearby Ousel Falls is a favorite), trout streams, biking trails, rock faces, protected lakes, whitewater canyons, and peaks 11,000 feet high.

These days, the check-in cabin is near the barn—a reminder that in the West, a horse is your best friend. From there, you head up through the meadow and over the small river bridge to your cabin, one of 25 built by Butler for his city guests. A basket of petunias hangs on the deck, near a stack of wood for the heating stove inside. Jack London's *Call of the Wild* and Henry David Thoreau's *Walden* rest on the bedside table. A record player and a stack of 331/3 rpms are nearby, though the idea of playing the Peter Frampton album on the table seems a bit jarring.

After a 2-hour horse ride through tall grass surrounded by mountains, having dinner at Lone Mountain Ranch's Horn & Cantle sounds so much better. Fondue, trout rillette, and rigatoni with wild-game bolognese are on the menu. Summer is prime time for families, with river rafting, fly-fishing, bull riding at the Tuesday-night rodeo, and balloon rides over Gallatin Valley. A herd of 100 horses is on hand for daily rides under the eye of watchful wranglers. Yellowstone National Park begins just 18 miles away; curious guests who want to deeply understand the caldera's steaming mud pots and spouting geysers can sign up for private excursions.

Bitterroot room at Lone Mountain Ranch.

Riding in Gallatin National Forest.

In winter, the land takes on a rugged magic. Horse rides give way to dog sleds, snowmobiles, and sleigh rides. Ice climbing takes over frozen Ousel Falls. Yellowstone's summer crowds disappear, and park visitors have the strange dichotomy of snow-rimmed hot springs to themselves. Downhill skiing at Big Sky and cross-country at Lone Mountain Ranch? There's that, too.

Planning a Trip

Lone Mountain Ranch is about an hour south of Bozeman, the closest airport, and an hour north of West Yellowstone. Bed and breakfast packages are offered some days, but often a minimum stay is required. Multiday packages including meals and activities are also offered.

FACING PAGE, TOP: *Fly-fishing at Lone Mountain Ranch.*
BOTTOM: *Horse stable at Lone Mountain Ranch.*

ITALY

In the Tuscan Hills

GREAT FOR	COST	WEBSITE
COUPLES, FAMILIES WITH CURIOUS CHILDREN	$$$	VILLA-LENA.IT

Forget the pigs. When hunting for white truffles in the humid forest soil of **Villa Lena,** dogs do the work because they're easier to manage. But even the keenest dogs may turn one way and find nothing, then come back the same way and alert. Explains owner Lena Evstafieva, "The truffle needed that extra 30 minutes to release the scent."

Autumn truffle hunts, walks in the forest, gardens filled with tulips and dahlias, and organically grown vegetables are part of the Villa Lena experience. At heart, this 1,200-acre estate is about art—art made by nature, and art made by man.

Evstafieva took over the crumbling Tuscan estate in 2007, envisioning a retreat where guests could engage with the creative process that inspired her own career as an art professional at a Moscow-based nonprofit and a commercial gallery in London: "I wanted people to experience that magic that I was seeing when I was working with the artists, that I felt was actually missing when the show went up on the walls in a gallery or museum."

When Villa Lena opened in 2013, it combined agritourism with artist residencies, providing workshops where guests could express their own creativity. Visitors sometimes collect flowers and make dyes before trying their hand at illustrations with a floral artist. A chef leads visits to the expansive garden, where guests gather produce and then return to the kitchen to transform it into a meal. When there's a writer in residence, they may take guests to a serene overlook to practice creative journaling. Resident artists live in the 19th-century villa, while guests stay in renovated rooms, villas, and apartments dotted across the estate.

At Villa Lena, the art of nature is always at hand. Guests bike and hike through the poplars, oaks, and cypress trees that create conditions needed for truffles. On forest walks, they look for stags and giant porcupines stretching more than 2 feet long. They picnic in the olive grove that produces the foundation for Villa Lena's own peppery olive oil and stroll the vineyards that give birth to the estate-made Sangiovese wine. Estate grounds include a medieval park at one of the highest points in Tuscany, where princes of the region once met to negotiate disputes. For those craving more inspiration, the museums of Florence and Pisa are just an hour away.

Planning a Trip

Airports in Florence and Pisa are about an hour away; the closest train station is at Pontedera, about a half-hour drive. The hotel can arrange transportation.

TOP LEFT: Arranging flowers at Villa Lena. TOP RIGHT: Exterior of Villa Lena. MIDDLE LEFT: View of olive orchards from Villa Lena. MIDDLE RIGHT: Pool at Villa Lena. BOTTOM LEFT: Entrance way of Villa Lena. BOTTOM RIGHT: Guestroom at Villa Lena.

TOP: *Mountain biking at Hacienda el Porvenir.*
MIDDLE LEFT: *Game room at Hacienda el Porvenir.*
MIDDLE RIGHT: *Cotopaxi Master Suite at Hacienda el Porvenir.*
BOTTOM: *Llama and boy, Hacienda el Porvenir.*

At a Historic Hacienda

GREAT FOR	COST	WEBSITE
COUPLES, FAMILIES, ACTIVE TRAVELERS	$	TIERRADELVOLCAN.COM

More than 100 years ago, when Jorge Perez's family bought Hacienda El Porvenir, south of Quito, only rancheros and herders ventured onto this rural Andean mountainside. While the mushrooming city is growing ever closer, Hacienda El Porvenir retains traditional ways.

Once a year, *chagras* from area farms gather in the corral. In leather chaps and wool ponchos, they honor Pachamama with a swig of locally distilled alcohol—and a health pour for Mama Earth. The ritual complete, they canter up the slope of Ruminahui Volcano to drive the farm's 380 cows to lower ground for the coming winter. Perez's family gathers by the fire in the antiques-filled living room, warming for the hearty barbecue that will follow.

In 1999, Perez and his wife, Maria Jose Andrade, opened the hacienda to adventure-oriented guests heading to snow-capped Cotopaxi, one of the world's highest active volcanoes and namesake of the national park just a few miles away. Boots lined up in the alcove hint at popular on-site activities—horse riding, hiking, and mountain and e-biking. On a clear day, the cones of four volcanoes are visible from the property.

Guest rooms rim the hacienda courtyard and include spacious suites in the historic house, doubles with private bath, and bunk rooms with shared bath. Rates include a hearty breakfast. Other meals are offered a la carte and feature sophisticated Ecuadorian fare with modern twists, including soups, steak, and vegetarian dishes.

An afternoon horse ride over the grassy slopes takes guests to a gusty 12,500 feet, where they'll be happy they dressed in the chaps and ponchos provided. With a lodge guide or on their own, they can drive to **Cotopaxi National Park** for a hike.

Or they could learn to cook an Andean dish from farm-grown ingredients. Cinnamon, sugar, and a cloud-forest fruit called *naranjilla* become the warm drink called *canelazo*. Chiles are ground in a mortar and sprinkled with coriander for salsa. Flour, salt, sugar, and milk are mixed into the stiff dough for empanadas and then filled with cheese and twisted closed for frying. With a little practice, the edges on the dough pockets are almost as pretty as the teacher's. Almost.

Planning a Trip

Ecuador maintains relatively even temperatures year-round, with highs around 60°F in Quito. Conditions widely depend on the altitude. In the Andes, clear views and strong winds are expected June through August.

Their company, **Tierra del Volcan,** has two other rural lodges. It offers trips throughout the country and historic home rentals.

MONTANA

Grab Your Stetson & Ride Along

GREAT FOR	COST	WEBSITE
COUPLES, FAMILIES	$$	320RANCH.COM

Here's the kind of thing you can learn at a place like 320 Guest Ranch from a guy like Morgan Cryster, who has worked here for decades: Mix one part silicon and two parts mineral spirits, and it can waterproof just about anything—boots and cowboy hat included.

His hat looks like it's seen a few miles. It's a Stetson, he confirms, but not a fussy one. Bought it years ago at Murdoch's, a no-nonsense ranch-supply store up the road in Four Corners.

Such practicality is a by-product of life in the Old West. Though the slick town of **Big Sky** is just 12 miles down the road, 320 Guest Ranch retains the feel of its 125-year history. To encourage settlement in the West, in 1862, Congress passed the Homestead Act that promised 160 acres of Montana land to anyone who lived on it for 5 years. A father and son each claimed their share in the **Gallatin Valley,** a total of 320 acres, and 320 Guest Ranch was born.

Some 40 years later, Montana's first female physician, Dr. Caroline McGill, bought the place as a medical retreat for her patients, where they could be soothed by nature. And while you don't need a doctor's prescription to come here now, 320 is still a place where a person can breathe in clean air and find a taste of simpler times.

Out by the barn, guests pet the friendly dog and mount well-schooled mares for a gentle trail ride through columbines and lupines. If they're lucky, they spot a moose or elk along a brook or amid the ponderosa forest. Hawks occasionally appear overhead, hunting for their next meal.

At the nearby farm pond, a boy shorter than his fishing pole learns to cast with the help of a ranch wrangler. Once he's sharpened his form and hooked a few trout, he is ready to try the brook that edges the property—the same stream used in the film *A River Runs Through It.*

The original log homestead is now McGill's Restaurant and Saloon, where guests throw their Stetsons on the table and dine on elk wontons with herbed cheese, arugula salad, and bison short ribs. When they ease up from the table, they can shoot a round of pool and chat with fellow guests.

When you move to your cabin porch, you begin to understand why they call this place Big Sky. Even a novice stargazer can pick out the Big Dipper, so close you can almost touch it. The Milky Way lights the path across the universe, a hundred billion stars sparkling along the way to restful dreams.

Planning a Trip

320 Guest Ranch is an hour south of the closest airport, in Bozeman, on the way to West Yellowstone; it's well suited to families with younger children ages 4 and up. Horse-riding reservations should be made as soon as you book your room. Activities and meals are a la carte. A weekly horse ride and barbecue is held Wednesdays in summer.

TOP LEFT: *Buffalo in Big Sky Montana.* TOP RIGHT: *Grounds of 320 Guest Ranch in Big Sky.* BOTTOM: *Horseback riding at 320 Guest Ranch.*

TOP: *Llamas and sheep in front of guestrooms at Iron Creek Bay Estate.* BOTTOM LEFT: *Tasmanian wombat.* BOTTOM RIGHT: *Guestroom at Iron Creek Bay Estate.*

TASMANIA, AUSTRALIA

On a Farm by the Sea

GREAT FOR	COST	WEBSITE
SOLOS, COUPLES, FAMILIES, GROUPS	$	IRONCREEKBAY.COM.AU.

The bucolic scene off the balcony includes ducks, sheep, llamas, alpacas, ponies, and a vineyard overlooking **Iron Creek Bay.** All I can think about is something I can't see: wombats.

A friend and I have spent the day wandering among wombats in the groomed green meadows of Tasmania's Maria Island, a former penal colony–turned–national park. Reached by boat, the island is a surprisingly peaceful place of sea-worn cliffs and eucalyptus trees and the drafty remains of brick barracks that once housed prisoners convicted of crimes including army desertion, political dissonance, and theft of a pan.

It's also a wildlife reserve, home to pademelon, birds, and the elusive Tasmanian devil. But it's the lumbering wombats—flat-faced hamsterlike creatures the size of a West Highland terrier—that fascinate. The sentiment obviously is not shared; the wombats continually turn their backsides to visitors.

Sleeping near them is out of the question; drafty on-island rooms house bunks only. Better to head back on the ferry.

An hour later, we arrive at Iron Creek Bay, a historic waterfront winery and farm east of Hobart. Settled in the 1830s, the family who owned the farm raised sheep, dairy cattle, and fruit. Its next owners added Riesling grapes for wine. In 2016, the current owners stepped in, adding 10,000 fruit trees, a restaurant, and stilted lodging units with private suites and hotel rooms finished in clear, smooth wood.

Vines lead to the paddock, where friendly sheep and llamas climb up to greet whoever wanders by. Alas, no wombats. For those, we must drive a half-hour to Bonorong Wildlife Sanctuary, home to Tassie devils, kangaroos, blue-tongued lizards, and echidnas. A naturalist there plays with a sweet, cuddly wombat, and I wonder what I've done wrong.

Then, she explains: This wombat is still a baby. After about age 2, wombats become downright snide. When threatened, they put their heads into their earthen dens, blocking the entrance with their hindquarters. Their rumps are so strong and thick that they can actually kill a predator by smashing its skull against the roof of the burrow.

Now we understand their island behavior. Best to keep our distance.

Planning a Trip

Iron Creek Bay is about 15 minutes from the airport. The farm animals are friendly to children, and the grounds include a play area. Its restaurant, Orani, is open for breakfast and lunch and seasonally for dinner.

PORTUGAL

A Night in a Barrel

GREAT FOR	COST	WEBSITE
COUPLES	$$	QUINTADAPACHECA.COM

Wineries are mystical places where humble fruit is transformed into exquisite potions, fit for a champagne farewell on a Casablanca runway or Hannibal Lector's discerning palate. Unlike produce eaten straight from the vine, wine requires time, finesse, and sorcery that can easily go sideways.

The mystery of this complex transformation explains the appeal of sleeping amid the vines. Wineries from Chile to California, France to Spain, offer art-filled boutique hotels where guests can sip on rare vintages chosen to accompany fresh gourmet fare. But at **Quinta da Pacheca**, they can actually sleep inside a barrel—a barrel-shaped room, that is.

These 240-square-foot curved wood-lined pods were built as guest rooms, with a king bed, bathroom, skylight for star-watching, and, yes, air-conditioning. The round window at the foot of the bed swings open to a deck set with a pair of chairs flanked by olive trees.

The barrel-shaped lodgings are unique, much like the pioneering woman who bottled the region's first private label wine in the 1730s, and for whom this place is named. In Portuguese, the feminine format "da" honors Mariana Pacheco Pereira. (If the owner had been a man, it would have been Quinta do Pacheco.) Today, these 175 acres overlooking the Douro River are filled with Touriga Franca and Tinta Barroca grapes and olives producing lusty oil.

Visitors focused on convenience may prefer the vineyard's **Wine House Hotel,** either in the original 18th-century building opened to guests in 2009 or the contemporary wing opened in 2020. But they miss the morning songs of chaffinches and treecreepers, the breeze cupping their face, and the scents of lavender and herbs.

Though the region is best known for its ports, guests can also taste Quinta da Pacheca's grand reserves, the red touriga and the white cuvée of Arinto, Gouveio, and Viosinho. The wines are deeper and smoother than we expect, and before long, we're ordering a case for delivery at home.

Good thing we're staying in a barrel instead of driving.

Planning a Trip

Quinta da Pacheca sits in the Douro River Valley, about 1½ hours west of Porto. Its 175 acres comprise the winery, vegetable garden, 37 acres of vines, tasting room, hotel with spa, and restaurants. Cooking classes are offered. In the fall, guests can help with the harvest.

TOP: Interior of Wine Barrel room at Quinta da Pacheca.
BOTTOM LEFT: Aerial view of Wine Barrel rooms at Quinta da Pacheca.
BOTTOM RIGHT: Wine Barrel room at Quinta da Pacheca.

TOP LEFT: Exterior of silo. TOP RIGHT: Bedroom in silo at Clark Farm. BOTTOM LEFT: Kitchenette inside silo guestroom. BOTTOM RIGHT: Aerial view of Clark Farm Silos.

MONTANA, USA

The Ultimate Bin

GREAT FOR	COST	WEBSITE
COUPLES, SMALL FAMILIES	$$	CLARKFARMSILOS.COM

At last, the amber waves of grain and purple mountain majesties appear. They're just outside the corrugated walls of your Montana silo.

From the chair on the small porch, guests watch as the Rockies darken into a blackberry blue. The wheatgrass around the vintage tractor shimmers in the waning light. As the sky turns red, a cow bellows in a nearby field. "It's so peaceful," says a neighbor, and I have to agree.

These 5 acres between Kalispell and Glacier National Park feel about as far from the hubbub as a person can get. That's exactly what Eli Clark had in mind when he set aside this patch from the 160 acres of his family's fifth-generation farm and brought five grain silos from Idaho to repurpose into lodgings.

From the outside, the silos look like soup cans topped with the Tin Man's cone-shaped hat. Inside, the bi-level layout reflects a thoughtful approach shaped by Clark's background as a graphic designer. French doors open to a kitchenette counter and a separate bathroom. A sofa and hassock are set beneath the curving wooden stair. In the loft, a king bed rests on the clean wood floor beneath the conical roof finished in the same light wood.

The location is 30 miles outside Glacier National Park, still ruggedly beautiful despite crowds and receding glaciers. The park's 1,580 square miles are the watersheds for the Atlantic, Pacific, and Hudson Bay, swooping from 10,466 feet to 3,150 feet of elevation, creating more than 200 waterfalls along the way. Soils crafted by volcanoes, glaciers, and water movement nourish a wide array of plants: ferns, conifers, grasses, pale ghost flowers, and bug-eating butterworts. Local residents include bighorn sheep, bear, elk, moose, and pygmy shrews.

Nearly 3 million people come here each summer to hike, fish, and drive the park's iconic Going to the Sun Road. In that busy time, the park lodges are nearly always filled; the best bets for serenity are camping in the rough or sleeping in chalets reached only by foot. Better to drive back to the silos and watch the hay grow.

Planning a Trip

Clark Farm Silos are open year-round. The closest airport is about 30 minutes away in Kalispell, home to restaurants, groceries, and drugstores. The silos are about 30 minutes from the entrance to Glacier National Park and a similar distance to upscale Whitefish.

Those driving into Glacier Park should reserve entry and any tours well in advance. Red Bus Tours in restored 1930s cars are especially popular; book at glaciernationalparklodges.com. Going to the Sun Road is open only in summer, and even then is sometimes closed due to weather and construction. The free park shuttle is the best bet for avoiding traffic. The park's website (nps.gov/glac) has updated information.

Puglia, Please

GREAT FOR	COST	WEBSITE
COUPLES, FAMILIES, FOODIES	$$$	MASSERIATORRECOCCARO.COM

A farmhand leads the way through the yard and points to the picturesque scene of goats in a pasture. A bar worker follows a guest across a plaza to be sure directions to the cathedral are clear. A police officer stops traffic to point the way to Roman ruins.

In Puglia, helpfulness is a way of life. So is food, gloriously delicious and just plucked from the fields and sea. Pass the fava beans drenched in local olive oil and ricotta topped with pickled celery, please.

Despite its recent growth in popularity, Puglia gets fewer than 10% of Italy's visitors. Most of those head for the UNESCO World Heritage town of Alberobello, a hilly 15th-century village where rows of pointy-topped houses called trulli—1,000 in all—sit hip-to-elbow up slopes and sharp ridges. (Their distinctive style derives from a medieval scheme to avoid taxes by building only with dry stone.)

Other nearby visitor meccas include the baroque marvels of Galatina and Lecce, with its Roman amphitheater. The Adriatic towns of Polignano a Mare and Bari are famed for history, beaches, and, of course, food. (Don't miss the ice cream in Polignano a Mare.) A highlight is the cave city of Matera, which is the third-longest continually inhabited city on the planet, in the neighboring region of Basilicata.

Above all, Puglia is an agricultural haven, which is why you want to stay in a *masseria*, a farmhouse converted to a countryside hotel where the cheeses are made by a neighbor, the carrots grown on the farm, and the olives from the tree outside your door.

At **Masseria Torre Coccaro,** those olive groves are 800 years old. They surround the pool, ringed by hand-set stone walls. Sauna and massage take place in an ancient cave. Dinner is served in a vaulted room that served as a 16th-century stable. Zucchini, fennel, artichokes, and eggplant were grown in a garden first cultivated in the 17th century.

I waddle to my private garden and think I should have chosen a tower room, where at least I'd get exercise climbing the stairs. At this rate, I'll never fit in my swimsuit or make it to the hotel's two beach clubs. The sacrifice is worth it.

Planning a Trip

Weather in Puglia is mild most of the year, though like the rest of Europe, it can be scorching in July and August. The closest airports are in Bari and Brindisi. To tour the region, you will need a car.

Masseria Torre Coccaro is one of a dozen highly rated farmhouses-turned-hotels in Puglia. Amenities include two beach clubs, spa, indoor and outdoor pools, and cooking classes. A number of other *masserias* have been converted to vacation rentals.

TOP: *Olive oil factory at Masseria Torre Coccaro.* MIDDLE: *Pool at Jasmine Villa at Masseria Torre Coccaro.* BOTTOM: *Entrance to cooking school at Masseria Torre Coccaro.*

TOP: Bathtub in guestroom at Rancho Santana.
MIDDLE LEFT: Sea turtles at Rancho Santana.
MIDDLE: Pink spoonbill at Rancho Santana.
MIDDLE RIGHT: The stables at Rancho Santana.
BOTTOM: Restaurant at Rancho Santana.

Colonial Style & Surf Breaks, Too

GREAT FOR	COST	WEBSITE
SURFERS, COUPLES, FAMILIES	$$$	RANCHOSANTANA.COM

If your family had a generations-old hacienda by the sea, it would be **Rancho Santana.**

The day begins the way it ends: with waves crashing rhythmically against the worn lava rocks, a surfer surveying the swells, and long-tailed songbirds whistling from the palms in the groomed garden outside your balcony. Just down the beach, a red wooden boat returns from a night of fishing; a half-dozen men haul it ashore.

This corner of Nicaragua is tucked in a wrinkle in time. In the nearby town of Tola, and even in bigger Rivas, farm carts are pulled by oxen; bicycles are loaded with firewood. Locals greet visitors with a friendly *buen dia*—a surprise, given Nicaragua's authoritarian government and travel warnings by the U.S. State Department.

Rancho is something of a world unto itself: 2,700 wooded acres with five pristine beaches, four restaurants, riding stables, livestock farm, organic garden, and its own K–12 school. An on-site wood mill and shop build furniture and custom homes.

It's a seismic shift from the 1990s, when five surfers came to the area on vacation and fell so in love with the place that they pooled resources to buy it from a local family. All five still have homes on property.

The 17-room stone inn bears the hallmarks of colonialism, with thick stucco walls, wood-beamed ceilings, and a central courtyard shaded by a "rain" tree whose leaves fold as a storm approaches. But looks are deceiving; the inn was added only in 2015, replacing a four-room hotel. Spacious rooms with high ceilings are filled with heavy wooden doors and dark wood furniture. Wide terraces are roofed for shade and angled for breezes and sunset views—an alternative for those too lazy to head to the beach.

A bridge across a narrow river links the hacienda to four two-story condo buildings added in 2023. Private homes are set on lots behind the inn, tucked into wooded grounds home to howler monkeys, yellow-bellied chickadees, and iridescent motmots.

Rancho's five beaches remain untouched, preserved for sea turtles, dune surfing, and the swells of some of the planet's most famous waters. The surf's always up.

Planning a Trip

The dry season of November to May is prime time throughout Nicaragua. Rancho Santana is near the beach town of Popoyo on the Pacific Coast, about 65 miles south of Managua and 50 miles north of the border crossing to Costa Rica. Rancho Santana can arrange private transportation from either entry point. A new Pacific highway scheduled to open by 2026 will speed the trip.

Nearby San Juan del Sur is the center of Pacific surf action, with waves up to 20 feet.

MONTANA

An Artful Ranch

GREAT FOR	COST	WEBSITE
ACTIVE COUPLES, FAMILIES WITH CHILDREN OVER 16	$$$$$	TRIPLECREEKRANCH.COM

An elk lingers by the covered wooden entryway. It turns out it's a welded metal statue by Russell Lamb—one of 1,500 Western artworks at **Triple Creek Ranch.**

The breadth and depth of the collection here could easily fill a museum. A 3-D painting of cowboys lurking for a gunfight, the twig horsehead inlaid with a geode, the cowgirl with the neon gun. Paintings by such classic artists as Charles M. Russell and Alfred Bierstadt.

But for most ranch guests, the art collection is a minor frill. They come here for the crisp scent of fresh pine and the creak of leather saddles and leather armchairs. For the adventures of cattle drives and whitewater rafting and steelhead fishing, and the hope that maybe, just maybe, they'll find something shimmering and flawless when they pan for sapphires. They come here to scrub off the city and get right with themselves.

When Craig Barrett, former Intel chair, and his wife, Barbara, bought Triple Creek in 1993, it already welcomed guests to the mountain-rimmed Bitterroot Valley west of Butte. The Barretts added 26,000 acres nearby, for a total of 27,000 acres where visitors can ride across grassy hills looking for elk and deer, learn leatherworking and candlemaking, and snowshoe in winter. They can even golf.

Lewis and Clark came through here as they charted a path to the West but ultimately found the "River of No Return," as they called Idaho's Salmon River, too challenging and switched routes. Ranch guests can get a hint of what that 1800s expedition might have experienced on a saddle-to-paddle day, riding above the tree line for views of the Continental Divide and then kayaking on the Salmon River. As in the explorers' time, eagles and osprey soar overhead while big-horn sheep clamber on the rocks. But modern guests get transportation and a sumptuous lunch that Lewis and Clark could only have dreamed of.

When the day is done, it's time to feast again, but this time, a gourmet menu of fiddlehead ferns and pheasant awaits in the lodge. If that seems like too much effort, the staff will deliver dinner to your log cabin in the pines.

Planning a Trip

Triple Creek Ranch is open year-round. It can arrange transportation for the 2-hour ride from the Missoula airport. Rates include all meals, on-site activities, and evening programs.

***TOP:* Dog sledding at Triple Creek Ranch.**
***MIDDLE LEFT:* Horses at Triple Creek Ranch.**
***MIDDLE RIGHT:* North Star cabin at Triple Creek Ranch.**
***BOTTOM:* Rafting at Triple Creek Ranch.**

CHAPTER 8

GLAMPING: CAMPING WITH COMFORTS

Everything is made out of Magic, leaves and trees, flowers and birds, badgers and foxes and squirrels and people. So it must be all around us. In this garden—in all the places.
— Frances Hodgson Burnett

I haven't been everywhere, but it's on my list.
— Susan Sontag

Aerial view of Open Sky (p. 219).

UTAH, USA

On the Staircase

GREAT FOR	COST	WEBSITE
COUPLES, FAMILIES, FRIENDS	$	OFLAND.COM

Signs for Grand Staircase-Escalante National Monument appear, and I keep wondering where it is. Then, I catch on: We've been on it for days as we've visited the North Rim of the Grand Canyon, Zion National Park, past the Chocolate and Vermillion Cliffs, over the Glen Canyon, to Bryce Canyon. "Steps" of as much as 2,000 vertical feet rise between plateaus, creating a 100-mile-long staircase stretching 150 miles wide. The sandstone cliffs and improbably balanced rocks and pinnacles are layers in a 50-million-year-long story of deposits, uplift, and erosion.

The Staircase has plenty of campsites, but few towns or lodgings beyond the national parks.

One of the few is Escalante, population about 825. Just 2 miles west is **Ofland Escalante,** an unconventional collection of tiny houses, self-contained cabins, vintage Airstreams, and campsites on 20 acres. A pool and hot tub, general store, and Wi-Fi make this a convenient base for exploring rugged landscapes.

It's a friendly place where visitors hang out under the covered pavilion and chat with people they otherwise might not meet: hipsters, bikers, families, seniors, between-jobbers who haven't yet decided what their next chapter might entail. Those without kitchens—which is most visitors—stop at the food truck or preorder a grill-it-yourself meal kit for two, with protein, veg, bread, and s'mores.

We're in a deluxe cabin—the top end of facilities here, with an en suite bathroom, comfortable queen bed, sleeper sofa, private outdoor shower, heating and air-conditioning, minifridge, and microwave. Parking is adjacent to our cabin. We take a look in the tiny cabins, which look just as comfortable, but smaller, and without a bathroom. The shared bath house is clean and spalike.

Conversation invariably turns to nearby natural sites—"Is Capitol Reef worth it?" "Oh my, yes! Don't miss the pie shop"—and the evening's featured movie at the on-campus drive-in (not a place you actually drive and park your car, but a pro cot lot where you buy popcorn from the Airstream snack stand and choose your seat in a convertible Corvair, pickup truck, apple-green Rambler, or lilac Studebaker, all from an earlier era).

At Ofland, we feel like we're, too, from an earlier, simpler era. It's a good thing.

Zion National Park.

Planning a Trip

Ofland Escalante is open from mid-March to late October. It is situated between Bryce and Capitol Reef National Parks. Several accessible units are offered.

DEFINING *GLAMPING*

As a term, *glamping* officially entered the English language in 2005, defined as "glamorous camping." In real terms, it's camping with the comfort of a bed, toilet, and shower. Whether those toilet and shower facilities will actually be in your tent or cabin is another subject.

Glamping resorts range from luxurious canvas cabins with plush robes, Frette linens, en suite bathrooms, and butler service to the motel equivalent of bare-bones rooms elbow-to-elbow, with a single shared bath house three rows away. Some cost less than $150 per night for a room and a cup of coffee. Others are priced at thousands per night and include three gourmet meals per day and guided safaris on private reserves.

Here are questions you should ask before booking. Often, you'll find the answers online, but be sure to ask about anything that is unclear:

- What is included in the rate?
- What are the camp's opening dates? (Some are year-round camps; others are seasonal.)
- What is the setting? How far are you from the road? (Some are so close to the highway that road noise is inevitable.)
- How many units does the camp have, and on how many acres? How far apart are tents/cabins? (You really don't want to hear your neighbors.)
- Are tents air-conditioned? Heated? Do they have fans or gas fires?
- Are sheets, pillows, and towels included? (In most cases, the answer is yes.)
- Where is the bathroom? Is it private or shared?
- Does the tent have electricity? Where can you charge devices?
- Is there Wi-Fi and cellphone coverage?
- Are pets allowed?
- Is there a pool? Clubhouse? Restaurant or bar? Programming, such as music or kids' games?
- Is it child-friendly or oriented toward couples?
- Is there an on-site concierge who can help arrange activities, or do you need to do that in advance?
- Is the situation suitable for people with limited mobility?
- Is there first-aid treatment on site?

***TOP LEFT:* Rock climbing at Devils Garden near Ofland Escalante.**
***TOP RIGHT:* Interior of room at Ofland Escalante.**
***MIDDLE:* Firepit at Ofland Escalante.**
***BOTTOM:* Drive-in theater.**

WISCONSIN, USA

Glass Houses

GREAT FOR	COST	WEBSITE
COUPLES, SMALL GROUPS	$$$	ANAWAY.COM

A firefly embraces a maple bough. A trillion stars glimmer overhead. The cabin deck is an amphitheater where every avian voice becomes a solo, clear and distinct, yet still part of a chorus.

These 110 acres outside the small town of Richland Center, Wisconsin, are an unexpected place for six exquisitely sculpted cottages. And yet here we are, in a curved hilltop cabin, listening to the cicadas and whippoorwills and lullabies of heaven-knows-what other birds, wondering how this two-story glass house landed here.

And it's not the only one. Just down the hill, amid the maples and walnuts, a cabin surrounded by glass sits beneath a vaulted wood ceiling, with a queen bed, kitchenette, and gas fireplace to keep guests cozy in winter. The bi-level Woodland House is a case of silo meets castle, with a tower and spiral staircase. And in the meadow, surrounded by wildflowers, sits a glass cottage as miraculous as Cinderella's crystal coach, minus the mousy footmen.

The original 80 acres of **Anaway Place** were a family legacy offered to four sons. Norbert, a contractor who lived locally, eventually bought out his brothers and sought to preserve the land, in part by creating rental cottages. A conventionally styled rental cabin became two. His rescue of 32 insulated glass panels spurred a different type of cabin that seemed to be part of the landscape itself. "This is a stupid idea," he recalls saying at the time. "But when that glass house hit the website, we suddenly were a thing. We were on to something. It was about getting really close to nature without being in it."

Each sensitive, precise design came from Norbert's long building experience, with interiors fashioned by his wife, Susan, and their daughter. Two more glass houses are in the works—but Norbert won't be building them. When retirement beckoned, he and his family sold Anaway to a Chicago-area couple, Chris and Lindsay, who were past guests. The new owners have created two new designs that have met with Norbert's approval. They've maintained the gourmet shop and coffee bar beneath the barn and added a small event space and massage studio.

In the next few years, guests headed for trout fishing, kayaking, hiking, orchard visits, or a tour to the nearby Frank Lloyd Wright–designed warehouse will return to Anaway to find eight cabins, a pond, the four barn bedrooms now available, and an additional four bedrooms in the farmhouse for groups.

***TOP:* Hillside room at Anaway Place.**
***BOTTOM:* Living room at Anaway Place.**

But if they're like Chris and Lindsay when they first visited, many guests will never leave the grounds. Notes Lindsay, "Most people are looking for a place where they can come unplug, where they can have a unique and beautiful experience and reconnect to the things that matter to them the most."

Planning a Trip

Richmond Center is about midway between Chicago and Minneapolis. The drive from either point takes about 3½ hours. Milwaukee is an hour closer. Two-night minimums are usually required.

FACING PAGE, TOP: Exterior of building at Anaway Place. BOTTOM: Sunset at Meadow House, Anaway Place.
THIS PAGE, TOP: Bathroom in guestroom at Anaway Place. BOTTOM: Glass house at Anaway Place.

ARIZONA, USA

Silence near the Canyon

GREAT FOR	COST	WEBSITE
COUPLES, FAMILIES	$$$	TRAVELBACKLAND.COM

The Grand Canyon is everything its name implies—and far too grand for a single visit. Every time our route passes nearby, my husband insists we veer to one viewpoint or another. Though I've seen the canyon from mule, helicopter, and footpath, I can never describe its vastness or its beauty. As astronaut Jack Schmitt said about both the canyon and space, you have to be there to know what it's really like.

Each year, some 5 million people come to see it for themselves. Though the national park covers 1,900 square miles, this place can feel less than serene—especially in summer. **Backland** offers the best of all worlds: proximity to the canyon and a sense of peace.

Your GPS won't get you there. A special app directs guests up an unpaved road through the ponderosa pines and meadows of the Kaibab National Forest. Twenty minutes in, a sign points to a private meadowland surrounded by pines. Floor-to-ceiling windows of the small lodge reflect the trees, clouds, and pond where the occasional fellow guest tosses in a fishing line or takes a spin in a kayak. A horseshoe of 10 canvas cabins sits a short stroll away. Another 14 are in the works, along with a wellness area with soaking tubs.

Tents here are shaped like a megaphone, slightly smaller near the entry and wider as they open to the terrace and outdoors. The generous space features a king bed, pull-out sofa, and discreet refrigerator. The bathroom is roomy enough that you can brush your teeth and grab that end-of-day shower without tripping over the spouse or kids.

Around the tents sits wilderness and nothing more. The 160 acres originally were a 1919 homestead, and the tiny cabin where the pioneers lived evokes an image of how grim it must have been to live out in the middle of nowhere. Eventually, a rail line brought logs from the forest to nearby Williams, but potatoes and root vegetables never really took hold. A few head of cattle still graze at a ranch down the road.

For those bent on an in-town restaurant, lively Williams sits 30 minutes away on the old Route 66. It's a long drive in the dark, and Backland's own restaurant proves surprisingly good. A charcuterie board, glass of pinot noir, cavatappi alfredo, and blackened trout leave us ready for an evening of stargazing, without a cloud in sight.

Planning a Trip

Backland is open March through December. Some suites feature a skylight over the king bed and bunks as well as the pull-out sofa. Rates include breakfast, nightly s'mores, and use of kayaks in the 8-acre pond. A children's menu is available.

TOP LEFT: Sunrise over Grand Canyon.
TOP RIGHT: Exterior of Backland dome.
BOTTOM LEFT: Bedroom in Backland.
BOTTOM RIGHT: Aerial view of Backland.

TOP LEFT: Interior of cabin at Eastwind Oliverea Valley. TOP RIGHT: Stairs leading to cabin at Eastwind Oliverea Valley. BOTTOM LEFT: Firepit at Eastwind Oliverea Valley. BOTTOM RIGHT: Airstream at AutoCamp Catskills.

Glamping in the Catskills

GREAT FOR	COST	WEBSITE
COUPLES, FAMILIES	$	AUTOCAMP.COM, EASTWINDHOTELS.COM

The Catskill Mountains have drawn New York City dwellers for nearly 200 years—some for the pastoral scenes depicted by the 19th-century Hudson River School artists, others for schmaltzy Borscht Belt comedy. Today, they come to escape the hustle and walk in the woods.

AutoCamp Catskills

Just west of the Hudson River, rows of sleek silver campers are set on a gravel path, each with its own small garden and sitting area. This is a place for people who want to be near the woods, but not its potential annoyances. Check-in is just like at a boutique hotel, but without the bell-hop. Guests say "hi" to their neighbors, then load up a cart with their luggage and weekend essentials: toys, groceries, hiking boots, dog food, and laptop.

If you've never been in an Airstream, you're in for a lovely surprise. Each is outfitted with a kitchenette with microwave and mini-fridge, futon sofa, tiled bathroom, towels and linens, and a separate bedroom beneath the rounded back window. Climate control? Check!

At the clubhouse, local folk singers tune their guitars for an evening performance. The music is so rousing that a grandpa is moved to clap and dance. Too bad the band has to leave.

AutoCamp resorts are dotted around the country. In addition to Airstreams, some offer cabins and accessible lodgings. Some offer outdoor pools; all are dog-friendly.

Eastwind Oliverea Valley

From the ever-popular Phoenicia Diner, a 20-minute drive along a wooded stream leads to **Eastwind Oliverea Valley** in the Slide Mountain Wilderness. At the end of the path sits the Scandanavian-style lodge, all light woods and windows, where guests fetch keys.

We've reserved something called a Lushna suite, a thoughtful two-level triangular cottage with a writing nook, airy sitting area, bathroom with shower, and lofted sleeping nook. The queen mattress is dressed in Frette linens. Mid-century how-to books hang from wall hooks above period furniture. On the outdoor deck, a gate allows the dogs to watch for squirrels but not chase them. From here, we can see a wooded hill set with a hotel wing and standard Lushna cottages, with private bathrooms in a separate structure.

On this rainy afternoon, we forget the 2½-mile hike up the McKenley Hollow Trail in favor of the sauna, then head to the restaurant. With a toddy in hand, we feast on gnocchi with brown butter sage and enjoy the soothing rain.

Eastwind operates Scandinavian-style nature resorts in Lake Placid and Windham, New York.

TENNESSEE, USA

In the Great Smoky Mountains

GREAT FOR	COST	WEBSITE
STELLARA RESORT: COUPLES	$$$	VISITSTELLARA.COM
GLAMP MINTY: COUPLES, FAMILIES	$	GLAMP.STAYMINTY.COM

Ferris wheels, cable cars, and Dollywood—that's what comes to most people's minds when they think of eastern Tennessee. Leave all that behind, and you're in the sweep of rolling hills known as the Great Smoky Mountains, where waterfalls are the main attraction.

A half-hour drive in the woods takes guests from Sevierville, the county seat, to the 85-acre woodsy hideaway called **Stellara Resort.** Here, a collection of treehouses and reflective mirrored cabins that opened in 2024 act as home base for forays into the forest and skies above.

Stellara Resort was designed for people unaccustomed to sleeping in nature. "We wanted to give them a little bit of a glimpse into the seasons and the phases of the sky and the phases of the universe—to have that moment where they say, 'Oh, wait, the moon is actually really cool,'" says Meredith Garrett, founder and CEO of Stay Minty, which owns Stellara Resort.

Hot tubs, a sauna, cozy beds, and indoor bathrooms come with lodging. Lunar phases, telescopes, and astrological readings are available as part of the star experience. Mountain views, horse rides across meadows, hikes, whitewater rafting, and gentle tube floats are offered nearby.

Thirty minutes down the road, sister resort **GLAMP Minty** at Dunn's Creek comprises 20 acres and eight geodesic domes—three for couples, five with child-friendly lofts. Each dome is themed to a Space Age song; "Lucy in the Sky with Diamonds," "Midnight Rider," and "Highway to Heaven" are all on the playlist. Essentials including beds, kitchen, bathroom, and vintage vinyl are inside the retro-themed domes.

Both resorts are a crow's fly away from Elkmont, a popular spot for viewing the annual light show of synchronous fireflies. While it may look like an alien form of morse code, the show is actually a firefly mating ritual. Each June, the males of the species *Photinus carolinus* start blinking their lights all at once. Scientists aren't entirely sure why, but it may be that, as with birds, the flashiest male gets the girl.

Planning a Trip

The closest airport to both resorts is in Alcoa, Tennessee, about 45 minutes from Stellara Resort. All units have kitchens, heat, and air-conditioning.

Aerial view of cabins at GLAMP Minty.

UTAH, USA

Gateway of the Gods

GREAT FOR	COST	WEBSITE
ACTIVE COUPLES, FAMILIES	$$$	ULUMRESORTS.COM

If there are more spectacular desert views than those near Moab, they must be on another planet.

For 200 million years, the cosmos has been at work here, splashing Earth with now-dry oceans, tumbling it with upthrusts and shifts, seasoning it with salt, sculpting it with wind and river, layering it like a wedding cake, and then wedging the slices apart. The result: vaults and tunnels, avenues surveyed by merciless sentinels, precariously balanced boulders, wide bay windows in seemingly impermeable walls, and arches that look like gateways of the gods.

Author Edward Abbey called Arches National Park "the most beautiful place on earth." Nearby Canyonlands vies for second place, with views stretching 100 miles across red and tawny canyons carved by the Green and Colorado Rivers. Dead Horse Point must surely take third; after all, it's here that filmdom's Thelma and Louise chose to end their fateful road trip.

Most visitors spend their Moab days hiking, rafting, and taking in the scenery from a car, ending up at a brewery and motel. **ULUM Moab** lets guests stay on the land while leaving crowds and dust behind.

The dirt road to the resort is so discreet that people routinely miss the turn. They know they've arrived when they round a cliff to find an angular building and pools shaded by angular sails. For those familiar with Under Canvas glamping resorts, this place will feel familiar; the two are sister brands. ULUM brings a decidedly upscale edge, with hot and cold dipping pools, handcrafted cocktails, seasonal menus with a Southwestern twist, and bespoke excursions into the desert. Fifty spacious tents are equipped with wood-lined bathrooms and cozy robes, electricity, wood-burning stoves, and cooling units.

What's most memorable, though, is the location. From the restaurant and pool, guests can see ULUM's private monument, Looking Glass Arch. Climb up, and you can see the valley and mountains beyond. It seems like a perfect place to propose a life together—and many visitors have done just that.

Planning a Trip

Moab is a typical desert environment. Temperatures from June through September are in the 80s and 90s Fahrenheit; highs are in the 40s Fahrenheit in December and January. The closest major airports are at Grand Junction, Colorado, about 2 hours away, and Salt Lake City, 4 hours away.

Sister brand Under Canvas also has a Moab resort geared toward families.

View of Moab Desert from ULUM Moab.

MINNESOTA, USA

Silence near the City

GREAT FOR	COST	WEBSITE
COUPLES, FAMILIES	$	CO.DAKOTA.MN.US

Whitetail Woods is scarcely 30 minutes from the home turf of Prince, Lizzo, and Dylan, not to mention the nation's largest mall. But here, the only music is the croak from a male pheasant and the hammer of a woodpecker's beak. Cedars, pines, and birches fill the window view. This might well be in Alaska.

The 450 acres of **Whitetail Woods Regional Park** are a wilderness of forest, wetlands, and dry hill prairie filled with tall grasses, goldenrods, and blazing stars. More than 10 miles of trails lead through birches and maples to Empire Lake, home to snapping turtles, green frogs, and muskrats. In summer, butterflies flit across cattails and trilliums; ospreys and bald eagles soar through the sky. Great blue herons and egrets step gingerly about the shore, looking for dinner. The occasional deer wanders by.

The park is edged by other public lands, with even more room to roam. Vermillion Highlands, 2,822 acres where research and recreation are combined, features horse and human trails, a pollinator garden, and information about prairie restoration efforts; hunting for turkey, deer, and other animals is allowed here by permit. The 1,500-acre Vermillion River Wildlife offers good trout fishing and bird-watching for species including geese, ducks, sandhill cranes, and belted kingfishers with their jaunty mohawk head feathers.

It's no wonder that the five camper cabins here are nearly always booked. The original three, built in 2014, blend with the forest they overlook. Interiors feature comfortable sitting chairs, a pair of bunks with full-size mattresses, table for four, pull-out queen couch, and a covered deck with Adirondack-style chairs. In 2020, two additional cabins with air-conditioning were placed overlooking the prairie. All cabins include Wi-Fi, heat, and electricity and are accessible to those with mobility issues. Picnic tables, fire rings, and the bath house with toilets and showers are located nearby.

If these cabins had kitchens, this wouldn't be camping at all. Grilling dinner is a reminder that this is still the great outdoors.

Planning a Trip

Whitetail Woods camper cabins are available year-round. Guests need to bring their own pillows, bed linens, and towels. In summer, a cooler is needed to store food.

Once-native bison have been reintroduced at nearby Spring Lake Park.

TOP: Cabin at Whitetail Woods.
MIDDLE: Interior of cabin at Whitetail Woods.
BOTTOM: Living room at Whitetail Woods.

Tent at Huttopia Sutton.

Dans Les Bois

GREAT FOR	COST	WEBSITE
COUPLES, FAMILIES, FRIENDS	$$	HUTTOPIA.COM

Two dozen preschoolers sit spellbound on the screened porch as an actor playing a skunk peeks shyly from behind a screen. A pair of hikers sip on end-of-day brews. A young couple battles at a foosball table. Three teens bursting into young adulthood blithely ignore health warnings and puff on cigarettes.

Moms, granddads, road-tripping girlfriends, and the occasional family are "camping" in ease at **Huttopia Sutton,** a collection of two-bedroom wooden chalets and canvas-tented cabins in the Quebec forest.

By day, guests head off into the surrounding 160-acre forest to hike, canoe, and cycle in these protected lands just 9 miles north of the Vermont border and 70 miles from Montreal in the Eastern Townships. Hikes can be challenging; Mont Sutton rises more than 3,000 feet, providing a popular base for winter skiing and snowshoeing. Those less inclined toward physical pursuits shop in the friendly boutiques and galleries of Sutton, just 1½ miles down the road. The 23 wineries on the 100-mile-long La Route de Vins are an easy drive away.

But the real point of being here is to smell the firs, listen to the cicadas, and get off-grid without the hassles of roughing it. Huttopia Sutton provides two options: Two-story wooden chalets feature a sitting area and two bedrooms, while canvas "trappeur" tents set on an enclosed wooden deck offer a queen bed in one alcove and a queen-with-upper-bunk in another, accommodating five. All include a wood stove, fridge, dining table, deck, pots and pans, propane grill, electricity, and sheets smoothed across inviting beds. And yes, an en suite toilet and shower with hot water are included.

For those who aren't up to grilling, a central reception pavilion features a food bar with fresh croissants in the morning and wood-fired pizza and sandwiches throughout the day. There are games and books, and yes, a fenced pool and children's play area are just beyond the decks.

The downhill walk from the pavilion leads through birches and maples and past dozens of tents. Parents and children gather around fire pits just off their deck, trying to smash roasted marshmallows between graham crackers before the gooey centers ooze out.

Crackling campfires create a lullaby that sings you sweetly to sleep. There's little solitude here, but plenty of good company in this cozy village amid the trees.

Planning a Trip

Huttopia Sutton is open from mid-May to mid-October. In the U.S., Huttopia offers similar camps in southern Maine, New Hampshire, New York, and California. All are open spring through fall.

COLORADO, USA

Rockies Without Crowds

GREAT FOR	COST	WEBSITE
SOLOS, COUPLES, SMALL GROUPS; CHILDREN ALLOWED ONLY ON FAMILY WEEKENDS	$$$	DUNTONDESTINATIONS.COM

In the Rockies, nature used to be the big draw. In the winter, that meant pristine powder in Breckenridge and Aspen, Telluride, and Vail. In the summer, it was horse rides into the mountains, hikes around Maroon Bells, and fishing in swirling rivers. These days, people come as much for fine living as the flora and fauna. That jeans-wearing couple at the next table are more likely to be wealthy art collectors, Hollywood executives, or Silicon Valley entrepreneurs than hikers and horsemen.

To get into the woods without a cast of dozens, you need to get to a place like **Dunton River Camp.** The two-lane road to the camp edges the West Dolores River and runs past hay fields, meadows, and farms wedged between a pine forest and the San Juan Mountains. The camp itself is nothing fancy—just a couple of farm buildings in the trees. Or so it seems. . . .

The office building—if you want to call it that—is a one-room 1800s cabin, now with a pool table and a countertop that serves as the bar. The other is the dining room, with a fireplace where meals are served when weather is too cold or windy on the deck. With only eight tented suites on 500 acres of a former cattle ranch, you don't need much infrastructure. You certainly won't find crowds.

Here, the aspens, firs, and river are just outside your deck. Catch-and-release fly-fishing is a big draw—there are anglers who come here just to knock off brown, brook, cutthroat, and rainbow trout in a single trip. Others come for rock hounding, rock climbing, horse riding, biking, and hiking through the hills and paddleboarding on the river.

Just a few miles up the road lies sister resort **Dunton Hot Springs,** a former mining town where 14 log cabins reflect history with a touch of whimsy. River Camp guests can come up for a hot soak when timing permits. (Yes, Tom Cruise once vacationed here.)

But often, camp guests simply snuggle into their plush robes, hang out by their gas fire, or nap on the duvet-covered king bed in their tents. Because they can.

Planning a Trip

The closest town is Telluride, about 30 miles over an unpaved road. The River Camp is open June to October; rates include three gourmet meals daily and mountain bikes. The Hot Springs resort is open year-round.

***TOP LEFT:* Fly-fishing at Dunton River Camp. *TOP RIGHT:* Bathhouse at Dunton Springs Camp. *MIDDLE LEFT:* Tented cabin at Dunton River Camp. *MIDDLE RIGHT:* Horseback riding at Dunton River Camp. *BOTTOM:* Dogsledding at Dunton Hot Springs.**

TOP LEFT: Grand Prismatic Spring in Yellowstone National Park.
TOP RIGHT: Bedroom at Under Canvas West Yellowstone.
BOTTOM: Glamping tents.

MONTANA, USA

Wonderland of the West

GREAT FOR	COST	WEBSITE
ANGLERS, COUPLES, FAMILIES	$$	UNDERCANVAS.COM

It's only 2 p.m., but the sky is dark as night, sending us to cover in the car to wait out the storm. Then, it's over, leaving nickel-sized hail on the boardwalks and around the boiling mud pot in a hot-meets-cold collision. A rainbow glimmers overhead.

Sudden weather shifts are part of life in a high, mountainous landscape marked by unsettled geology. It's just one of so many wonders that make Yellowstone one of America's most-visited national parks—and my personal favorite. Geysers, travertine terraces, and frothy hot springs ringed in turquoise, yellow, and orange create a sense of awe. Every bend in these 3,500 square miles brings a different view: waterfalls, marshes, grazing bison, a 12-point buck. When our vintage touring car comes to a dead stop, we think it's because of the torrential rain—until we see the grizzly standing on its hind legs.

With some 4.5 million Yellowstone visitors a year, lodging can be in short supply, pushing many visitors to park-edge motels with few amenities, little privacy, and basic dining options. **Under Canvas West Yellowstone** offers a peaceful alternative. Just 10 minutes from the park's west entrance, its 102 safari-style tents are set well off the highway in a 40-acre prairie filled with tall grasses and wildflowers and rimmed by pine-forested hills.

This is where the Under Canvas glamping brand got its start in 2012; since then, the brand has added another dozen locations convenient to other national parks. West Yellowstone is a family favorite; all tents here are spacious enough for four and feature wood-burning stoves, en suite bathrooms with showers, plenty of indoor-and-outdoor seating, and battery packs for charging devices.

Level paths link tents to one another and the welcome lounge, where guests find electricity, a fire for s'mores, bar, live music, and an activities concierge who can arrange horse riding, fly-fishing, hikes, and river excursions. Under Canvas West Yellowstone also features a full-service dining room that serves charcuterie boards, salads, and entrees including seared trout.

Strolling to my tent, I imagine I'm part of a wagon train heading to my own little home on the prairie. But I'm glad someone else is making the wild game bolognese.

Planning a Trip

Under Canvas West Yellowstone is open mid-May to early September. Tent styles include stargazer options with an open panel above a king-size bed. Camps book well in advance, as do popular activities. Under Canvas also operates a resort near Yellowstone's north entrance at Paradise Valley.

CALIFORNIA, USA

In the Redwoods

GREAT FOR	COST	WEBSITE
COUPLES, FAMILIES, GROUPS	$	MENDOCINOGROVE.COM

From the north, U.S. 101 leads through a miles-long tunnel of towering redwoods, past the town of Leggett, California, with its drive-through sequoia, over emerald rivers mirroring the forest green. The highway hits the coast, edging seaside cliffs above rocks rearing from the sea like a giant shark fin.

A lane leads into the forest and up a hill to 37 acres of redwoods, oaks, and ferns. Tucked within the trees are 60 crisp white tents and rare comforts: espresso bar, ice delivery, massage service, sauna, and breakfast cooked by someone else.

At its best, camping combines solitude with the solace of community. **Mendocino Grove** delivers on both. Our tent-for-two high sits above the highway, where we can't see or hear another soul. The surf crashes against the beach just across the road; a low rhythmic foghorn warns ships from the shore. From our deck, we can almost see the village of Mendocino, that, for all its fame, retains the unassuming air of a farm town.

A 2-minute walk up the lane leads to the central meadow, where kids who were just strangers are teamed up for touch football. There's a friendly, welcoming vibe. Flowers are set on tables throughout the camp and in the farmhouse-style bath houses. Fellow campers say "hello" as we pass. Gas grills are convenient to camping areas; the most critical grilling tools hang from the handle. A campfire valet delivers firewood with kindling and ensures we understand how to use the bear box.

Even in summer, the evening is chilly. We pull on our puffy vests and huddle around the fire ring, setting aflame the marshmallows that are meant for s'mores. Our dogs are already snug on the pet bed provided, and we're quick to follow. With a heated bed and warm blankets in our tent, why are we sitting outside?

The morning is misty, and temperatures are slow to warm; a visit to the espresso bar is in order. The mellow scents of fir trees, coffee, and campfires ward off the chill. "It's really majestic, isn't it?" says a neighbor waiting for a latte. So it is.

Planning a Trip

Mendocino Grove has options for couples, groups, and families, including campers with mobility issues. The camp is open late April through November.

Year-round highs are in the 50s Fahrenheit; mist is common. Airports in San Francisco and Oakland are about 3 hours away.

***TOP:* Hiking trail at Mendocino Grove.**
***MIDDLE:* Canoeing at Mendocino Grove.**
***BOTTOM:* Tent at Mendocino Grove.**

TOP: Riding through Zion National Park.
MIDDLE: Outdoor shower at Open Sky.
BOTTOM: Tent at Open Sky.

UTAH, USA

Far from the Crowd

GREAT FOR	COST	WEBSITE
COUPLES, FAMILIES, SMALL GROUPS	$$$	STAYOPENSKY.COM

Zion National Park is set in a canyon that grows ever slimmer the farther you go. A tram eliminates automobile traffic but does little to slow the throng of eager summer visitors. I get it: The wet hike through the Virgin River into the 20-foot-wide Narrows with its thousand-foot-high rock walls is unforgettable. The fast-flowing river and slippery rock floor are exhilarating, if a bit scary.

Still, after a day of side-stepping fellow hikers and queuing for the shuttle, we crave a retreat. From the highway, a discreet dusty road leads past a ravine, an orchard, and a cheerful farm, deep into a valley surrounded by cliffs. Three miles in, we come to a small gate opening onto an elbow. Set amid the sandy stones and brush are a handful of tented safari camps surrounded by juniper bushes. We've reached **Open Sky Zion.**

Our wood-framed safari tent offers every comfort we want after a hot, rigorous day. The cool stone terrace leads to a glass door securing oh-so-welcome air-conditioning and the plush king bed. Behind the bed wall, the indoor bath features a glass door leading to an outdoor shower surrounded by rocks. Our entire camp is surrounded by rocks and cliffs, creating privacy that is so needed after a day in the busy park. The setup is designed for stargazing without light spill from neighboring tents.

Each of the 11 camps offers the same basic amenities: microwave, mini-fridge, soft robes and slippers, heated bathroom floors, coffeemaker, Wi-Fi, and outdoor gas fire pits. Yet each is slightly different. Some have multiple bedrooms; others have hot tubs and overbed skylights and giant curved bathtubs. One unit offers easy access for those with mobility issues. One even has bunks for kids.

Each features a covered terrace. From a swing, I watch hummingbirds and a bright blue spark lark flit in the juniper bush. The flat, sandy path from our camp leads to a rock-lined pond, and for a minute, I flirt with the idea of a plunge. But dinner at the on-campus, chef-run restaurant Black Sage beckons, and soon we are sipping on pinot noir and a dish called "smoked meatloaf" that is too delicately seasoned for such a humble name.

By the time we return to our terrace, the full moon is shining overhead, obscuring all but the brightest stars. We snuggle into our swing and breathe in the moment. The Milky Way will have to wait.

Planning a Trip

Temperatures are coolest between September and May. Summer and winter months can be crowded, despite the nearly 90°F temperatures of July and August. The closest large airport is in Las Vegas, about 3 hours away.

ILLINOIS, USA

River, Prairie & Bricks

GREAT FOR	COST	WEBSITE
COUPLES, FAMILIES	$$$	CAMPARAMONI.COM

Central Illinois is mostly flatland, a vast plain of soybeans and corn. The 18 canyons of Starved Rock State Park come as a surprise. In the spring, when the snow melts, the park's 2,600 acres are dotted with waterfalls plummeting over cliffs, logs, sandstone folds, and rocky layers stacked up like pancakes. When the water dries, the canyons become stone labyrinths and earthen bowls. The grim name is said to come from an ancient tribal rivalry, when Illiniwek people were trapped atop a cliff and left to starve.

A trolley ferries park guests to the Starved Rock Lock and Dam on the Illinois Waterway linking the Mississippi to the Great Lakes. With all the advances in technology, it's amazing to see that river locks still function much as they did in the early 20th century, when the Army Corps of Engineers built this one.

After a day of exploration, a camp staffer with an electric cart whisks our luggage to our canvas cabin. Each of **Camp Aramoni**'s 11 tents is slightly different. Ours, Foxglove, feels like a farmhouse suite, with a sofa and pale rug in the spacious living area. A wrought-iron bed against a paint-washed wall dominates the bedroom; the bathroom and shower are tucked behind. From our elevated deck, we watch a sight too rare these days: a dad playing kickball with a gaggle of kids.

Rooms here come with breakfast and dinner, which prevents worry about where to eat. Cocktails are offered at an Airstream-turned-bar outside the dining barn. For dinner, we dig into a bourbon-brined pork chop in blackberry compote and cornmeal-crusted flounder that compete with anything we could have found in the nearby town. The almost-full moon lights the way to the tent, where s'mores and the fire pit await.

We wake to a cool breeze fluttering through the prairie off the deck, rippling the purple clover and blossoms of white, gold, and yellow. With 93 acres, there's plenty of room for walks in the woods and a bike ride along the Vermillion River. The land encompasses a former brickyard, where 100 men once made 12,000 bricks per day. Though the century-old operation ceased in 1981, Aramoni's owners have preserved what remains in tribute to its history.

With the help of binoculars and a little patience, we spot an eagle and a hawk. Patience isn't our favorite habit, but in a place this pretty, it's a skill worth practicing.

Planning a Trip

The camp is open May through October. Chicago's two airports are less than 2 hours away.

TOP: Starved Rock State Park. MIDDLE: Picnic at Camp Aramoni. BOTTOM: Tents at Camp Aramoni.

CAMP ARAMONI

NEW YORK, USA

Simplicity & Cider

GREAT FOR	COST	WEBSITE
COUPLES, FRIENDS	$	FIRELIGHTCAMPS.COM

A highway runs by the entrance, and for a minute, I'm wondering just how "natural" this upstate New York glamping resort can be. Once we drive down the slope to the check-in tent at **FireLight Camps,** the picture becomes clearer. The "lobby," if you want to call it that, and 19 safari tents sit on the edge of a forest. From here, a gentle 20-minute hike takes guests to Ithaca's Upper Buttermilk Falls, one of the most beautiful strolls in the area.

Buttermilk is well worth the walk—but far from the only waterfall in the Finger Lakes. From here, you're perfectly positioned to drive to check out the Genesee River falls and gorge dubbed "the Grand Canyon of the East," the 19 falls along the trail at Watkins Glen State Park, and the 215-foot-drop at Taughannock Falls. Or you could hit those other kinds of trails, lined with wineries, cider houses, and distilleries.

First stop: our comfortable billowy tent, secured with log poles covered in bark. Oriental rugs lie on the plank floor next to the big, warm bed. A pair of rocking chairs on the deck are positioned for views of the pine forest. A folding canvas chair and wooden desk provide a place to write—as long as the laptop battery lasts. Most tents are electricity-free, though you can charge devices at the welcome tent.

FireLight Camps feels like it was born from the forest itself, without a trace of corporate slick. That's because it's owned by a couple who have created the kind of friendly sanctuary they love themselves. Guests use a communal bath house 2 minutes from their tent. They bring their own burgers for the shared grill, chat with tent neighbors around a campfire, or challenge their partner to a game of checkers.

The chilly night encourages a snuggle beneath warm covers. It seems like only minutes have passed before warblers and goldfinches are whistling a wake-up tune. It reminds us that the Cornell Lab of Ornithology is on our must-see list before we head off down the road.

Planning a Trip

FireLight Camps offers a fresh, healthy breakfast daily and bar with local libations. Live music and a pizza truck are available on Tuesday evenings. Only a few tents offer electricity and heaters. The communal bath house offers showers and flush toilets. Yoga is offered in summer.

TOP LEFT: *Rainbow Falls in Watkins Glen State Park.*
TOP RIGHT: *Exterior of tent at FireLight Camps.*
MIDDLE: *Living room in tent at FireLight Camps.*
BOTTOM: *Interior of a glamping tent at FireLight Camps.*

TEXAS, USA

Wine & Wildflowers in Texas Hill Country

GREAT FOR	COST	WEBSITE
SOLOS, COUPLES, SMALL GROUPS	$$	WALDENRETREATS.COM

The German immigrants who founded Fredericksburg, Texas, would scarcely recognize the place today. While a few schnitzel houses and a shop filled with beer steins pay tribute to the past, boots and Stetsons and enough wineries to rival Sonoma have taken over. Sheep and longhorn cattle are wedged between the vineyards and stylish tasting rooms.

On a blue-sky afternoon, a charcuterie board and wine tasting beneath the live oaks may be the place to be. Then, it's time to retreat to your sanctuary above the Pedernales River, overlooking the hardscrabble lands that produced the crusty 36th U.S. president, Lyndon Baines Johnson, and his ever-gracious wife, Lady Bird.

The ranch that shaped Johnson's views is now a national historical park, home to bison, cattle, and sheep. Terracing, crop rotation, and water storage maximized yields in this dusty land and encouraged similar land practices on other ranches. In the spring, these 142 acres are dotted with wine-cups, spiderworts, and Indian paintbrushes—native wildflowers and untamed landscapes that Lady Bird Johnson sought to preserve across the U.S.

Up a narrow road—past cattle crossings, a few cows, and a deer lingering by the road—you arrive at **Walden Retreats.**

A vulture soars across the deck, dancing on the winds above the dry grasses, junipers, and cedar elms. A glass-paned door provides entry to the tented suite, a spacious haven with a fully equipped kitchen, sitting area with a pair of leather chairs, and a duvet-covered king bed. Like the landscape outside, the room is a study in beige. A copy of Henry David Thoreau's *Walden* rests on the bed, a subtle reminder that the salve of nature is the reason for coming.

A wistful whistle blows just outside the tent flaps, unfurled for sunset views of the landscape beyond. Come nightfall, the winds of the day give way to a full-blown storm. Gusts batter the tent, setting the curtains aflutter and the deck creaking. It's no night for lighting the fire you've set in the pit outside. Better to sit snuggly by the wood stove inside.

By dawn, the furious winds subside. Streams of light give promise to a calmer time. It's not a day for the steep trail to the riverbed below, perhaps, but a gentler stroll among the cedar elms and grasses on the hill behind the tents. Just the metaphor for life Thoreau intended.

Planning a Trip

Walden Retreats sits on a ridge about 30 minutes east of Fredericksburg and 90 minutes from Austin. Tents feature bathrobes, heat and A/C, and en suite bathrooms. Accessible tents are available.

TOP: *Tent at Walden Retreats.*
MIDDLE: *Fly-fishing near Walden Retreats.*
BOTTOM: *Interior of tent at Walden Retreats.*

On Ice

GREAT FOR	COST	WEBSITE
COUPLES WITH DEEP POCKETS , ACTIVE FRIENDS	$$$$$+	WHITE-DESERT.COM

As a hard-core explorer, Patrick Woodhead has summitted previously unclimbed mountains in the Himalayas, kayaked uncharted streams in the Amazon, and crossed the Atlantic in record time. But his great passion is what he calls "the real Antarctic," the interior of the White Continent that even few explorers and scientists ever see.

In 2005, he set out to change that. For the past 20 years, **White Desert** has brought small groups of guests to camps in Antarctica's interior, where the facilities are a heck of a lot more sumptuous than the three tents Whitehead and his cofounder started with.

The journey starts in Cape Town, South Africa, where a private jet whisks guests (and sometimes scientists and supplies) over the Southern Ocean to Wolf's Fang, a runway and transit camp with medical and firefighting teams located on a glacier in Queen Maud Land, Antarctica. Guests are transported to one of two 12-person camps.

At Whichaway, six heated polar pods with fluffy beds and private bathrooms overlook the freshwater lakes of the Schirmacher Oasis. After a day of ice-climbing, visiting emperor penguins, or traversing blue-ice tunnels, guests return to the cozy champagne lounge, sauna, and dining room provisioned via weekly flights from Cape Town.

Echo Camp's six glass-fronted Sky Pods look like they were beamed down from another planet. Amid jagged peaks, guests ski, ride fat-tire bikes, and rappel from rocky cliffs.

Keeping the camps operating takes extensive planning. Fuel is delivered by a research vessel each season and then transported on snowplow-towed sleds to Wolf's Fang. Power is provided by a combination of solar and diesel generators. Waste from the dry-flush toilets is removed from the continent. The 2 tons of food needed per week to supply guests and the 100-person staff come in by plane.

At the end of each Antarctic summer, camps and even the runway are dismantled. By the time the first snow comes, even footprints have disappeared.

Planning a Trip

White Desert's camps accommodate a maximum of 12 guests at one time. Most trips last 7 nights; a 1-day trip also is offered. Rates include charter flight from South Africa, transportation via light aircraft on the continent, activities, and meals.

***TOP:* Living room at White Desert.**
***MIDDLE:* Exterior of dome at White Desert.**
***BOTTOM:* Penguins near the resort.**

CALIFORNIA, USA

Omakase & a Yurt

GREAT FOR	COST	WEBSITE
COUPLES, FAMILIES WITH CHILDREN 13 & OLDER	$$	TREEBONES.COM

"It was here in Big Sur that I first learned to say 'amen,'" wrote Henry Miller in 1957. This rugged stretch of California coast has struck a lot of people that way, from Jack Kerouac to Dennis Hopper, Ansel Adams to Joan Baez, and the founders of the legendary Esalen Institute. It's the setting that does it: the Pacific crashing against granite cliffs, sea otters and seals in the surf, the zigzag road along the mountain edge, the tidal falls by the beach.

Landslides often block the two-lane road, restricting access to one end or the other for as far as you can get. When the way is open, Highway 1 from Carmel in the north to San Simeon is only 90 miles long. Making it in a single day means sticking with the car instead of getting out to watch the elephant seals crowding the beach or taking a hike down to the water.

It's an argument for staying a night or two—especially if you can do so in the thick of nature. That has always been the way of things at **Treebones Resort Big Sur.**

Before *glamping* officially became a word, John and Corinne Handy grabbed onto the concept of camping in comfort. In 2004, the former Mattel executive and his wife opened Treebones Resort Big Sur on 10 acres of hillside overlooking the sea. Today, 16 spacious yurts sit on redwood decks amid wildflowers and firs, each outfitted with a comfortable bed, sitting area, and sink with running water; bathrooms and showers are in the nearby lodge. A treehouse is reached via a swinging bridge. Two twig lodgings—a hut and a human nest—come with private campsites, as neither is weatherproof. Newest are a pair of autonomous tents, each with its own bathroom and Nespresso machine, and a self-contained 3-D-printed tiny house with a soaking tub.

The Handys' original idea of "perching lightly on the edge of the world" remains the guiding principle. Treebones Resort Big Sur is solar-powered and off-grid, with limited Wi-Fi but no cell service. That doesn't mean that dining is an afterthought—far from it. Treebones Resort Big Sur features two restaurants: an intimate Omakase restaurant with a 15-course tasting menu—don't worry, dishes are small—and the lodge dining room with a four-course dinner menu.

If the idea of fine dining seems incongruous with sleeping in a yurt without a bathroom, consider this: Treebones Resort Big Sur continues to win luxury travel awards year after year. It must be doing things right.

Planning a Trip

Treebones Resort Big Sur is about 110 miles south of Carmel; be sure to check coastal road closures to plot the best route. Highs are between 60° and 70°F year-round; the warmest months are June through October.

TOP LEFT: Deck of Treebones Resort Big Sur. TOP RIGHT: Dining at Treebones Resort Big Sur. MIDDLE: View of the Pacific Ocean from Treebones Resort Big Sur. BOTTOM: Interior of tent at Treebones Resort Big Sur.

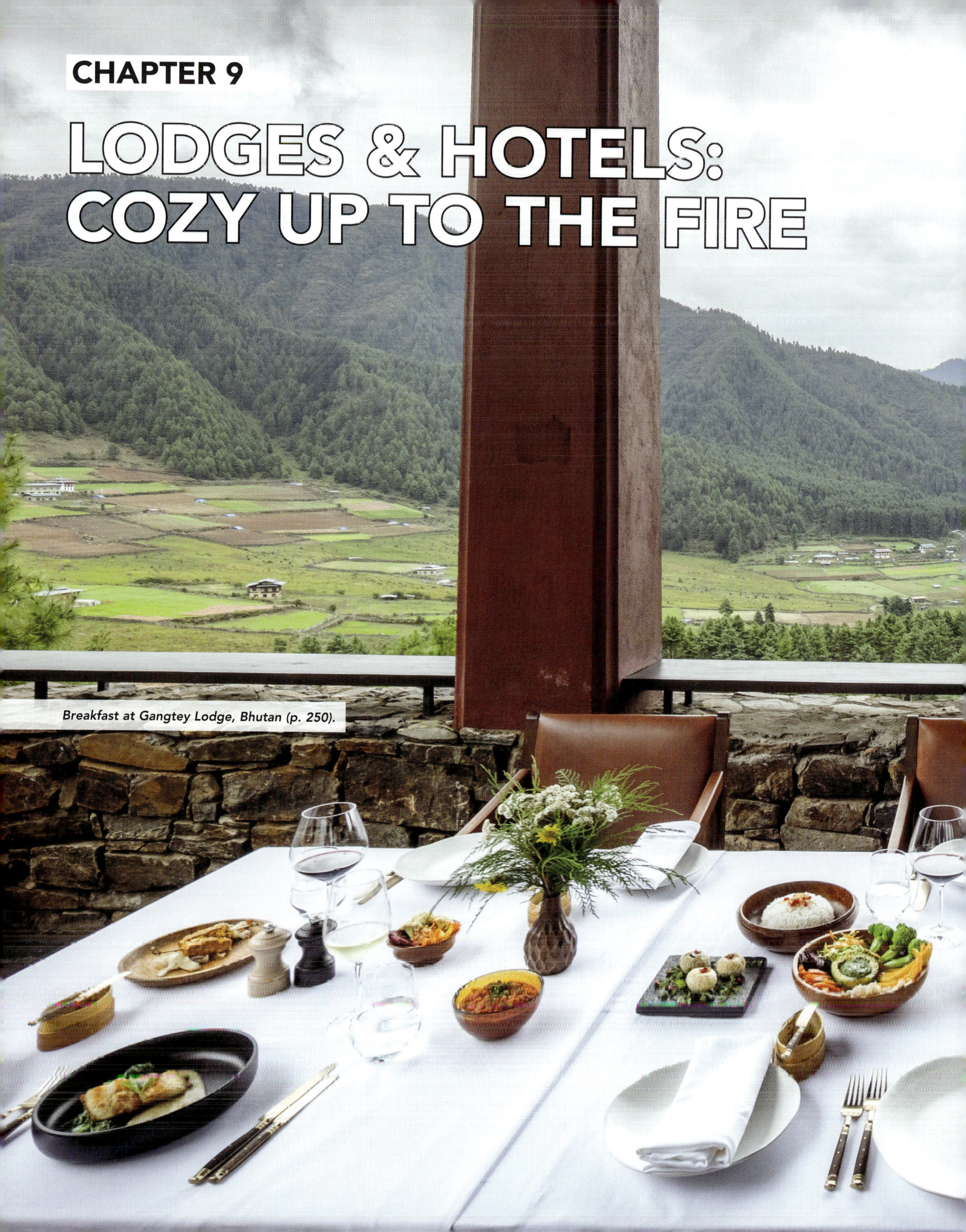

CHAPTER 9

LODGES & HOTELS: COZY UP TO THE FIRE

Breakfast at Gangtey Lodge, Bhutan (p. 250).

Study nature, love nature, stay close to
nature. It will never fail you.
— Frank Lloyd Wright

Wilderness is not a luxury but a necessity
of the human spirit, and as vital to our
lives as water and good bread.
— Edward Abbey

"Sleeping in the Forest"
I thought the earth
remembered me, she
took me back so tenderly, arranging
her dark skirts, her pockets
full of lichens and seeds. I slept
as never before, a stone
on the riverbed, nothing
between me and the white fire of the stars
but my thoughts. . . .
— Mary Oliver

View of Snoqualmie Falls and Salish Lodge.

The Mist That Carries Prayers

GREAT FOR	COST	WEBSITE
COUPLES, FAMILIES	$$	SALISHLODGE.COM

Spray from the Snoqualmie Falls may seem a predictable result of the 20,000 cubic feet of river water per second cascading over a 270-foot drop. But for the Snoqualmie people who have lived here longer than memory can mark, these are mists that carried prayers from early beings to the Creator. Legend has it that the First woman and First man were created here, so it was natural that this would become a sacred site for burial and renewal.

Visitors can feel the droplets from boardwalks overlooking the cascade at a small park just downstream. Better still, they can sleep above them in the hotel known to *Twin Peaks* fans as the Great Northern.

Salish Lodge & Spa, as it is properly called, is dramatically perched above rocks in the Snoqualmie River just before it plunges over the granite ledge.

Lodge guests survey the falls from a spa and two restaurants—not unlike the tribal people who gathered seasonally in this fertile land to hunt, forage, feast, and trade before the settlers came. The 86 handsome guest rooms are designed to blend with the spruce and cedar forest blanketing the Cascade Mountains.

Today's lodge represents a long-fought victory for the Snoqualmie people. Under an 1855 treaty, the land beneath it was ceded to the U.S. government in exchange for a reservation that never materialized. The natural beauty and commercial possibilities drew white settlers to the area. Soon, logging and the railroad moved in, and in 1899, the world's first underground hydroelectric plant was installed here. The original eight-room Snoqualmie Falls Lodge opened in 1916 and soon became famed for its generous breakfasts.

After a series of expansions and renovations, the Salish Lodge reopened in 1988 as a luxury hotel, complete with a rooftop hot tub. In 2007, it was acquired by the Muckleshoot Tribe. A dozen years later, the two nations reached an agreement, transferring the lodge and 45 surrounding acres to the Snoqualmie.

Despite its tumultuous history, the lodge and the falls remain a place where you can hear the thundering water, feel its mist, and renew. "Spend some time there, breathe deep, listen and be still before the Creator," Snoqualmie elder Lois Sweet Dorman has written. "It is a place of healing, a place for celebration, a place to mourn, a place to reconnect to the great mystery. It is an exchange of spirit."

Planning a Trip

Salish Lodge is about a 30-minute drive from Seattle. The weather is temperate and rainy much of the year; the warmest and driest months are June through September.

AUSTRALIA

Fiery Skies of Tasmania

GREAT FOR	COST	WEBSITE
COUPLES, FAMILIES	$$$$	SAFFIRE-FREYCINET.COM.AU

Sunset comes early in the fall month of May. It's just before 5 p.m. when the sun slips beneath a thin line of clouds hovering over the Pacific coast of Freycinet National Park, burning yellow and then orange before bursting into a fiery red that sets the sky aflame. Seconds later, it evaporates, leaving curving white beaches, eucalyptus trees, and granite peaks in a deep, quiet darkness.

Those searing sunsets and rich, regional deposits of sapphires gave name to **Saffire Freycinet,** 20 meticulously designed suites angled to showcase views across Coles Bay and the jagged peaks of the Hazards Mountains. The roof of the main lodge swoops over floor-to-ceiling windows, an interior stream and waterfall, lounge, and restaurant offering vegetables grown in a rooftop garden.

The dramatic architecture can be mesmerizing. So is the outdoors.

Along with dramatic views, visitors to Saffire's 27 acres are sure to see endangered Tasmanian devils. A cancerous facial tumor disease has decimated devil numbers; studies estimate that half of the population has been lost since the late 1990s. To safeguard those that remain, the government and private entities have stepped in. The sanctuary at Saffire is run by a Hobart-based institute working to develop vaccines and cures for the cancer. For now, many of the fierce red-eared, black-and-white marsupials live in protection.

On the other side of Coles Bay, a peninsula of 41,000 acres is home to the smooth sands, peeling eucalyptus trees, and jutting pink granite cliffs of Freycinet National Park. A 3-mile drive beyond the visitor center leads to Hastings Caves, a huge space of massive columns, delicate stone spirals, and drapery-like formations.

Elsewhere in the park, paths lead down to beaches amid granite boulders, and up along the hillsides to reveal the sheltered white sand rimming the park's iconic Wineglass Bay. From the boardwalk at Cape Tourville, you can sometimes spot sea eagles, dolphins, and whales.

Peering down at the idyllic coastal scene, it's difficult to imagine that aggressive whaling practices once turned this blue water red. Demand for whale oil led to the near-extinction of the southern right whale, a mammoth weighing in at 80 tons. In these more eco-conscious times, the whale population has rebounded. From May to July, you can see them breach in the waters below Freycinet's Cape Tourville as they migrate through the Tasman Sea. One more reason to visit Freycinet.

TOP: Yoga on Freycinet Saffire Beach.
MIDDLE: Tasmania Suite at Freycinet Saffire.
BOTTOM: Marine Farm Experience at Freycinet Saffire.

Planning a Trip

Temperatures are moderate year-round.

All meals and some experiences are included in rates.

The National Park is home to friendly **Freycinet Lodge** (freycinetlodge.com.au), a cost-wise alternative. Its showcase shelters are Coastal Pavilions, glass-walled cottages immersed in the forest, featuring broad private decks and outdoor bathtubs. Some offer water views. Its other stylish one- and two-bedroom units are cottages with decks and sea views; some are tucked into the bushland and feel like a New York loft, with leather couch, TV, and duvet-covered beds. All feature hard-wood floors and coffeemakers and are convenient to the lodge restaurant and bar, where meals are served in front of the spectacular water view. Breakfast is included in the room rate.

FACING PAGE, TOP & BOTTOM: Freycinet Lodge within Freycinet National Park.
THIS PAGE, TOP LEFT & RIGHT: Guestroom with outdoor tub, Freycinet Lodge.
BOTTOM: Tasmanian devil.

NEW YORK, USA

Living Like the Rockefellers

GREAT FOR	COST	WEBSITE
COUPLES	$$$	THEPOINTRESORT.COM

Even before 24/7 news and social media alerts, urbanites sought the solace of nature. They gazed across the glassy lake to the towering spruce, picnicked on a patch of million-year-old granite, and curled up by the fire with a book and a tipple. If they lived in New York during the early 19th century, they headed to the lakes, forests, and mountains of the Adirondacks.

The Point is a testament to the Gilded Age, when Vanderbilts and Guggenheims and Rockefellers retreated from the city to "rough it" in lakefront homes made from local logs and stone. William Avery Rockefeller II, a grandson of the Standard Oil cofounder, built this place in 1933 on Lake Saranac, dubbing it Camp Wonundra. Then-rare amenities included eight stone fireplaces, steam heat, running water, and interconnected phone service, according to the *Plattsburgh Daily Republican*. The outrageous cost was $100,000, worth about $2.4 million today.

Since that golden time, many other historic Adirondack camps have fallen into disrepair or disappeared altogether. Fortunately, Rockefeller's 75-acre outpost was refashioned in 1980 as an 11-room inn and renamed The Point. Sitting in your room by the huge stone fireplace flanked by generous armchairs, you can sometimes hear laughter from the lake, much as in Rockefeller's time.

Now, as then, this is a camp for adults. In summer, visitors canoe or kayak on the lake, play croquet, hike through maples and spruces, or visit other historic camps around the lake. Winter invites snowshoeing or cross-country skiing followed by hot toddies by a bonfire at the lake. Guests often gather in The Pub for pool, poker and puzzles, and televised sports games. Rates are all-inclusive, leaving you to order a round of brews or hoist a whiskey without a second thought. And yes, you can even bring your dog.

Dinner is served as it was in Rockefeller's day, at communal tables in the vaulted great room, where you discover the small world of friends-of-friends. Guests dress for dinner; on Sundays and Wednesdays, that should be black tie for the seven-course wine-paired meal. Attire is more casual on other evenings, when the menu is limited to a mere four courses. When the saffron risotto with Parmigiano Reggiano and Australian winter truffles arrives, you understand why The Point is noted for its cuisine. Be prepared to loosen your belt.

Planning a Trip

The Point Resort is located amid the patchwork of public and private lands of New York's Adirondack Park. The closest airport is Saranac Lake, served by Cape Air from Boston and New York. Larger airports in Burlington, Vermont; Albany, New York; and Montreal, Canada, are 2-plus hours by car. Rates include meals, activities, and libations. Children under 18 are not allowed.

TOP: *Adirondack chairs overlooking Lake Saranac.*
MIDDLE: *Guestroom, The Boathouse at The Point.*
BOTTOM: *The Great Hall at The Point.*

Guestroom, Eden Boutique Hotel.

Amid the Kasbahs

GREAT FOR	COST	WEBSITE
COUPLES, FAMILIES	$$	EDENBOUTIQUEHOTEL.COM

The rug sellers and spice stalls of Marrakech fade into the rearview mirror as the car drives east into the High Atlas Mountains on the Road of a Thousand Kasbahs. Half-crumbled towns fashioned from red mud are surrounded by palm and olive trees. Some desert villages remain in ruins; those that have been restored look like movie backdrops set in hills and steep valleys—and often appear in films. While the citadels and desert are genuine, other scenes are the product of the huge, fenced film lot of Atlas Studios, where an $8 ticket buys a tour of sets where *Gladiator* and *Game of Thrones* were shot.

The mountains and rock formations here date back roughly 200 million years—an irresistible temptation for adventurers. Hikes and quad tours take visitors off-road to the limestone river canyons of the Todgha Gorges, a favorite with casual walkers and serious rock-climbers, who can been seen dangling from rappelling lines. Day hikers head for the Dades Gorge, whose 1,000-foot-high walls seem to glow red and orange on sunny days. Ambitious trekkers often go for multiday walks to Mount Toubkal, at 13,670 feet the highest peak in northern Africa.

Along the way, they may see storks roosting in mud towers and endemic bird species feeding on wild figs and argan trees whose nuts produce Morocco's famous skin oil. They will surely meet friendly locals living as the Indigenous Berber people have for centuries, farming olives and tomatoes, weaving carpets, and crafting pottery. A trio of women haul huge bundles of sticks on their backs, smiling at waving visitors.

Stops for short forays have pushed us behind schedule. By the time the sun slips behind snow-capped peaks and date palm plantations, it's time for a hotel. *Any* hotel.

When we finally arrive, we understand why this particular auberge was so worth an extra few minutes in the car. A gentle staircase through a rose garden leads to the stately palace entry. Carved wooden doors open through an arch to the library, a tall-beamed space set with sofas and hassocks and tables inlaid with age-ringed wood.

Vintage wooden radios and black-and-white photos make us think that the hotel has been here for decades. But despite its beamed ceilings and intricately carved doorways, **Eden Boutique Hotel** is new, opened in 2024. Over 7 years, two brothers who grew up in a family of nomads built this oasis near the Dades Valley midway between Marrakech and the Merzouga Desert, just across from a strange rockscape dubbed The Monkey's Fingers, popular with hikers. Local carpenters, weavers, and woodcarvers crafted every table, bed, lantern, ringed door pull, and built-in chest in the 18 guest rooms tucked along stairways, around corners, and overlooking gardens.

A third brother, Mohammed, is the rave-worthy chef. Dinner starts with a plate that looks like an artist's palette dotted with salads, baked fish, and pureed herbs. The steak is perfectly

Pool at Eden Boutique Hotel.

seared, with a coulis of local berries on the side and topped with crisped potatoes. Come morning, breakfast presents a feast of Berber omelets, pancakes, and fresh yogurt—more than enough to fill your stomach for the day.

A pair of English women at the next table declare their intention to forgo touring plans and instead spend the day at Eden. We wish we could join them.

Planning a Trip

Fall and spring are the best times to visit. The closest airport is at Errachidia, about 2 hours away. The hotel has no elevator, and guests with mobility issues may find the stairs a challenge.

***FACING PAGE, TOP & BOTTOM LEFT:* Exterior, Eden Boutique Hotel.**
***BOTTOM RIGHT:* Lounge, Eden Boutique Hotel.**

TOP LEFT: Campfire at Urban Cowboy.
TOP RIGHT: Bathtub.
BOTTOM LEFT & RIGHT: Guestrooms.

Mountains & Woods, Slicker-Style

GREAT FOR	COST	WEBSITE
URBAN SINGLES, COUPLES, FRIENDS, FAMILIES	$$	URBANCOWBOY.COM

Even on a Sunday night, the great room at the **Urban Cowboy Lodge** feels like a party. A guy on the sofa sports a T-shirt emblazoned with "Emotional Cowboy" beneath his Stetson. A dozen other people are gathered in front of the giant stone fireplace, old-fashioneds in hand. The taxidermied bear is wearing a top hat; a disco ball hangs from the deer-antler chandelier. A family munches on impossibly huge fried-chicken sandwiches. Every seat in sight is covered in a Pendleton-style print.

Imagine what it's like on Fridays, when a DJ spins tunes from Miranda Lambert, Luke Combs, and Taylor Swift. Manhattan sits only 2½ hours away.

This is the wilderness? Well, yes, almost 70 acres of it, in the Big Indian Wilderness in New York's Catskill Mountains. The lodge is so deep in the hills that it gets no cell service. Once guests shift from the Main Lodge over to one of 28 suites in one of the side buildings, they get the picture. From the window over the copper-lined claw-footed tub, hills covered in maples, balsams, and birches stretch as far as the eye can see.

It won't take long to grab our boots and head out for a walk along the decks at nearby Kaaterskill Falls—at 260 feet, even higher even than Niagara—or the more challenging hike to 4,200-foot Slide Mountain, New York's tallest. (Sharp-eyed hikers can see porcupines and deer.) The trail to Giant Ledge promises some of the Catskills' most impressive views. The kids might prefer the views from the nearby gondola ride at Belleayre Mountain or a tube on the Esopus River that edges Urban Cowboy's property.

Urban naturalists may want to check out historic sites related to the Hudson River School of Art, then get in their steps on the Hudson River Skywalk pedestrian walkway linking the Thomas Cole Historic Site and Frederic Church's Olana.

Then, it's back to the room to immerse in cowboy culture. Sloped roofs and fretted railings recall the hotel's previous life as an alpine-style lodge. Today's glossy style is designed to bring city sensibilities to the backwoods. Bedside sconces are made from wooden snowshoes; easy chairs hewn from logs are topped with brown leather cushions. The walls—and even ceilings—are hand-printed with geometric patterns inspired by the American West; the fabric of the fluffy bathrobes matches. That giant bathtub calls. Be sure to leave the wine bottle where you can reach it.

Planning a Trip

Urban Cowboy Lodge is a 2½-hour drive from New York City. The Albany, New York, airport is about 35 miles away. Children and pets are welcome. Urban Cowboy also has themed lodgings in Denver, Colorado, and Nashville, Tennessee.

IRELAND

Amid the Faeries

GREAT FOR	COST	WEBSITE
COUPLES, FAMILIES	$$	GREGANS.IE

The narrow road twists past hills and harbors, weathered graveyards, and walls of stone painstakingly set by hand. At first glance, the view across the **Gregans Castle** garden looks like so many in the Irish countryside: rolling emerald meadows dotted with the spindly legs and wooly puffs of unshorn sheep.

As the early mist clears, the rounded rocky cap on the hill becomes clear. This is the Burren, home to one of Ireland's six national parks and geology so unique that it is recognized as a UNESCO Global Geopark.

Even if you've never heard of it, you're likely familiar with its most famous feature, the dramatic Cliffs of Moher rising above the Atlantic along five miles of County Clare. In weather fair or fearsome, the parking lot is filled. Stiff winds push waves against the rockface; fulmars and guillemots soar over its grassy cap. From a banjo comes a jaunty tune as a busker plays for tips. A walk along the mostly flat path can last an hour or a day.

After a visit to the cliffs, most foreigners hop back in their cars and head for Limerick or Dublin. They miss so much: Wide plains of limestone pushed up from the sea, crackled by ice and swept by wind and glaciers. The 24-foot stalactite hanging chandelier-like in Doolin Cave, which may recall ever so slightly the Cave of Gollum. Ruined remains of Neolithic settlements as old as the temples of Egypt.

Exploring the cultures here, ancient and modern, requires walks amid cairns, wildflowers, and fields home to shaggy Highland cattle. A drive over the hills leads to Burren Smokehouse, which offers tastings of its smoked salmon and smokehouse tours. The truly peckish stop in at the Burren Perfumery's cafe for smoked mackerel, vegetarian soups, and fresh scones, set next to the workshop filled with herbal scents and cosmetics. I the evenings, fiddlers crank up Irish tunes in pubs from Lisdoonvarna to Lahinch.

A stay at Gregans Castle combines history with contemporary style, part of owner Simon Haden's long effort to encourage appreciation of the Burren while preserving its ecology and traditions. Since the 1750s, a house has stood on this very spot as a summer refuge from the cities. In the 1940s, the owners began accepting paying guests, including *The Lord of the Rings* author J. R. R. Tolkien. Alas, those visits were before Haden's parents bought the place in 1976

Fireplace at Gregans Castle.

Since taking over in 2003, Haden has imbued the 21-room hotel with a savvy sense of comfort, mixing antiques with bold colors and whimsical touches. The multicourse dinner sourced from the hotel garden and local purveyors books out well in advance. After you taste the cured Atlantic scallop with pickled kohlrabi, roast cod with mussel sauce, and caramelized white chocolate with blackcurrant jam, you'll be reserving your next visit.

Planning a Trip

The Burren experiences mild temperatures and frequent rain year-round; summer months are warmest and driest.

The closest airport is at Shannon, about an hour's drive away. Getting to Dublin Airport takes about 2½ hours by car.

FACING PAGE, TOP LEFT: *Breakfast, Gregans Castle.*
TOP RIGHT: *Garden, Gregans Castle.*
BOTTOM: *O'Loughlan Suite, Gregans Castle.*
THIS PAGE, TOP: *Galway Bay Bathroom Window.*
BOTTOM: *Stairway.*

BHUTAN

Happiness in the Himalayas

GREAT FOR	COST	WEBSITE
COUPLES, FAMILIES WITH OLDER CHILDREN	$$$	GANGTEYLODGE.COM

The monastery at Tiger's Nest looks like it might fall any moment from its 10,000-foot-high rock ledge. That's unlikely; Bhutan's most famous monument has sat firmly in the Himalayas since 1692. For flatlanders like my husband and myself, the hike takes almost 6 hours round-trip. On this iconic trail, we have plenty of company, from fellow foreign hikers to the occasional monk with his shaved head.

The dramatic views are well worth the effort. But we prefer the relative serenity of the bowl-shaped Gangtey Valley ringed by the 16,000-foot-high Black Mountains. Streams cross wide meadows dotted with wildflowers and Buddhist flags fluttering in the breeze. In the fall, revered black-necked cranes fly overhead as they migrate to the warm valley. Friendly villagers working terraced farms wave and smile. Pines and maples thicken as we hike upward along rocky paths on a 3-day trek to the town of Wangdue.

In Bhutan, reverence for nature is a part of the culture that is celebrated daily with flags and prayer wheels and at elaborate festivals in the spring and fall. We end our trek with a mile-long run down a steep mountain path to Wangdue monastery, where the traditional fall festival is just beginning. Cymbals and drums hammer a discordant pace for intricate dances dedicated to Buddhist traditions and a reverence for all living things. A dancer in an elaborate deer mask twirls into the temple courtyard, tossing his head, twisting, stepping high to ripple the layered scarves of his skirted costume. The courtyard is jammed with locals seated on picnic blankets. Crimson-cloaked monks watch from a wooden gallery festooned with yellow and red banners.

Each fall and spring, annual festivals bring elaborate pageants, archery contests, and processions throughout Bhutan. But at every time of year, Bhutan is a place of color, nature, and spirituality that combine to create the national measurement scale of Gross National Happiness.

That unique blend led Khin Omar Win and her husband, Brett Melzer, to open **Gangtey Lodge** in 2013, on the edge of the Phobjikha Valley, as Gangtey is also known. Inspired by a house owned by a Queen Mother, the couple created a 12-room stone lodge that disappears into the landscape. The terrace and floor-to-ceiling windows overlook the Black Mountains and the Gangtey Monastery, where 100 monks perform daily prayer rituals with chants, genuflection, and meditation.

TOP: Nature trail, Phobjikha Valley.
BOTTOM LEFT: Breakfast, Gangtey Lodge.
BOTTOM RIGHT: Main Lodge, Gangtey Lodge.

Lodge guests are invited to participate in morning prayer and other activities that are part of Bhutanese daily life, such as potato harvests, archery, and cheese making. "We wanted to create a place where you would have luxury but not forget where you are," says Win. "We also wanted it to be like a home, where you could go out and explore and then recharge."

That translates into a wood-beamed lodge with columns painted with traditional designs, suites featuring in-room fireplaces and curved bathtubs, and familiar dinner dishes like risotto and grilled fish. The scent of local spices and the views always remind guests where they are. Whether a hike lasts days or just hours, it's a welcome haven.

Planning a Trip

The drive from the Paro airport to Gangtey Lodge takes about 5 hours; the hotel can arrange transportation.

The best times to visit are the spring and fall. Most festival dates vary each year; however, Gangtey's annual Black Crane Festival is always held on November 11.

FACING PAGE, TOP: *Monk painting Gangtey Lodge.*
BOTTOM LEFT: *Monks at Gangtey Monastery and Shedra Monastic College.*
BOTTOM RIGHT: *Guestroom, Gangtey Lodge.*
THIS PAGE, TOP: *Monks in Phobjikha Valley.*
BOTTOM: *Monks at Gangtey Monastery and Shedra Monastic College.*

ALASKA, USA

America's Last Frontier

GREAT FOR	COST	WEBSITE
ADVENTURE-ORIENTED COUPLES & FAMILIES, FOODIES	$$$$$	WITHINTHEWILD.COM

Come May, the snow on the shore edge gives way to hungry bears and moose. From the lodge deck, guests aim their binoculars at sandhill cranes and blue herons. Eagles soar overhead; sea otters bob in the bay. Puffins live on a nearby island reached by a short boat ride.

This forested edge of Kachemak Bay lies beyond the end of the road, so far from cities and cruise ships that it's hard to believe they're all in the same state. But then, Alaska is twice the size of Texas.

From Homer, a boat delivers guests to **Tutka Bay Lodge** on 40 waterfront acres thick with old spruce. Each of the six cabins affords views of trees, snow-crusted mountains, and whales that swim daily through the bay. A boardwalk links them to the cozy lodge, a meeting point for cocktails and conversation.

Socializing is a bonus. People really come here for two things: the serenity of the wilderness and the bounty of fine cuisine crafted from the freshest local ingredients.

The day starts with yoga on the central platform, followed perhaps by a naturalist-led shore walk, kayaking trip, or flight-seeing. Helicopter tours glide over glaciers and mountains, rocks and rivers where you can set down and walk the edge, looking for brown bears fishing for salmon. Other outings may take all day; for guests heading out for halibut fishing or a long hike into the surrounding hills, the scenery will chill the chakras.

What no one wants to miss is the afternoon cooking class or dinner. Chefs trained at Le Cordon Bleu and Thomas Keller–run kitchens mix passion with the bounty of fish, crustaceans, garden-grown vegetables, wild berries, and foraged greens. The results appear on plates filled with salmon bacon, rhubarb muffins, smoked oysters, and king-crab beignets. Reindeer and beef tenderloin farmed nearby are often on the menu.

At Tutka Bay, the culinary program has been key ever since Kirsten Dixon, a nurse, and her husband, Carl, an audiologist, gave up their Anchorage hospital jobs in 1983 and moved to the wilderness to open a fishing lodge. Kirsten always loved cooking and became the chef. Along the way, she published a cookbook and attended Le Cordon Bleu. In 2004, the couple and their two daughters moved to the region near Tutka Bay, where they purchased the lodge in 2009.

Says Kirsten, "Our mission is to bring people into the natural world and do our part to preserve and protect natural spaces. We hope they are inspired."

Planning a Trip

Tutka Bay Lodge is open from May to September. Rates include all meals and some activities.

TOP: Bear family near Tutka Bay Lodge.
MIDDLE: Tutka Bay Lodge.
BOTTOM LEFT: Glacier tour.
BOTTOM RIGHT: Tutka Bay Lodge's cooking school.

TOP: Fire pit at Areias do Seixo.
MIDDLE LEFT & RIGHT: Guestrooms.
BOTTOM LEFT: Beach at Areias do Seixo.
BOTTOM RIGHT: Cycling along the river near Areias do Seixo.

Chic on the Beach

GREAT FOR	COST	WEBSITE
COUPLES; VILLAS ARE SUITABLE FOR FAMILIES WITH CHILDREN	$$	AREIASDOSEIXO.COM

Birds tweet sweetly throughout the outdoor yoga session—loudly enough to distract from a poor attempt at a tree pose. Hey, it's been awhile. This grassy land on the Portuguese coast seems a good place to reengage.

Areias do Seixo was created as a quiet refuge from city life without going too far physically or psychically. From Lisbon, the drive takes just an hour. It's a graduated detox from highway to small roads, through villages and farmland, to a discreet bunkerlike building that makes you wonder whether you've found the right address.

The scene inside is photoshoot-ready. Bleached wooden tables set with tall, clear candle-holders and wispy wildflowers provide seats for lunch (a quinoa bowl or steak sandwich) or a meeting. A chandelier hangs over a wooden piano—clearly an art installation—in front of the bar. Comfortable chairs and sleek coffee tables surround a fireplace hanging from the 20-foot ceiling by the glass wall overlooking the grounds and ocean. Finishes are raw, reflecting the landscape beyond.

Beyond the wood seat of a rope swing, gentle steps lead down to a stone-lined corridor, next to a luggage cart made from driftwood. Inside four spacious "love" rooms, low beds are set on concrete platforms, making the ceiling feel even taller. Bedposts are fashioned from unfinished logs, while massive shower rooms are lined with the same beige rock as the private courtyard. A terrace off the bedroom allows long views across the pool and garden toward the ocean. Each room features a fireplace and enough stacked wood to last the winter.

A stroll to the dunes, bike ride down the coastal path, massage, or dip in the pool could be in order. Whatever the choice, the chef's tasting dinner is a must. Small, beautifully arranged dishes feature mousse between two house-baked biscuits served on a pile of black rocks, seared eggplant and pepper slices rolled into a blossom, a trio of tropical sorbets, and turbot in a light cream sauce. A plate offers blanched vegetables from the garden. Tastes and textures are delicate, complex, and delicious—much like Areixo Do Seixa itself.

Planning a Trip

Areias do Seixo features 13 sea-view rooms and one land-view room, plus a tented glamping shelter; all are limited to adults and children over 16. Afternoon tea and a generous breakfast are included.

Villas above the hotel feature private pools and are great for families and groups.

Just a few minutes south, casual Noah Surf House (noahsurfhouseportugal.com) features bunks, bungalows, and a restaurant from the same owners.

CHILE

The Stunning Blue Towers

GREAT FOR	COST	WEBSITE
COUPLES, ACTIVE FAMILIES	$$$	EXPLORA.COM

The vast region of Patagonia covers some 300,000 square miles, sprawling across the southern parts of Chile and Argentina. Its peaks reach to 13,000 feet, home to ice fields that feed 48 glaciers and countless lakes. Its roaring rivers are considered some of the world's most challenging whitewater. Seventeen national parks lie within its boundaries. Among its most famous is Chile's Torres del Paines, or "blue towers," 700 square miles of dramatic peaks named for the tint to the granite.

At **Explora's Torres del Paines lodge,** there's no need for art on the walls. Saw-toothed spines called the Horns create a landscape so unique that fliers can spot from the air.

The peaks and the glacier-fed lake splayed at their feet dominate every view: from the comfy chairs of the blond-wood lounge; from the 50 guest rooms; through the window in the granite bathrooms that have been hewn from the same rock that forms the mountain spines. Everywhere, that is, except the hot tub and the pool, tucked into their own building down a winding path overlooking yet another lake.

"It's almost too perfect, too beautiful," says a fellow traveler.

As tempting as it is to simply stare at the view, there's so much else to do. The day's activities appear on a chalkboard: rugged hikes in the peaks across the lake, short walks along the glacial shore, horse rides for beginners and experienced equestrians, and serious climbing for mountaineers.

I go for the horses. On this sunny day, five of us head off on horseback, cantering across iridescent fields and rushing rivers swollen with spring melt-off, through trees decorated with yellow balls called false mistletoe and a lacy moss called old man's beard that grows only in the purest air. Above, wispy mists swirl above darker cirrus clouds, giving way to the spaceshiplike lenticular clouds that occur only in places like this, with high winds and altitudes.

Come evening, tuna with carrot puree and short ribs grace the menu, paired with plenty of Chilean wine. Awe is an unwritten ingredient. Here, man is a vagabond, trespassing on lands that belong to gods.

Planning a Trip

The lodge is open year-round. June to August are coldest, with temperatures around freezing. The closest airport is at Puerto Natales. Rates include all meals and guided activities. A minimum 3-night stay is required. The 108-room **Rio Serrano Hotel & Spa** (rioserrano.com) offers a price-wise alternative with good views.

Explora was a pioneer in luxury adventures; it now has locations at Torres del Paine, Patagonia, Easter Island, Atacama, and Peru's Sacred Valley. Its newest offerings are point-to-point expeditions in Peru, Tierra del Fuego, and Iceland.

FACING PAGE, TOP: Torres Del Paine National Park.
MIDDLE: Hanging bridge at Explora Torres Del Paine.
BOTTOM: Living room at Explora Torres Del Paine.

TOP: Bar and lounge of Tu Tu' Tun Lodge.
BOTTOM LEFT: Scallop dish, restaurant at Tu Tu' Tun Lodge.
BOTTOM MIDDLE: Rafting on the Rouge River.
BOTTOM RIGHT: Guestroom at Tu Tu' Tun Lodge.

OREGON, USA

In the River's Bend

GREAT FOR	COST	WEBSITE
COUPLES; HOUSES ARE AVAILABLE FOR FAMILIES	$$$	TUTUTUN.COM

Gold Beach, Oregon, is home to two entirely separate kinds of beach: one a rock-filled shore facing the Pacific Ocean, and the other just a few miles inland, on the Rogue River. Here in Siskiyou National Forest, mountains, coast, and inland forests come together in a crush of 400-million-year-old rocks and soil, home to 3,500 plant species. Relatively few people make it to its backcountry wilderness, which might help explain the survival of a dinosaur-age pink-blooming heath related to azaleas. Carnivorous cobra lilies and droopy Brewer's spruces are found only here.

On the sloping bank of the Rogue Rivers sits **Tu Tu' Tun Lodge.**

A doe and fawn grazing beneath an apple tree pay no mind to the occasional human walking by. People have been coming to the two-level cedar lodge since 1970 to fish for steelhead trout and salmon, kayak a waterway lined by Douglas firs and blue oaks, relax by the pool, and smell the cedars.

For decades, they did so in the 16 rooms and two suites of the original lodge, all with tongue-and-groove cedar ceilings and terraces or balconies facing the river. In the last few years, a new owner has reclaimed a stream and land next door, adding four family-size houses plus a dozen glass cabins that reflect the trees and brook around them. Four new houses—two with two bedrooms, two with three—are set up for families.

Restaurants are few along this stretch of the river, and even nearby towns are limited to seafood, steak, and pizza. The lodge restaurant brings a sophisticated edge, focusing on local organic ingredients with international twists, like burrata with beets, Granny Smith apples and macadamia nuts, and chicken-leg confit with cippolini onions. Somewhere among the 6,000-bottle wine list, you're sure to find a grenache Syrah blend to please the palate.

Guests have a choice of dining alone or joining a communal table. Do so, and you're likely to meet couples who have come here for years to celebrate anniversaries, birthdays, or just a weekend away from the kids. The conversation turns to the osprey someone spotted and the trout that got away. Soon, you're finishing that last glass of wine by the fire with new friends.

Planning a Trip

Temperatures are moderate throughout the year, with winter lows in the 40s Fahrenheit. The lodge is open year-round.

The airport at North Bend, Oregon, sits about 2 hours to the north. The airport in Eureka, California, lies about 2½ hours to the south.

SPAIN

A Curve in Time

GREAT FOR	COST	WEBSITE
COUPLES	$$$	HOTELNAFARROLA.COM

The eucalyptus forest begins just a few miles outside Bilbao. Scarcely a quarter-hour after leaving Louise Bourgeois's 20-foot spider sculpture outside the Guggenheim Museum, you're twisting through the forest and up a mountain, then down past a field of sheep in front of a stone farmhouse. Just over the next crest sits a terrace overlooking the Bay of Biscay.

The wood-and-stone house behind it dates back almost 400 years, to a time when the structure was located farther down the hillside. The Basque culture it reflects is far older, perhaps to the beginning of spoken language.

That heritage is what led Josu Goikoetxea Larrauri, a polymer engineer, and his brother Gaizka, a chef, to open the eight-room **Hotel Nafarrola** just outside the village of Bermeo in 2021. "We love this place," says Josu, whose family has lived in the region for generations. "This is a way of transmitting its history."

Hikes, cycling, picnics in the mountains, and massages in the pines are part of the experience. Nafarrola sits in the Urdaibai Biosphere Reserve, a unique ecosystem of forest, wetlands, cliffs, beaches, and traditional villages tied by Euskara, the primary Basque language. Gaztelugatxe, Josu warns, has been overrun since it was transformed into the *Game of Thrones* Dragonstone Castle. Better to head toward the bird center in Gautegiz Arteaga to look for Eurasian spoonbills, Laga Beach and the cliff at Ogono, and the museum dedicated to iconic fashion designer Balenciaga at Getaria. He'll put together an itinerary. Oh, and don't miss the wine cellar at the restaurant Rekondo.

Not that anyone's in a hurry to leave Nafarrola. The hotel's own menu features grilled oysters and slow-cooked octopus, veal cheeks with potatoes in a red wine sauce, cake made from local hazelnuts, and a Basque cheesecake rich enough to draw tears.

From the hot tub in your stone-wall guest room, a skylight in the beamed ceiling reveals the Big Dipper twinkling in the darkness. A cow bellows from the field next door, a reminder of the continuity of then and now.

Planning a Trip

Temperatures are moderate year-round; the warmest and driest months are in the summer, reaching the high 70s Fahrenheit. The closest airport is about 30 minutes away at Bilbao. San Sebastian is about 90 minutes away.

TOP: ***Hiking at Hotel Nafarrola.***
BOTTOM LEFT: ***Massage treatment.***
BOTTOM RIGHT: ***Guestroom.***

tectake

Pool at Sun Mountain Lodge.

WASHINGTON, USA

In the Cascades

GREAT FOR	COST	WEBSITE
ACTIVE COUPLES, FAMILIES	$$	SUNMOUNTAINLODGE.COM

A startled deer takes off through the yellow thistles. The trail leads through tall grass and down the hill along fluttering aspens and lodgepole pines whose needles cushion the ground. Though it's a gentle hack, the lead wrangler turns in his saddle to check on the novices and the guardian who rides behind. And then the mares are climbing, climbing across the scrub-covered hill to the crest 1,000 feet above the valley floor. The Cascade Mountains sprawl as far as the eye can see—which on a cloudless day feels like forever.

Sun Mountain Lodge transports guests to a fearless time of endless summer days, novels printed on paper, and cool dips in a lake. A taxidermied bison stands just inside the door, its nose shiny from affectionate pats. Like the wild boar and pronghorn heads hung throughout the lodge, the bison comes from a historic hunting collection of non-endangered animals. Fires crackle in stone hearths. A group of preteens cheers as a friend slams his father at the foosball table.

A vast wilderness fills every window. Sun Mountain's 1,500 acres sit amid the mountains of North Cascades National Park, home to more glaciers than any other park in the Lower 48. Guests in 112 wood-lined rooms have a choice of views: mountains or the fertile valley or Patterson Lake, edged by 16 cabins designed for families. Endless orchards of gala, honeycrisp, and Granny Smith apples lie in the fields below.

Almost 70 miles of hiking trails crisscross the area, some on lodge grounds, others stretching into the Okanogan-Wenatchee National Forest filled with firs and spruces. In the winter, hills and ridges and lakes are painted in white, creating a playground for snowshoers and skiers and an almost impenetrable camouflage for snow hares. Dark-hued pine martens are easier to spot. Anglers can try their luck at any season. In the summer, that means fly-fishing in the Methow River for cutthroat and rainbow trout. In the winter, an ice hut provides shelter for hearty fishers aiming for bass.

In the summer and winter, guests dine in a windowed room that feels like a treehouse. The choices are tough. For dinner, will it be dry-aged ribeye, braised lamb shoulder, or steelhead trout from the Columbia River?

Surrounding conversations turn to memories of visits past and plans for return trips. In these times, simplicity is a rare treat.

Planning a Trip

Sun Mountain Lodge operates year-round, offering a wide array of seasonal activities. The drive from Seattle takes 4-plus hours, with spectacular views of the Columbia River. Facilities include a spa, petting zoo, pool, pickleball court, and stables. Fly-fishing excursions, guided nature walks, ax throwing, wagon rides, and mountain biking are also available.

MONTENEGRO

The Hidden Canyon

GREAT FOR	COST	WEBSITE
COUPLES, FRIENDS, FAMILIES	$	ECOVILLAGENEVIDIO.COM

Traversing Nevidio Canyon calls for fortitude, fearlessness, and perhaps a touch of foolhardiness. Those with grit find an experience that is, quite genuinely, unlike anything else. For 3 hours, they clamber, hike, swim, leap, rappel, and climb through almost 2 miles of waterfalls, thousand-foot rock walls, and serpentine mazes so tight that you have to wiggle sideways. Its very name means "hidden"—fitting for a geological wonder that was only officially "discovered" in 1965.

For adventure seekers, Nevidio may top the list of thrills in the 150 square miles of Durmitor National Park. But it's not even the park's deepest gorge. Those honors go to Tara, Europe's deepest canyon, at 4,265 feet. In the spring, visitors can raft through its Class IV rapids in water clean enough to drink; in the summer, they zip-line over the Tara River at speeds that reach 75 miles per hour.

Seasoned mountaineers find their challenges on one of the 6,600-foot-plus peaks in the park (there are 48 of them). Ascending the tallest, 8,278-foot Bobotov Kuk, takes a reasonably fit hiker about 6 hours round-trip over 6¼ miles, first through a grass valley and then up across brittle limestone boulders. The rewards are stunning views across sawtooth pinnacles all the way to the Adriatic Sea.

Clearly, a visit to Durmitor can take more than a couple of days. That's why Dragan Gašo Lalović, a renowned mountaineer, opened **Eco Village Nevidio** in 2010 above a small village near the canyon entrance. Today, it offers lodging in nine stone traditional-style cottages that look like gingerbread houses. All have two levels, the ground floor for living space and the second a sleeping loft. Both levels have terraces overlooking the forested mountains.

Though Lalović died in 2017, his family continues to operate the hotel with his passion for sustainability. Solar panels provide the power; all materials are natural; ingredients for the restaurant come from the local area. While cottages have electricity and Wi-Fi, they are not air-conditioned.

There's no TV—and no time to watch it. Biking and hiking through the European Black Pines brings the beauty of glacial lakes and stark massifs. The hotel can arrange horse-riding jaunts and rafting trips on the Tara River. Bungee and base jumping off the historic arched Tara River bridge are offered, along with zip-lining and Jeep tours.

Or just sit back and rest. You deserve it.

Planning a Trip

Eco Village Nevidio is open April through October. Breakfast is included. Airports at Tivat and Podgorica, Montenegro, and Dubrovnik, Croatia, all lie within a 2½-hour drive. Closest in driving time is the Podgorica airport.

TOP: *Cabins at Eco Selo Nevidio.*
BOTTOM LEFT: *View of Šavnik village from Eco Selo Nevidio.*
BOTTOM RIGHT: *Canyoning in Nevidio Canyon.*

Lobby at Cloud Camp.

COLORADO, USA

A Century in the Clouds

GREAT FOR	COST	WEBSITE
COUPLES, FAMILIES	$$$$	BROADMOOR.COM

At 9,100 feet, Cloud Camp's name says it all. To the north, Pike's Peak's 14,000-foot summit seems like a kissing cousin. To the south, the communications towers atop the NORAD military installation sit almost at eye level. The broad valley of Colorado Springs unfolds beneath the lodge deck, a cozy perch amid firs, rocks, and hawks' nests.

When Zebulon Pike arrived on this mountain in 1806, he was aiming for the 14,100-foot peak that now bears his name. He never made it there.

Pike climbed the hard way. Today's options are easier on the thighs. After you arrive by white Chevy Suburban, mule—yes, that's an option!—or on foot (one seriously long walk), you travel from the century-old **Broadmoor** hotel through the Cheyenne Mountain Zoo, past the tapirs and rhinos, then up a series of ever-rising switchbacks past the mule barn. If it all seems a bit odd, consider the Broadmoor's flamboyant founder, Spencer Penrose, who commissioned the zoo to house his personal menagerie of elephants and giraffes. The steep road above was built in 1925 by mule, pickax, and dynamite—a notable engineering feat at the time—to provide access to Cheyenne Mountain Lodge, as it was then called.

From the beginning, it was a party place in the sky, far from the eyes of those inclined to enforce Prohibition. For $3 or $4, guests who'd had one too many could overnight here.

That original lodge was closed in 1961 and later demolished. The 8,500-square-foot stone-and-timber lodge that replaced it opened in 2014 with seven rooms, 15 comfortable cabins surrounded by rocks and forest, and a fire-tower suite high above the rocks. All are decorated with Western fabrics.

Even in the summer, crisp air and bird chatter draw guests out of their wooden cabins for a guided hike, archery, or pickleball match. A graying sky is a hint that rain could be on the way—an excuse to walk along the wooded path to one of the two hot tubs. If a downpour really does occur, Western art hung throughout the expansive great room calls attention: a Sioux dress decorated with curving rows of elk teeth, evocative paintings by Charles Russell and Frederic Remington, and the shirt worn by Kevin Costner in *Dances with Wolves.*

Every day ends the same way: with a ceremonial lowering of the flag and a patriotic song. Guests sit together at long tables for hearty meals of steak au poivre or coq au vin and house-made lemon raspberry tart. It's a reminder that regardless of differences, these states are united.

Planning a Trip

Cloud Camp is open May to October. It is part of the Broadmoor Resort in Colorado Springs. Rates include all meals.

The closest airport is in Colorado Springs. The Denver Airport is a little over an hour away.

SWEDEN

An Almost-Polar Plunge

GREAT FOR	COST	WEBSITE
COUPLES, SMALL FAMILIES	$$$	ARCTICBATH.SE

The poles stand askew, as if some Nordic giant dropped his pick-up sticks in the middle of the snow. On approach, the drifts seem to flatten; a wooden walkway comes into view. A few feet along the path, it becomes clear that the "sticks" adorn a round building frozen in the winter ice of the Lule River.

Images of the dramatic floating lodge captured my imagination long before the place actually opened. What was inside the circular space? What happened in the middle of the donut hole? Could you really visit in the winter? And, perhaps most confounding: Why was this spectacular design in the tiny town of Harads, population 500?

Arctic Bath, it turns out, is just 2 miles down the road from the famous Treehotel (p. 21). It was there, over dinner, that the idea for Arctic Bath took shape. Initially, the owners—unrelated to Treehotel—planned a floating sauna in a glass cube. The idea morphed into a ring piled with pine, a reference to the river logjams that were once common in the 18th and 19th centuries, when Lapland became a timber center.

Ten years after that first conversation, **Arctic Bath** opened in 2020, with the circular lodge as its hub. Guests sleep nearby, in snug floating cubes or lofted glass-fronted cabins with wide river views.

On this cloudless March day, the floating hotel is mired in ice. The walkway leads to the smooth wooden interior of the restaurant, sauna, steam room, and changing rooms. The idea: Don a swimsuit, bake in the sauna, and then dash outside onto the snow-covered deck and plunge into the lake. Fly up the stepladder and run madly for the hot tub (which isn't feeling so hot). Grab a robe and a furry reindeer throw and bolt back into the warmth of the sauna.

The tiny town is short on eateries, making Arctic Bath's own restaurant an obvious choice for hotel guests. The inventive cuisine is locally sourced, and even on a clear day like this, the creamy smoked soup topped with caviar is a welcome addition to the artistic multicourse dinner. Then, I'm back to my cabin to lounge during what turns out to be a full-moon night.

I'm up early for a dog-sledding excursion, long on my personal "must" list. There's no view from the window. Winter's wrath has blown up overnight; just getting to breakfast takes a sturdy spine. Mushing will have to wait. Oh dear, I'll just have to come back for another visit.

Planning a Trip

Despite its name, Arctic Bath lies slightly south of the Arctic Circle. The hotel can arrange activities suitable for the season, from summer kayaking to winter snowmobiling. The airport at Lulea is about an hour away by car on smooth roads that are well cleared in winter.

TOP: Spa at Arctic Bath.
BOTTOM LEFT: Suite cabin at Arctic Bath.
BOTTOM MIDDLE: Hot tub in the middle of the spa.
BOTTOM RIGHT: Guestroom.

TOP: Dining room at Amanjiwo.
BOTTOM LEFT: Stupas at Borobudur World Heritage Site.
BOTTOM RIGHT: Borobudur village tour.

On Sacred Land

GREAT FOR	COST	WEBSITE
COUPLES, FAMILIES	$$$$	AMAN.COM/RESORTS/AMANJIWO

Amanjiwo in Dalem Jiwo.

We arrive before sunrise, climbing to an upper level with the help of a flashlight. A few minutes later, when the sun rises over central Java, the 9th-century Buddha statue before us is haloed by light, as if glowing from within—fitting for a temple designed as a map to Enlightenment.

Borobudur is the world's largest Buddhist temple, and one of the most beautiful. But it's not just the harmony of 72 bell-shaped stupas encircling the central dome that brings wonder to a quiet morning. The confluence of this distinctive culture with the nature that frames it is a potent cure for modern life.

Groomed gardens melt into a jungle of palm, tamarind, and bodhi trees. Wide terraces of rice paddies step down mountainsides. Thirty miles to the east, the volcanic cone of the ever-active Mount Merapi rises into the sky. Stress evaporates.

A 25-minute bike ride ends at **Amanjiwo,** a 36-room resort set at the foot of the forested Menoreh Hills. The templelike design mirrors Borobudur, which feels inspiring and slightly overwhelming. Should we whisper? Our reverence is soon lost to a mid-morning nap on the platform bed amid marble columns and smooth wood walls of our walled villa.

Then, my husband and I are off to explore. The hiking trail into the hills starts just behind the hotel and leads up to a perch where the view unfolds: the hotel, then the temple and the wide green plain. Coffee and flowering bushes edge the path. Along the way, we discover earthly features that have evoked legends; here is the cave where a 19th-century prince sought wisdom; there is the spring where a future king stole the clothing of a bathing nymph.

In this rural place, the fates of man and land are intertwined. Our immediate destiny is a dip in the pool overlooking the rice fields, followed by a martini with gin infused with local lavender. Meditation on the lawn can wait until tomorrow.

Planning a Trip

The best time to visit is the dry months between May and October, when highs are around 80°F. Borobudur and other area temples are crowded on weekends.

Amanjiwo is located on Java. Rates include round-trip transportation from Yogyakarta Airport, about 90 minutes away; breakfast; daily yoga; afternoon tea; and shuttle to Borobudur.

CHAPTER 10

SHORT STAYS: DINING & DAY TRIPS

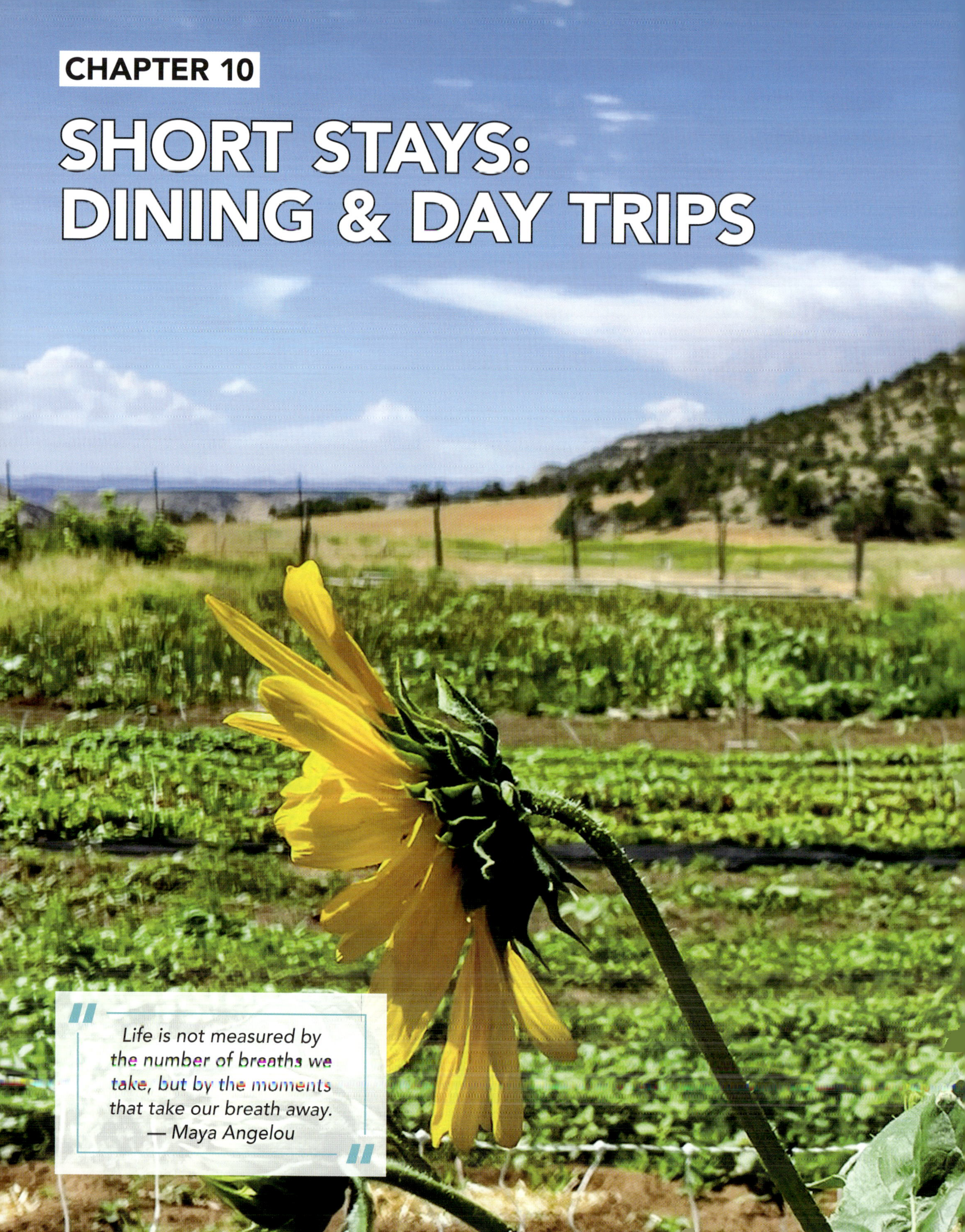

> Life is not measured by the number of breaths we take, but by the moments that take our breath away.
> — Maya Angelou

Sunflowers at Hell's Backbone Grill & Farm (p. 280).

SOUTH DAKOTA, USA

Chasing Bison

GREAT FOR	COST	WEBSITE
FAMILIES, HISTORY BUFFS	$	CUSTERRESORTS.COM

The canopied Jeep bounces over the dirt road, wind rushing through the windows. The chase is on. This isn't a hunt with a gun or bow and arrow, though permits are offered. This is a 2-hour wildlife-watching safari, South Dakota–style. Though the woolly mammoths that once ranged these prairies disappeared some 12,000 years ago, the buffalo still roam.

A herd of shaggy-faced, humped-back creatures ambles past, grazing and moving, moving, moving on a nightly migration led by a cow that can weigh 1,000 pounds. Bison society is matriarchal, says your guide.

Call them buffalo or bison, the huge-shouldered beast is the same. About 1,500 live here in the South Dakota Black Hills at Custer State Park. Each fall, some 14,000 visitors come for the annual roundup, when wranglers drive the beasts across the valley to corrals. Some 500 will be culled and sold for breeding.

Nearly 400,000 buffalo once roamed North America. By the late 1800s, the numbers had dwindled to about 800. In 1915, buffalo were brought to the land that soon would become a public park—an added attraction to the park's 71,000 acres of glacial lakes, grazing meadows, and jagged rock formations. Together, they create a raw grandeur that has appeared in films including *How the West Was Won* and *National Treasure II*.

Nearby are Wind Cave National Park, an underground trove of rare honeycomb formations, and the Badlands, whose forbidding name belies the stark beauty of the wind-and-water-carved hills. (Also in the area are the Minuteman Missile National Historic Site and the Mammoth archeological site.)

Just down the road sit man's own larger-than-life attempts at sculpting this harsh land. At Mount Rushmore, the granite faces of Presidents Lincoln, Washington, Roosevelt, and Jefferson stand 62 feet tall—an ingenious early-20th-century tourism ploy that still creates awe. Even more inspiring is the Crazy Horse Memorial, a 75-year project that's a testament to one family's tenacity in a sound-bite world.

Planning a Trip

The best time to visit is May to September, when highs are in the 70s and 80s Fahrenheit and all park lodges are open. The region is jammed during the Sturgis motorcycle rally each August.

Custer Park offers simple comfort at the **Sylvan Lake Lodge** and cabins—some overlooking the Needles. The historic **Game State Lodge,** which served as Calvin Coolidge's 1927 summer white house, was recently renovated. East of Mount Rushmore, **Under Canvas** glamping resort offers 52 comfortable glamping tents in a hillside pine forest; some offer views of the presidents.

TOP: Buffalo at Wind Cave National Park. MIDDLE: South Dakota Black Hills, Wind Cave National Park. BOTTOM: Sylvan Lake Lodge, Custer State Park

Dine on the Land event at Locavore Farm.

Farm, Food & the Family You Choose

GREAT FOR	COST	WEBSITE
COUPLES, FAMILIES	$$$	LOCAVOREFARM.COM

A guy in jeans and ballcap waves cars into a field already packed with dusty farm trucks and shiny city cars. Even at $165 a person, this is clearly a hot ticket.

Mason jars filled with sunflowers and dahlias dress up the 110-foot hand-crafted wood table stretching across the lawn. When everyone has arrived, 100 strangers will settle in with beer and smoked bourbon lemonade for **Locavore Farm's** monthly Dine on the Land celebration. They'll leave as a community.

"That's what we're trying to do here, to bring people together," Rachael Jones says as she fusses with an armful of hydrangeas. "My hope is that we learn from one another."

Restlessness, a love for meeting people, and their own search for meaning drove Jones, a municipal economic development director, and her husband, Chris, a biomedical engineer, to pack in their comfortable suburban Chicago lives in 2014 and move to 5 acres in rural Illinois. They had two children and adopted two more.

When it became clear that 5 acres wasn't nearly enough to fulfill their vision of food, family, and community, they crowd-funded the down payment on another 35 acres with a dilapidated house. Friends, family, and neighbors pitched in to help transform it into this busy farm, with goats, chickens, pigs, and acres of vegetables. That once-shabby house is now an airy guest cottage.

In summer, Locavore hosts children's camps focused on farming and healthy foods. On Thursdays, neighbors gather for casual suppers with live music and homemade dishes, such as smoked pork tacos and blackberry charred crumble. Monthly, on Saturdays, the Joneses host the multicourse Dine on the Land feasts in collaboration with well-known chefs who fashion fresh-from-the-earth veggies and house-smoked meats into a multicourse feast.

The goal is to satisfy a hunger that goes beyond the belly.

"Hospitality creates moments and flavors and space where people can be revived. They remember what feels good, what tastes good, what feels worth it," says Rachael. "That's my desire for people who come on the farm, so they feel that for a moment and emulate it in their lives."

Planning a Trip

Locavore Farm is located an hour south of Chicago in Grant Park, Illinois. Dine on the Land events are on select Saturday evenings, June through September. Reservations and casual shoes are a must. Casual Thursday dinners run May to October and are a la carte; reservations are advised.

UTAH, USA

Dining Along a Rocky Spine

GREAT FOR	COST	WEBSITE
COUPLES, FAMILIES, GROUPS	$$$	HELLSBACKBONEGRILL.COM

Utah's Route 12 twists into a hairpin, then hugs a towering red rock wall before dipping and soaring again along the ridge of the Grand Staircase-Escalante. The views are awe-inspiring, the driving terrifying. And you've not even hit the gravel roadway dubbed Hell's Backbone.

Good news: **Hell's Backbone Grill & Farm** is right there on the paved road at Boulder, elevation 6,600 feet, though it feels about as far off the grid as a human can get. Drive at the 40mph speed limit, and despite the fluttering Buddhist flags, you'll blow right past it.

This tiny Mormon town of 243 is a curious place for a James Beard-finalist fine-dining restaurant that's been winning kudos since it opened more than 25 years ago. Co-owner and chef Blake Spalding stumbled on this place in 2000, when her then-boyfriend was repairing the Boulder Mountain Inn. For Spalding and co-owner Jen Castle, friends and chefs for rival Grand Canyon outfitters, the inn's closed grill offered an affordable opportunity to open the place-based restaurant they'd imagined in a stunning landscape.

Towers and cliffs plummet to gorges and chasms, then flatten and roll to reveal swirls of red, copper, and sand 4 billion years in the making. The national monument stretches as far as you see.

"It's my life's work, helping people understand that we belong on this planet," says Spalding, a Buddhist. "We're helping people connect with the wilderness. Most people, if they can't see a night sky, they forget that you're in an animal body that craves being connected to earth and sky. . . . We want to make people feel good here."

Diners enjoy organic fare featuring herbs, tomatoes, apricots, cherries, squash, and beans grown on their own nearby farm. Most meats come from a local farmer. The only fish are trout from the region.

The bounty is transformed into bison and green chile meatballs, pan-seared chicken breast with a lemony sauce, and vegetarian posole with corn, black beans, and butternut squash. While the menu changes with the season, two much-loved dishes are always on offer: bison-and-beef meatloaf and the nightly variation on a "Jenchilada" in a habanero cream sauce. "We tried to take them off, and customers lost their minds," said Spalding.

Planning a Trip

Hell's Backbone Grill & Farm is open for dinner March to November. In late 2024, the chefs purchased the Boulder Mountain Inn, which operates year-round. Boulder is located 90 minutes north of **Bryce Canyon** and an hour south of **Capitol Reef.**

TOP LEFT: *Aerial view of Boulder Mountain Lodge.*
TOP RIGHT: *Beet dish, Hell's Backbone Grill & Farm.*
BOTTOM LEFT: *Founding owners Jen Castle and Blake Spalding.*
BOTTOM RIGHT: *Entrance, Hell's Backbone Grill & Farm.*

Pool bar at Tabacón Thermal Resort & Spa.

A Soothing Soak in Thermal Springs

GREAT FOR	COST	WEBSITE
COUPLES, FAMILIES	$$	TABACONSPRINGS.COM

Arenal Volcano rises a mile above the leafy rainforest, its perfect cone visible for hundreds of miles. Hikers and horse riders come to its 500,000-acre national park for white-faced monkeys, delicate orchids, and some 950 bird species in colors bright enough to make Big Bird jealous.

Though the volcano has been dormant for the past 15 years, Arenal's geothermals still warm the springs that bubble through the surrounding jungle. After a long hike or jarring ATV ride, a leisurely soak may be just the antidote you need.

For more than 3 decades, **Tabacón Thermal Resort & Spa** has welcomed day visitors to its 163-acre gardens. Red ginger blooms sway near the spring-fed brook that cascades down rock-lined pools surrounded by bromeliads. Water pools into nature's answer to a hot tub before slipping over a curved edge to create a diaphanous curtain that looks like a scene from an episode of *The Bachelor.* Toucans whose colorful beaks look like abstract paintings sit in Guarumo trees. Iridescent motmots with long brushy tails look like sweepers on their way to clear paths from some invisible pollen. As dusk approaches, a sloth may creep through the trees.

The garden is crisscrossed with bridges and decking that are easy on bare feet. Handy railings are conveniently stationed to steady languorous guests as they emerge from the warm water. Temperatures are regulated by nature, ranging from a tepid 75° to cozy 105°F. If soaking isn't enough to recalibrate the psyche, guests can add spa treatments using local ingredients. Body wraps are infused with lemongrass, volcanic mud, or wild berries. Exfoliation is aided by pineapple or chocolate. Massage treatments involve Himalayan pink salt stones or olive oil and honey. Exfoliating facials use grounds from locally grown coffee. New are balneotherapy journeys for detoxing the body and calming the spirit.

The cocktail menu is jammed with rum and tequila options along with zero-proof concoctions that will keep the kids hydrated while parents snag a nap. After spiced rum with gin and coconut cream, they may need it.

Planning a Trip

Tabacón Thermal Resort & Spa is about 15 minutes west of La Fortuna on Route 142. Use is complimentary for guests of the highly rated Tabacón Resort hotel just across the road.

Nonresidents can book a day pass online or on-site that includes entrance to the springs area along with a towel, lockers, and showers. You can add lunch or dinner for an additional fee. The number of nonresident guests is limited. Children under 5 are free; those ages 6 to 12 pay a reduced rate.

ARMENIA

Wildlife & Wine

GREAT FOR	COST	WEBSITE
COUPLES, GROUPS UP TO 8	$$$	2492.TRAVEL/WILDFOOD

France, Italy, and Portugal are most closely associated with wine production. But long before Greece, Egypt, and Rome ruled the ancient world, wine was already being produced in the countryside of modern-day Armenia, near the village of Areni. After Armenia broke from the Soviet Union in 1991, a handful of locals worked to regain their wine-making heritage.

Visitors can taste the results at restaurants throughout the country. But no eatery is more dramatic than the tented dining table at the edge of the stark red Areni cliffs, in view of the two-story Noravank monastery. The church is known for its spectacular design and the backstory that inspired it. Promised the hand of the princess if the church was completed on schedule, the architect Momik was murdered just before the last stone was set.

More than 700 years later, another couple is sharing this heritage with tourists at **The Winemaker's Table,** one of seven Wild Food Adventures offered by 2492 Travel.

Guests meet their guide in the Areni village center, where husband-and-wife team Mariam and Anushavan make their Sar wine. An off-road vehicle whisks them away on a (seriously) bumpy 25-minute ride into the nearby protected wildlife area. You settle into your chair on the gorge for a glass of sangria and a three-course meal of tarragon salad (Mariam's family recipe), pumpkin hummus, lentils, trout wrapped in lavash with grilled pepper puree, grape leaves stuffed with beef, and grilled fruits—and, of course, a glass or two (or three) of wine.

Nearby, rangers have set up a scope for wildlife sightings. Seeing a Persian leopard is unlikely; they're elusive and rare. Chances are better for bezoar goats. Thanks to the rangers, there's a good view.

Happy and full, you brace for the ride back. It doesn't seem so outrageous this time. Must be the wine.

Planning a Trip

2492 Travel is an offshoot of **One Armenia,** a nonprofit designed to create jobs in rural areas. One of its successes is Areni's lauded Momik Wines, which offers tastings in its vineyard.

For a really wild ride, try **Mountaintop Eats** in **Yeranos,** east of Yerevan. A vintage Russian SUV takes you on a 90-minute off-road ride with views of the Azat Reservoir and Turkey's Mount Ararat, said to be the post-flood resting place of Noah's Ark. The Armenian barbecue starts with a cocktail made from the local almond vodka.

***TOP LEFT:** Surb Astvatsatsin church at Noravank Monastery.*
***TOP RIGHT:** A table with magnificent views.*
***MIDDLE:** Guests, Wild Food Adventures.*
***BOTTOM:** Appetizers, Wild Food Adventures.*

TURNER

MAINE, USA

A Barn Supper on Ancient Land

GREAT FOR	COST	WEBSITE
COUPLES, FAMILIES	$$$	TURNER-FARM.COM

Guests hop aboard the charter boat that sails from the mainland town of Rockland across Penobscot Bay, past the Rockland lighthouse and stone islets, to 200-acre North Haven and its weekly barn supper. They can also take the early ferry that docks in the town center, so they can see what's new at the art gallery and the community center bulletin board. Except for cozy Nebo Lodge, there's little commercial buzz in the village. Still, watching people come and go allows you to guess which are the locals—farmers, lobstermen, and oyster growers—and which are the Boston millionaires whose families have summered here for generations. Everybody pretty much dresses the same.

I've done it both ways. This night, I arrive by charter, rambling past the free-range chickens, eight pigs, and vegetable garden to the barn atop the hill. From here, I can see miles of indigo water, red spruces and balsam firs, and one single farmhouse. No wonder this dinner was featured on National Geographic TV's *Restaurants at the End of the World.*

The barn doors stand open, revealing a bar offering a choice of cabernet, chardonnay, or a Southshore cocktail of mint lemon soda—with or without gin. Two long tables are set with place cards on the white tablecloths and vintage china that remind you of Grandma.

Platters appear, filled with freshly baked focaccia, carrots and lettuces and beets, roasted radishes, smashed potatoes with walnut relish, and grilled tenderloin with salsa verde. The produce tastes like it just came out of the garden because, well, it did.

To my right sits a local town commissioner. To my left, an L.A. film executive and her lawyer husband whose family has had a place here for decades. Everyone talks about how they ended up at this table and, in that six-degrees way, discovers they're connected by friends of friends.

That's the way of this land. As long as 6,000 years ago, the Indigenous Wabanaki people gathered here for great feasts, say archeologists. In 2016, the Barn Suppers revived the tradition to help preserve the 153 acres now owned by the American Farmland Trust and to keep that community spirit alive.

Planning a Trip

Turner Farm hosts Barn Suppers on Thursday and Friday nights from mid-June to mid-September. Round-trip service aboard the *Equinox* from Rockland to the farm sells out quickly.

***TOP LEFT:** Free-range chickens, Turner Farm.*
***TOP RIGHT:** Dining event, Turner Farm.*
***BOTTOM LEFT & RIGHT:** Barn at Turner Farm.*

CHAPTER 11

ON THE SEA: EXPEDITION & ADVENTURE CRUISES

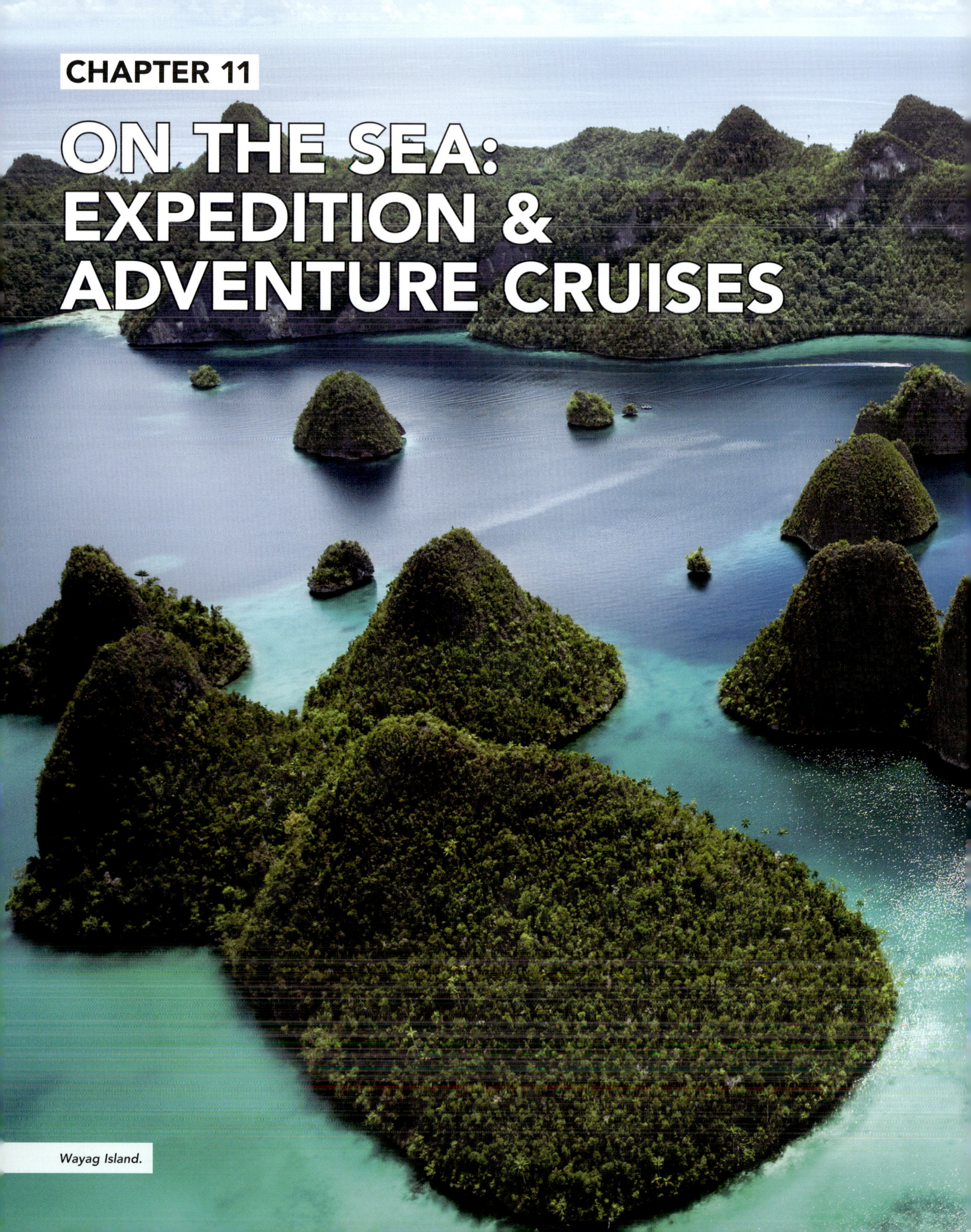

Wayag Island.

> The real voyage of discovery consists not in seeking new landscapes, but in having new eyes.
> — Marcel Proust
>
> We can't care for something we don't understand. This is the purpose of why we explore and why we voyage.
> — Nainoa Thompson
>
> Twenty years from now you will be more disappointed by the things that you didn't do than by the ones you did do. So throw off the bowlines. Sail away from the safe harbor. Catch the trade winds in your sails. Explore. Dream. Discover.
> — H. Jackson Brown

NORWAY

Searching for Polar Bears in the Far North

GREAT FOR	COST	WEBSITE
COUPLES, FAMILIES WITH ADULT CHILDREN	$$$$$	SCENICUSA.COM

North of Scandinavia, east of Greenland, west of Russia, and high above the Arctic Circle, the islands of Svalbard are so remote that international scientists use them as an insurance policy against disaster, storing 4.5 million crop seeds deep in the frozen earth. For travelers on expedition sailings, the primary attraction is polar bears.

But nature is in charge here, and viewings aren't guaranteed. On one cruise, you might see a single bear. On another, a pair of chunky cubs gambol near their 300-plus-pound mother—just one of a half-dozen bear sightings on the 10-day voyage. But even from the Zodiacs, the bears are often mere specks, hardly distinguishable from clumps of ice on the rocky beach. Better views come through the scope on the ship's bridge, where naturalists help you tune the focus and snap photos through a super-magnified scope.

Threatened by a melting habitat, polar bears have been deemed a vulnerable species. As the planet's prime territory for polar bears, this isolated archipelago is tightly protected. Only ships carrying fewer than 200 guests can land ashore. International regulations enforced by Norwegian administrators require humans to keep their distance. A bear-human encounter can result in tragedy for all.

And as you quickly learn, there's so much more to this archipelago than polar bears. Twice-daily excursions on land and by Zodiac take you to tundra with reindeer grazing on miniscule forests, rocky beaches filled with snoozing walruses, and soaring basalt cliffs jammed with 200,000 fledgling Brunnich's guillemot chicks that leap into the icy sea for their first swimming lessons. Kayakers paddle among ice flows, seeking bearded seals and intimate views of calving ice. If conditions are right, your captain may detour to beyond the continental shelf, where fin whales, humpbacks, and minkes circle the ship.

Aboard the *Scenic Eclipse*

On the *Scenic Eclipse*, more than two dozen experienced naturalists are always on hand, explaining the ecosystem and ensuring safety. The line's open-bridge policy promotes conversation about the ship's stabilizing design and the rigors of navigation. Use of *Scenic*'s helicopters and submarines—so popular in other regions—is prohibited in this fragile place.

On board, guests find a blend of classic and expedition features. They can sip top-brand whiskeys (Macallan, Glenfiddich, and Glenmorangie) at the stylish bar, hit the sauna and spa, gather for a nightly wildlife briefing or entertainment, and snuggle on their headrest of choice from the pillow menu. All suites feature verandas, king beds, and marble bathrooms.

Polar bear in Svalbard.

TOP: Eclipse verandah suite.
BOTTOM LEFT: Cooking demonstration, Eclipse.
BOTTOM RIGHT: The Scenic Bar, Eclipse.

Zodiac expedition at Brepollen Longyearbyen.

But what keeps everyone chattering is the cuisine served in eight distinctive venues, remarkable on a vessel whose maximum capacity is 228 passengers. Shall you have crispy frog legs in the French restaurant, Lumiere; hamachi at the sushi bar; fresh local fish with ginger and miso at Koko's Asian fusion eatery; steak in the Eclipse dining room; or the roll-up ice cream dessert in the Night Market? (If you snag a coveted invitation to the Chef's Table, you're in for a star-worthy experience.)

Unlike Antarctica and higher Arctic regions blanketed by vast ice, the beauty of Svalbard is subtle. That can mean a smoother journey, without the potential tumult of the Drake Passage leading from Argentina to Antarctica. It also means you must look closely to begin to understand Svalbard's complexity.

"Which do I like better, the North or the South?" says Andrus, a shipboard naturalist who has completed more than 130 polar voyages. "That's like saying, 'Which do you love more, your son or your daughter?'"

Planning a Trip

Svalbard cruises last more than 2 weeks and operate only in the summer months. Scenic offers only a few sailings each season, starting from Bergen or Oslo, Norway. Passenger flights between Longyearbyen, in Svalbard, and Oslo are included.

Other small-ship brands sailing in the region include Aurora Expeditions, Atlas Ocean Cruises, HX Hurtigruten Expeditions, Lindblad Expeditions-National Geographic, Oceanwide Expeditions, Ponant Cruises, Poseidon Expeditions, Quark Expeditions, Seabourn, and Silversea Cruises.

Tropical Islands to Warm Blue Seas

GREAT FOR	COST	WEBSITE
COUPLES, FAMILIES WITH OLDER CHILDREN	$$$$$	SEABOURN.COM

By air, getting to Papua New Guinea's Asmat region requires multiple flights and a 7-hour motorboat ride. An expedition cruise is by far the most comfortable way to go. Even then, your ship must moor in depths that are far from shore, and it takes an hour in a Zodiac before reaching landing for the 200-plus guests aboard the *Seabourn Pursuit.*

When you see the welcoming committee at the village of Per, you'll likely decide it's well worth the journey. Four hundred feather-crowned villagers surround you, fiercely beating paddles against their wooden canoes. Another 1,000 greet you on shore: old men with white painted faces and bones through their nose, grannies dancing in grass skirts, young children staring wide-eyed. You witness an elaborate ritual to whisk the spirits of deceased warriors to the afterlife. Afterward, you're invited into the men's house, where customs are conveyed from one generation to the next.

Then, it's back to the comfort of your ship: champagne and complimentary afternoon caviar on your suite balcony, martinis at the bar with new-found friends, soft-shell crab or filet mignon for dinner. A massage if you're feeling lazy; the gym if you absolutely must. Staffers seem to always remember your name and your penchant for pinot noir.

Aboard the *Seabourn Pursuit*

The ship is your base camp, enabling visits to the Solomon Islands, New Guinea, and the rich reefs of Raja Ampat in a single voyage. On board *Pursuit*, you'll sail 3,400 nautical miles over 2 weeks from the Solomons to Darwin, Australia, seeking cultures little changed over the centuries, a chance to see birds of paradise in the wild, and an underwater region home to the earth's richest biodiversity.

You'll have plenty of days at sea when you expect to nap or read, only to be lured from laziness by talks on underwater volcanology, avian mating rituals, and World War II history by members of the 24-member expedition crew. Whoever guessed that marine reproduction could be so downright bizarre?

***TOP LEFT:* Zodiac tour, Wayag Island.**
***TOP RIGHT:* Welcoming ceremony, Agats.**
***MIDDLE LEFT:* Resident, Alotau.**
***MIDDLE RIGHT:* Welcoming ceremony, Kitava.**
***BOTTOM LEFT:* Snorkeling tour.**
***BOTTOM RIGHT:* Kopar Village Ceremony.**

Divers and snorkelers are in their own blue heaven, chasing turquoise parrotfish and orange-striped clowns across vibrant corals waving in the current. A cuttlefish, so cartoonish with its tentacle face, hides beneath a brain coral. A school of angelfish sweeps you into its flow.

Birders slip into their own particular trance, staring through binoculars at turquoise-toned kingfishers and crimson-colored lories. A few hearty souls rise well before dawn for a chance to see the rare red bird of paradise, found only in these islands.

While the world you'll explore is pristine in many regards, you witness firsthand the damage wrought by warming seas, poachers, and the plastic that gathers on the shore. The world—and we—are more fragile than we know.

Victoria crowned pigeon, Papua New Guinea.

Planning a Trip

The Papua New Guinea sailing is one leg in a series of *Seabourn*'s South Pacific expeditions from Santiago, Chile, via Easter Island to Tahiti, Fiji, Guam, Guadalcanal, and on to Western Australia's Kimberley region. Most passengers sign up for more than one leg. Other lines offering expeditions in the region include Aqua Expeditions, Lindblad Expeditions, EYOS, Ponant, and Coral Expeditions.

FACING PAGE, TOP: *Panorama Veranda Suite, Seabourn Pursuit.*
MIDDLE: *Champagne surprise for Zodiac passengers.*
BOTTOM: *Kayak tour of Misool.*

MAINE, USA

Into the Wind

GREAT FOR	COST	WEBSITE
COUPLES, SOLOS, FAMILIES WITH CHILDREN WHO WON'T MISS INTERNET ACCESS	$$$	SCHOONERLADONA.COM

Some sign up for windjammer voyages to take in wind and waves, others for the pain-free glory of sailing to Penobscot Bay's scattered isles without the hassles of swabbing the deck. Others come out of nostalgia for Maine's centuries-long shipbuilding heritage and a nod to the commercial fleet that once hauled iron and ice to the south.

Occasionally, a porpoise breaks the surface; a group of seals suns on boulders. A whitewashed lighthouse crowns a crag high above the water. Granite doughnuts seem to bob on the sea; on closer inspection, they prove solid and unmoving, islands trimmed with spiky puffs of firs.

Traditional ways persist here. Shingled cottages dot the land. Islands are hard to reach; those that are accessible are more likely linked by ferries than roads. Slick is frowned upon, and even the occasional obscenely priced summer home has a timeless feel. Nets and lobster traps spill from the beds of pickups owned by lobstermen battling high fuel prices and bait costs. You sit mesmerized, watching this wild, rocky coast slide by.

On all windjammers, you are invited to help heave halyards that hoist mainsails, topsails, or mizzens up the masts. Or you can simply go about the day's business: reading, snoozing, visiting a lighthouse or fishing village, or taking a daring dip into the chilly water.

Aboard the *Ladona*

The schooner *Ladona*'s beginnings were more refined than those of most tall ships in the region. Built as a private family yacht in 1922, she vacationed along the eastern seaboard and sometimes raced. When World War II erupted, she served her country, patrolling for U-boats. She worked as a fishing dragger, then a training vessel, and finally as a tourist-carrying windjammer called the *Nathanial Bowditch.* Wharfed by disrepair, her history might have ended without captain Noah Barnes; his wife, Jane; and partner J. R. Braugh. The trio gutted and refitted the 82-foot ship and returned her to her original name and elegance.

Today, she is part of the **Maine Windjammer Fleet,** nine individually owned classic sailing ships offering a lazy version of adventure. None has a pool, spa, cigar club, Internet connection, or president's suite—or even en suite toilets. This is sailing—and sailing into the past, at that.

TOP: Windjammers in Penobscot Bay.
BOTTOM: Customer takes the wheel of the Ladona.

LEWIS R. FRENCH
LADONA

***Cabin aboard* Ladona.**

Ladona is more polished than most, with naturally lit cabins featuring hot running water, USB power outlets, and bathrobes. The three heads are lined with marble.

Before sunset, the sails drop. Wines and a charcuterie board featuring house-made duck prosciutto and artisan cheeses like Jasper Hill Bayley Hazen Blue and Montboissie Morbier appear. The table is set for 17 for Chef Anna Miller's nightly alfresco feast of quail or perhaps poached halibut. And on one night each sailing, a lobster bake with all the trimmings. This is Maine, after all.

Planning a Trip

Maine windjammers offer a variety of 3- to 12-night sailings from May through October, beginning in the nearby towns of Camden and Rockland. All are casual.

The *Ladona* caters to guests seeking sophisticated cuisine, upgraded cabins, and a casual house-party ambiance.

Eight other tall ships in the Maine Windjammer Fleet (sailmainecoast.com) offer similar sailings, each with its own personality. The Barneses also own and operate the *Stephen Taber.* Noah Barnes is a popular local musician who often plays aboard the *Ladona.*

FACING PAGE, TOP: *Maine Windjammers.*
BOTTOM LEFT: *Dining aboard a Maine Windjammer.*
BOTTOM RIGHT: *Hoisting the sails.*

Exploring an Ancient Rockscape

GREAT FOR	COST	WEBSITE
COUPLES, SOLOS, PARENTS WITH ADULT CHILDREN	$$$$$	SILVERSEA.COM

In Australia's rugged northwest, waterfalls go sideways. Rocks are older than cellular life. And the Wandjina—the spirits that created this land—still shape beliefs and customs.

The burnished cliffs of Australia's Kimberley region may remind you of such American parks as the Grand Canyon and Capitol Reef. But the Kimberley is far more remote, wedged between the Timor Sea and the Australian desert. Roads are few and indirect. An expedition cruise is the easiest option.

Our Silversea ship idles in Talbot Bay, awaiting the tidal change that can swing more than 35 feet thanks to the topography above water and below. When the time comes, we move deep into the bay, then load into Zodiacs, the stable inflatable boats used for expedition excursions.

The bay narrows, allowing close-up views of the surrounding cliffs that once sat on a seabed. Over the past 1.8 billion years—yes, *billion*—minute tectonic gyrations have caused the rock strata to bend, fold, and literally stand on their heads. The fiery red rock is too ancient for fossils.

As you near the falls, the water roils with the force of 1 million liters per second rushing through a narrow gap. Sir David Attenborough has called this one of the world's greatest natural phenomena. The locals call these roiling rapids "angry waters." You may simply say, "Wow."

On the *Silversea Silver Cloud*

On other days, the Zodiac transports us along mudbanks and into gorges in the care of the 24-member expedition team. Dolphins play in the water. Bright orange-flame fiddler crabs forage on a mudbank beneath mangroves, while mudskippers twirl and leap to attract mates.

Tawny beaches stretch across coves where we visit some of the planet's oldest rock paintings, drawn by the local Worrora people. While these people have lived here some 65,000 years, the rock art itself is only—only?—about 4,000 years old. But the stories they tell of the Wandjina date from the beginning of time.

Just 15 feet below the sea's surface, the Montgomery Reef presents another rare phenomenon. The Zodiac visit is timed for the tidal ebb, when water roars down the reef's clefts and crevasses. In mere minutes, the tide drops 10 feet or more, and the submerged sandstone appears. Egrets, heron, and stone curlews swoop down to hunt for fish and crabs in the newly formed puddles. Green turtles pop up their heads, periscope-like, often so fast that you can scarcely spot them.

***TOP:* Zodiac cruise at Montgomery Reef, off the Kimberley Coast.**
***BOTTOM:* Talbot Bay.**

On the sea, Montgomery Reef offers up a feast for marine creatures. On the *Silver Cloud,* you dine on expert talks on rock art and natural phenomena. Culinary feasts are delivered by butlers (suite service and afternoon canapes), La Terraza (the lunch buffet of sushi, salads, roasts, and more desserts than ought to be legal), and The Restaurant (lobster in a light cream sauce and filet mignon with bearnaise). The reservations-only La Dame offers a four-course French menu: caviar, escargot, blazed duck breast or pan-fried dover sole, and pistachio soufﬂe. So worth the calories.

Planning a Trip

Kimberley sailings are offered between June and August. While a few large ships sail the waters off the Kimberley, only small expedition vessels can access sites inside rivers and tight coves. Other lines offering similar itineraries include Seabourn, Coral Expeditions, Ponant Cruises, and True North.

TOP LEFT: Hunter River, Kimberley.
TOP RIGHT: The Silver Cloud.
MIDDLE RIGHT: The Restaurant, the Silver Cloud.
BOTTOM LEFT: Saltwater crocodile in Kimberley.
BOTTOM RIGHT: Aboriginal art in Kimberley.

SILVER CLOUD

GREENLAND

Where Icebergs Are Born

GREAT FOR	COST	WEBSITE
COUPLES, SOLOS, PARENTS WITH ADULT CHILDREN	$$$$$	TRAVELHX.COM

It's well past midnight, but the sun is still gleaming behind jagged peaks, washing the sky with a rosy shimmer. A waterfall gushes from a rocky cleft edging Disko Bay. Light glints off the ice floes like sequins scattered on the calm water.

If you can't bear to go to bed, you'll have company. Fellow travelers, too, are mesmerized by this surreal universe north of the Arctic Circle.

The voyage in western Greenland's Disko Bay takes you into a culture where the "grocery" lies beneath the ice and whale hunting is a survival skill. You can hike atop the oldest of Earth's crusts and trod on its second-largest ice cap. The glories of a fleeting frozen landscape surround you.

As expedition cruising has increased worldwide, an increasing number of foreign visitors are coming to this 770,000-square-mile island, the world's largest, as ships sail from Svalbard, Norway, to Iceland. Given its remote location between the Arctic and Atlantic Oceans, Greenland is hardly overrun. There are no roads; the 130,000-plus annual visitors come by air or sea.

Aboard the *Fridtjof Nansen*

It's the ice visitors come to see. The world's fastest glacier, Jacobshavn, flows more than 100 feet per day through the Icefjord, a UNESCO World Heritage site near the tourist-friendly town of Illulissat. From the town and from the ship's deck, you see the vast chunks fall into the sea. In the relatively shallow water here, they mire like SUVs on a freeway at rush hour. The result is an ice jam of Matterhorns and Space Mountains, amphitheaters and Gibraltar Rocks—all curved and swept, carved, and etched in ice. When the massive bergs finally do break loose, the chunks often drift into the Labrador Current and sail south into the Atlantic, like the iceberg that pierced the *Titanic*.

The sight inspires awe—and serious concern. As the planet warms, Greenland's mile thick ice cap and glaciers are diminishing. Greenland's melting glaciers are some of the main contributors to global sea rise, according to scientists at NASA and elsewhere. The result is obvious: Greenland melts; the U.S. floods.

TOP: Kayaking through icebergs in Ilulissat.
MIDDLE: Nuuk Fjords.
BOTTOM: Icebergs off the town of Qeqertarsuaq.

WINCH
ONLY

Despite the ice, it is snug on the 490-passenger, hybrid-powered ice-class ship, the *Fridtjof Nansen*. For more than 130 years, owner Hurtigruten has sailed in northern waters, first providing mail service along the Norwegian coast and now sailing worldwide. *Fridtjof Nansen* is the newest of the five ships in its expedition division, HX. Its Scandinavian heritage is evident in its clean design, European duvets, and menus featuring local dishes of fish and reindeer that you won't readily find elsewhere.

Wide windows offer expansive views from cabins (about half have balconies) and lounges. But the centerpiece is the science center, where guests interact with the expedition team, attend talks, and even participate in research.

Unlike other expeditions, Disko Bay itineraries include scheduled stops in communities where remote locations and harsh conditions have shaped traditional Inuit ways. Hunting is a necessity here, where dog-drawn sleighs are a hedge against unreliable snowmobiles. Don't be surprised when you find seal meat and reindeer steaks in the butcher shop of Sissimut, Greenland's second-largest city. If weather allows the ship to land in a small town like Ukkusissat, all 150 residents will come out to meet it.

Other days, cruisers may hike among rocky massifs ashore, kayak amid the twisted ice, or spend the day at sea, catching lectures by the ship's knowledgeable expedition staff. Change is constant in this part of the globe, and even if you've been north of the Arctic Circle before, you'll find that Greenland is a different world altogether.

Planning a Trip

Increased air service and a new airport in Greenland's capital of Nuuk have eased travel from Iceland and Denmark, which oversees Greenland. Additional airports in Ilulissat and Qaqortoq are set to open in late 2026.

Greenland sailings are limited to summer months. HX—Hurtigruten Expeditions—offers just a few sailings in Disko Bay each year.

Other lines offering Disko Bay sailings include Poseidon Adventures, Ponant Cruises, Quark Expeditions, Aurora Expeditions, Albatros Expeditions, Lindblad-National Geographic, and Polar Quest.

TOP LEFT: *Sauna, the MS* **Fridtjof Nansen.**
TOP RIGHT: *Science lecture, the MS* **Fridtjof Nansen.**
MIDDLE: *Aerial of MS* **Fridtjof Nansen.**
BOTTOM: *Hot tubs and infinity pool, MS* **Fridtjof Nansen.**

In Darwin's Footsteps

GREAT FOR	COST	WEBSITE
COUPLES, SOLOS, FAMILIES WITH CHILDREN OLD ENOUGH TO SWIM	$$$$$	CELEBRITYCRUISES.COM

A tawny sea lion sprawls in the middle of the path leading from your Zodiac to the crest of this arid isle. To get to the nesting grounds above, you'll have to go around him, then dodge a blue-footed booby with turquoise webbed feet.

Make that dozens of webbed feet. In the Galápagos Islands, wildlife is denser and closer than you expect. As hard as you try to maintain the required 6-foot distance, the thousands of resident birds, sea lions, and iguanas don't always allow it. Thank goodness the giant tortoises move too slowly to get in the way.

It's no wonder that Charles Darwin was awestruck when he landed on these rocky, sea-flooded volcanoes 600 miles west of the Ecuadorian mainland in 1835. Though he spent just 5 weeks here during the HMS *Beagle*'s 5-year voyage, his Galápagos visit reshaped scientific thinking forever.

This isolated location and a rare convergence of currents create a unique meeting place of species— some unique in themselves. Cold-water creatures, including penguins, fur seals, sardines, and anchovies, join migrating whale sharks and humpback whales, flightless cormorants, red-lipped lava lizards, and bright red Sally Lightfoot crabs. Male frigate birds puff out red under-chin pouches, while boobies flash their blue feet in a cancan—all to attract females. Spiky-headed land iguanas the size of schnauzers line up like a casting call for the next Godzilla reboot.

Aboard the *Celebrity Flora*

In recent years, more than 300,000 visitors have come here annually to re-create Darwin's experience, though in considerably greater comfort. Among the larger vessels sailing here is the 100-passenger *Celebrity Flora*. Built especially for these waters, the 333-foot ship offers panoramic views, all-suite staterooms, and a dedicated glamping area for those who want to sleep out under the stars. Yes, there's local seafood on the menus at its two restaurants, though not fruits with seeds (banned by local regulations).

Flora's 10 onboard naturalists play a dual role: ensuring that the fragile habitat is undisturbed and explaining this singular ecosystem. From them, you may learn that Galápagos tortoises can live more than 100 years and that marine iguanas can dive more than 30 feet deep. And who knew that despite their elaborate geek-dance mating ritual and reputation of partnering for life, albatrosses aren't necessarily monogamous and do sometimes divorce?

TOP: ***Seal with the*** **Celebrity Flora.**
BOTTOM: ***Penthouse suite, the*** **Celebrity Flora.**

***Seaside Restaurant,* the Celebrity Flora.**

Even these experts can't quite prepare you for the magic of snorkeling in these seas. Green sea turtles paddle by languidly, undaunted by human presence. Tropical penguins dart through the waters, past white-tipped sharks and eagle rays. But none are as enchanting as the young sea lions that dash in close to your mask, then playfully zip away in classic fake-out moves. The mothers hover nearby, and you can almost hear them chiding the pups. Like most teens, they pay no mind.

Planning a Trip

Galápagos sailings occur year-round. Bird mating times vary by species; June is prime time for viewing rituals for frigate birds, blue-footed boobies, and albatrosses. Turtles hatch between December and April; the most active time for bird hatchlings begins in July. Sea pups appear in August.

All Galápagos cruises require transit through Quito or Guayaquil. Ships range in size from 12 to *Flora*'s 100 guests. The larger the ship, the greater the amenities.

The *Celebrity Flora* offers 7-night sailings with add-on tours to Machu Picchu or Quito. It features all-suite accommodations, lounges, and two restaurants featuring floor to ceiling windows.

Other major companies offering Galápagos cruises include Lindblad-National Geographic, Silversea, Aqua Expeditions, Avalon Waterways, and Metropolitan Touring.

***FACING PAGE, TOP LEFT:* Day trip, the Galápagos. *TOP RIGHT:* Blue-footed booby. *MIDDLE LEFT:* Sea lion, San Cristobal Island. *MIDDLE RIGHT:* Discovery Lounge, the Celebrity Flora. *BOTTOM LEFT:* Giant tortoise, Santa Cruz Island. *BOTTOM RIGHT:* Iguana.**

ANTARCTICA

Voyage to the White Continent

GREAT FOR	COST	WEBSITE
COUPLES, SOLOS, FAMILIES WITH OLDER CHILDREN	$$$$$	EXPEDITIONS.COM

I bound onto the icy ledge—pronounced sturdy and safe by the watchful naturalists— joining shipmates on the crusty sheet where the captain has moored Lindblad's ice-hardened *National Geographic Explorer*. In this moment, I am Scott and Amundsen and Shackleton combined, explorers in a vast untouched universe.

The two dozen naturalist guides are appropriately hypersensitive about safety for guests and wildlife. The rules: Stay 15 feet from a penguin, farther from a seal, and avoid nesting grounds and other sensitive areas. In this fragile, fickle landscape, nothing can be taken for granted.

The inflatable Zodiacs that ferry guests ashore unload into gusts forceful enough to throw an average-size person—or 2-foot penguin—to the snow-packed ground. The katabatic blasts don't last long, and soon you tromp along the ice-packed "people paths" to a rookery of chinstrap penguins where brushy-tailed parents take turns warming a pair of eggs. The locals occasionally waddle over to check you out, getting far closer than anyone expects.

Aboard the *National Geographic Explorer*

Today's Antarctic trips are far more comfortable than the polar explorers of 100 years ago, and even 50 years ago, when Lindblad Expeditions, which runs the *National Geographic* sailings, pioneered tourism here. The 148-passenger ship features a spa, gym, fluffy duvets, Schnapps-laced hot chocolate, and home-baked cheesecake plated on a chocolate crunch. Thanks to fly-cruise programs, you can even dodge the unpredictable 36-hour voyage through the Drake Passage between Tierra del Fuego and the White Continent.

One way or another, you finally arrive on the ice-crusted shores of Antarctica.

You've come here for the penguins—gentoos, rockhoppers, chinstraps—that live only here. Flapping, the birds waddle purposely along until they belly-flop into the snow or fling themselves into the sea. Images don't quite capture the strangeness, but you will give it, literally, your best shot. At each point of interest—near the Weddell seals or the rookery—a National Geographic naturalist/photo instructor helps with settings on cameras ranging from SLRs to cellphones and suggests new angles.

Antarctic days unwind according to the dictates of ice and weather: landing, hiking to a colony of smelly red-lipped gentoos, cruising amid icebergs in your rubberized skiffs or kayaks. Some days, guests stay on board their 350-foot home base, plowing through ice sheets with their hardened hull and staring awestruck at hundred-mile-long ice chunks towering 150 feet above the sea. The ice, the quiet, the otherworldly vastness of it all enthralls.

A gentoo penguin colony on Cuverville Island, with the National Geographic Resolution *in the background.*

NATIONAL GEOGRAPHIC
RESOLUTION

But wildlife can be fleeting and trumps all. Whatever talk we're attending or meal we're eating is set aside so guests can dash on deck to follow a pod of orcas or a humpback cow that swims so close to the ship, we can hear her breathe. The bridge, always open, becomes a place to bring a hot chocolate and chat with naturalists and the captain, review the bird and mammal list for the day, and track our voyage.

Says company founder Sven Lindbald, "I believe the more people can get out and be exposed to these places, it creates awareness. It changes the way people see the world."

Planning a Trip

Antarctic voyages are offered from late November through March. The shortest lasts 12 days, beginning in Buenos Aires with a flight to your port in southern Argentina. Only cruise ships with 200 or fewer passengers are allowed to land in Antarctica.

Several lines, including Lindblad, offer flights to the White Continent, eliminating the Drake Passage on one or both legs of the voyage.

Emperor penguins are best seen in November and December in the Weddell Sea at Snow Hill Island, offered only on select itineraries. Most lines offer 3-week sailings that include the Falkland Islands and wildlife-rich South Georgia.

Lindblad Expeditions, partner with National Geographic, is known for its naturalist and photography experts. It operates four vessels in the region.

Other lines operating in the region include Aurora Expeditions, Atlas Cruises, Exodus Travels, HX-Hurtigruten Expeditions, Ponant Cruises, Scenic Cruises, Seabourn Cruises, Silversea Cruises, and Quark Expeditions.

WHAT TO KNOW ABOUT EXPEDITION CRUISING

An expedition voyage is the best or only choice for exploring many of the planet's remote bucket-list destinations.

Not so long ago, expedition cruises had only barebones cabins on vessels built primarily for scientific survey. But in the last decade, companies like Lindblad/National Geographic, Seabourn, and others began offering "bucket list" cruises for travelers interested in visiting remote locations and willing to pay hefty prices for the privilege . . . with the right onboard amenities. Today's voyages generally come with the comforts of room service, fluffy duvets, gourmet dining, bars, and a gym and spa. Most modern ships were built specially for polar waters, with ice-hardened hulls and state-of-the-art stabilizers, though many also offer warm-water itineraries. Only ships that carry 200 passengers or fewer are allowed to land in many sensitive places. (Some larger vessels sail in these waters but cannot land.)

Nature is the star, and it determines the schedule. Unlike classic cruises with ports advertised in advance, expedition itineraries depend on currents, tides, wildlife, and strict regulations aimed at environmental protection. And unlike classic cruises, there are no covered tender boats, no handy piers, no dress-up nights, no musical reviews, no casinos, and few shopping opportunities. While some vessels carry helicopters and submersibles, their use is limited by local regulations.

TOP LEFT: Zodiac returning to the **National Geographic Resolution.** *TOP RIGHT: Deck, the* **National Geographic Endurance.** *MIDDLE: Cabin, the* **National Geographic Endurance.** *BOTTOM LEFT: Icelandic meal, Charlie's Table restaurant, the* **National Geographic Endurance.** *BOTTOM RIGHT: Onboard igloo viewing area.*

On most lines, excursions involve transportation by the small, tough, inflatable boats called Zodiacs that take passengers among icebergs, into rivers, and up close to wildlife and waterfalls. Getting in and out of them takes a basic sense of balance and reasonably sturdy legs. Some companies require a doctor's statement of fitness and travel insurance.

On board and off, programming focuses on the destination. Most mornings and afternoons are dedicated to nature walks, hikes, kayaking, and wildlife viewing from the Zodiacs in the company of expert naturalists charged with keeping guests safe and explaining the local ecology. Each evening wraps up with a briefing where you learn about the next day's weather, tides, and plan for forays into the landscape. On sea days, naturalists offer presentations on topics ranging from marine mating habits to capturing great wildlife photos. While families are welcome, activities generally are oriented toward adults.

Such exclusive experiences come at a price. Meals, excursions, parkas, and other gear typically are included with fares that start around $1,000 per person per day for double occupancy; Galápagos cruises cost as much as 25% less. Many lines offer favorable fares for solo guests, who generally find like-minded travelers to share their time.

Brands offering high-quality expedition and adventure cruises include Aqua Expeditions aquaexpeditions.com, Atlas Ocean Voyages (atlasoceanvoyages.com), Aurora Expeditions aurora-expeditions.com, Coral Expeditions (coralexpeditions.com), Oceanwide Expeditions (oceanwide-expeditions.com), HX/Hurtigruten Expeditions (travelhx.com), Lindblad/National Geographics (expeditions.com), Ponant (us.ponant.com), Poseidon Expeditions (poseidonexpeditions.com), Quark Expeditions (quarkexpeditions.com), Scenic Ocean Cruises (scenicusa.com), Seabourn (seabourn.com), Silversea (silversea.com), and Uncruise (uncruise.com).

CHAPTER 12

PRACTICALITIES

While many aspects of nature travel are similar to other types of trips, exploring the wilderness comes with its own issues. Here are things to consider as you plan and prepare for your trip.

Packing

Casual, comfortable clothing is appropriate for most nature destinations, even at lodges with fine dining. Packing lightly is not only recommended, it may be necessary: Some trips, like African safaris, involve flights with strict weight limits.

That said, you want to be sure you take what you really need. Ask your travel supplier about specific packing and gear recommendations. Many lodgings give guests reusable water bottles. Keep sufficient water with you at all times—even if it means you'll need to make more pit stops. The advice "hydrate or die" isn't a joke.

Comfortable shoes suited to the terrain you're visiting are essential. For hiking, that means sturdy water-resistant boots. For cruises or marine adventures, you may need water shoes for wet landings that are still sturdy enough for trail walks.

Wet bags that protect your camera gear are always a good idea. If your cellphone is your primary camera, consider a clear plastic gear bag made specially for this purpose.

Jungle trips call for eco-friendly bug repellent and clothing with UV protection.

In cold climates and deserts, you want lightweight microfiber clothing that wicks moisture, packs easily, and can be layered for days that start and end cool but become warm during the day. A puffy vest and/or jacket that rolls tightly is a great choice.

For all destinations, add to your list a hat, tall socks, sunglasses, a lightweight water-resistant day pack, and eco-friendly sunscreen.

Many deep-in-nature lodges and expedition cruises include the use of boots and jackets. Some also offer long lenses for digital cameras that use interchangeable lenses. Most will note this on their websites, but to be sure, you should call or email for details.

Getting There

BUYING A TICKET If your trip involves flying, start looking for airfares months in advance, so you have a reference point. To check historical data on prices, **Google Flights** (google.com/travel/flights) is one of the easiest places to compare current flights (you can choose "best" or "cheapest" tabs). Below those results, you can click a tab to see historical pricing, so you know whether to wait. Multiple sites (including **travelocity.com, expedia.com,** and **smartertravel.com**) allow you to sign up for alerts when prices drop. Rates also often drop after a stock market sell-off or when negative news hits the region you're planning to visit.

Each year, Frommers.com publishes a guide to best airfare booking sites. The winners as we went to press? Sister sites **Momondo.com** and **Kayak.com** found the lowest prices most consistently. My advice: Use those multi-airline booking sites to compare fares, then book directly with your chosen airline. If something goes wrong, you're likely to resolve the issue more quickly if you've booked directly—especially if you're a loyalty program member.

It's worth noting that fares are sometimes cheaper on a partner airline, even on the same route. You will still earn mileage with your "home" airline, but you may not be eligible for upgrades and some other perks if you booked via the partner airline.

When you're traveling in remote or off-the-track locations, using a single airline and its partners isn't always viable. In such cases, a big, well-known agency (such as Expedia or Travelocity) is often the best choice. Be sure to keep the customer service number in your phone, along with itinerary details, in case something goes awry.

If you're looking for Economy Plus or Business Class fares, it's worth a call to **Skylux** (skyluxtravel.com), an agency that tracks and negotiates these types of fares. It can often find favorable prices, especially to Asia, Africa, and the Middle East, that you may not find on your own.

USING AIRLINE MILES One key advantage to using air miles is that if you need to cancel your flight, most airlines now will reinstate your miles for free.

Flyers often complain that they're unable to book with their miles. I've been all over the world on miles multiple times. Here's how I've made it work:

- Be flexible on dates.
- Travel during shoulder seasons. (Holidays and midsummer generally are expensive because so many people are traveling.)
- Don't count on flying nonstop or via the most direct route. Paying for a night in an airport hotel can be worth the money if you save thousands per ticket by using miles.
- Book well in advance. On many airlines that's 331 days before your flight.
- Didn't plan that far out? It's worth taking a look anyway. Airlines sometimes release frequent-flier seats when flights aren't fully booked.

USING CREDIT CARD POINTS Credit cards, such as **Capital One, American Express, and Chase,** award points that can be used at any time on many airlines. Points correlate to the actual dollar price, so a high-season flight requires more points than a low-season flight.

However, flights available for points can be limited to specific routes or specific flights, depending on the program. Also, refund policies vary by airline. If you cancel, you probably will get a credit with the specific airline you booked rather than getting points returned to your account.

Some experts recommend moving your points to a specific airline program to get the best value for them. But airlines closely regulate the number of "miles" seats available on each flight, so that doesn't always work either.

Bottom line: Every scenario is different. It's worth comparing availability of and routes before you hit "buy."

PRICE GUIDE

While most glamping resorts and many lodges price accommodations and meals separately, others include all meals and most activities and drinks. The symbols below are a general guide to lodging and cruises featured in this book.

$—Under $200 per night for lodging only.

$$—Under $400 per night for lodging only.

$$$—Under $1,000 per night for two people; may include meals and activities.

$$$$—Under $2,000 per night for two people; includes meals and activities.

$$$$$—More than $2,000 per night for two people; includes meals and activities.

Travel Advisors

Advisors today often specialize in luxury experiences. If you're traveling on a moderate budget, you're better off with a good guide book (we have one brand we recommend above the others, ahem). The same applies to straightforward trips with airfare, hotel, and car rental in a single destination.

But if you're considering luxury travel with a complex itinerary, remote locations, or multiple group members, you might want to consider a travel advisor who specializes in the location you're visiting. Note that often, the advisor will charge a planning fee—with good reason. Creating custom itineraries takes time, knowledge, and industry relationships. Those attributes should translate into upgrades, exclusive and behind-the-scenes experiences, and hard-to-get tickets. Also, if something goes awry during your trip, the travel advisor should step in and make needed changes.

HOW TO FIND A TRAVEL SPECIALIST

- **Virtuoso:** Most advisor-members of this luxury travel consortium specialize in a specific location or style of travel, such as safari. Search its website, virtuoso.com, and click on "travel advisors."
- **Magazines:** Condé Nast and Travel + Leisure publish annual lists of top travel advisors by specialty. Search for them online.
- **Wendy Perrin:** Travel journalist Wendy Perrin (wendyperrin.com) connects travelers with experienced advisors and publishes a list of on-the-ground operators who can arrange destination-specific custom itineraries.

A good agent should ask in-depth questions about your travel preferences: How quickly do you like to move on a trip? What trips have you enjoyed most, and why? Who will you be traveling with?

You may also want to ask them:

- How many times have you traveled to the location, and how recently?
- Describe your typical client.
- What did you like best about the destination? Are there any types of travelers you don't think would enjoy it?

CRUISE ADVISORS Cruise lines still work regularly with travel advisors and pay commissions, meaning their services generally are free to travelers. A knowledgeable advisor can steer you toward the itinerary and experience you want (see caveat below)—which might be a better fit than the one you've seen most advertised. They can often get you free upgrades, alert you to sales, and advise you on cabin categories and location.

And now, the caveat: Cruise advisors are often preferred agents for specific brands. That doesn't mean they get paid more by that brand, but they can be biased toward that brand. On the plus side, they also may have access to amenities that aren't generally available. (Yes, an advisor can be a preferred agent for more than one brand.) Well-known agencies include **Cruises.com, Cruise.com, CruiseOne** (cruiseone.com), and **CruisesOnly** (cruisesonly.com).

Here are the questions to ask:

- How long have they been booking cruises?
- How many cruises has the advisor been on personally, and on which brands?
- What do they do to keep current with cruise offerings? For instance, do they go to conferences, ship launches, and onboard events?
- How many clients do they have who match your own profile (couple, family with teens, adventure lovers, budget-conscious, special-occasion splurge)?

Fitness

Many nature-immersion experiences are perfect for travelers who want to sit on the deck and soak up the atmosphere. Others involve hiking, horse riding, snorkeling, and other active pursuits—sometimes at high altitudes. For travelers who aren't typically active, a vacation isn't the time to suddenly push normal limits. It's best to discuss plans in advance with a medical professional familiar with your history.

Insurance

Companies that operate expedition cruises and trips to remote places often require guests to purchase some forms of travel insurance. Others simply encourage it, but with good reason:

They won't reimburse you or rebook you. Sure, travel providers will do what they can to help in an emergency, but they're also running businesses.

Depending on your age and where you're going, travel insurance can be pricy. It can also save your bacon, especially if someone in your group is older, you have parents at home in fragile health, or you have to be medevacked out of a remote location to a hospital (a pricy, pricy trip).

There are three basic types of travel insurance:

- **Flight insurance:** Many airlines offer this at time of booking, but you only need it if you book a Basic Economy seat. Almost all other fares can be changed.
- **Medical/evacuation insurance:** Medicare *does not* cover care outside the U.S. The same goes for some low-priced health care policies. (See "Medical/Evacuation Insurance," below.)
- **Comprehensive trip insurance:** These packages include travel delays, cancellation, medical care, evacuation, and more. (See "Comprehensive Trip Insurance," below.)

If you're traveling inside the U.S. and the trip cost isn't great, you may not feel you need insurance. If you're traveling far from home and the trip cost is more than you're comfortable gambling, consider insurance.

PREMIUM CREDIT CARD INSURANCE Not so long ago, nearly all credit cards offered some type of insurance, such as rental car damage, if you booked with the specified card. Now, only premium cards, such as **American Express Platinum**, **Chase Sapphire Preferred**, **Chase Sapphire Reserve**, and some business cards, offer any insurance. Reimbursement amounts are limited; the highest-limit coverage typically is for car rental. Bottom line: Double-check your policy to be sure you know exactly what is—and isn't—covered.

COMPREHENSIVE TRIP INSURANCE These policies cover one specific trip. Most policies include medical and dental care, medical evacuation, trip delays, and cancellation. Pricing and inclusions vary widely, but comparing them is easier than you might think thanks to online insurance marketplace sites (see "Insurance Resources," below). My advice: Compare policies online, then call the phone number on the website and make sure you're looking at the right policies for your circumstances.

Here are some factors to consider:

- If one of the people in your travel group (friends or family) had to cancel because of health, would you also want to cancel your trip?
- If a family member at home died, would you want to curtail your trip? What is the relationship (parent, uncle, etc.)?
- Would you want to cancel if your home got hit with an extreme weather event?

Important Note Policies exclude preexisting medical conditions that occur during a "look-back period" that varies by policy. The exclusions are waived if you book the insurance within a short time of making your first trip payment, typically 10 or 14 days.

MEDICAL/EVACUATION INSURANCE Check your regular medical insurance. As noted above, Medicare, Medigap, and many low-cost plans do not provide coverage outside the U.S. Some don't include coverage outside your home state. And few, if any, include evacuation if you get sick or injured outside the U.S. The limits on credit-card policies are low.

There are several types of insurance for medical care and medical evacuation. Many are sold on an annual basis, which makes them ideal for people who take several trips outside the country each year.

Each has a coverage limit that may depend on age:

- **Medical evacuation:** Generally for this to happen, the patient must first be at a local hospital. The policy will then medically evacuate the patient according to the level of care and support needed in the particular case. In the case of a broken hip, that might be Business Class on a commercial flight; in the case of a severe heart condition, that might be on a medically equipped plane with nursing care. Some policies provide transportation to your home hospital; others provide transportation only to the nearest qualified facility.
- **Medical care & evacuation:** I've seen and written about so many incidents where travelers found themselves faced with the complexities of unfamiliar situations and huge bills. Case in point: My husband slipped on ice in Sweden, where the medical system is vastly different from the U.S. Our multitrip GeoBlue Trekker Preferred policy (purchased through insuremytrip.com) provided advice; handled translations; monitored his progress; arranged a qualified nonmedical escort and transit for both of them from the hospital in Lulea, Sweden, to our home hospital in the U.S.; and paid for his care in Sweden. The advisors told me what I needed to hear, not what I always wanted to hear. Priceless.

INSURANCE RESOURCES

Comprehensive & Medical-Only Policies: These websites allow you to easily compare products from multiple insurance companies and provide live phone support during the purchase process:

- **ardy.com**
- **insuremytrip.com**
- **squaremouth.com**

Medical & Safety Evacuation: These are the best-recognized companies offering annual evacuation policies:

- **globalrescue.com:** Policies can be annual or cover a specific time period. For an additional fee, it will cover travelers ages 75–84.
- **medjetassist.com:** Short-term and annual policies are offered. Travelers ages 75–84 are covered at an additional fee subject to medical history and approval.

INDEX

PHOTO CREDITS

Front cover: Courtesy of Treehotel / Ragnar Th. Sigurdsson; p. i: Courtesy of Green Safaris / Stevie Mann; p. vi: Courtesy of Finn Lough / Will Archer; p. 1: Courtesy of Treehotel / Malin Eriksson; p. 3: Courtesy of Moose Meadow Lodge / Carolyn Bates; p. 4: Courtesy of Seth Peterson Cottage / Kip Hogan, Courtesy of Seth Peterson Cottage / Kip Hogan, Courtesy of Seth Peterson Cottage / Kip Hogan; p. 7: Courtesy of Spyglass Sonoma / Devon Fox; p. 8: Courtesy of Spyglass Redwoods / Carson Linforth Bowley, Courtesy of Spyglass Redwoods / Carson Linforth Bowley; p. 9: Jane Wooldridge; p. 11: Courtesy of green o, Courtesy of green o, Courtesy of green o; p. 12: Courtesy of The Resort at Paws Up / Stuart Thurlkill, Courtesy of The Resort at Paws Up / Stuart Thurlkill, The Resort at Paws Up / Dan Goldberg; p. 13: Courtesy of green o; p. 15: Courtesy of Hope Glen Farm / Kelly Anne Grundhauser, Courtesy of Hope Glen Farm / Kelly Anne Grundhauser, Courtesy of Hope Glen Farm / Kelly Anne Grundhauser, Courtesy of Hope Glen Farm / Kelly Anne Grundhauser; p. 16: Entre Cîmes et Racines, Entre Cîmes et Racines / Marco Bergeron, Entre Cîmes et Racines; p. 19: Courtesy of Iron & Vine, Courtesy of Visit Rainier, Courtesy of Iron & Vine / Lux and Ember Photography / Paul Roderick, Courtesy of Visit Rainier / Henri Halle, Courtesy of Iron & Vine; p. 20: Courtesy of Treehotel, Courtesy of Treehotel, Courtesy of Treehotel; p. 23: Courtesy of Hapuku Lodge + Tree Houses, Courtesy of Hapuku Lodge + Tree Houses, Courtesy of Hapuku Lodge + Tree Houses; p. 24: Courtesy of Hapuku Lodge + Tree Houses, Courtesy of Hapuku Lodge + Tree Houses / Joshua Holko; p. 25: Courtesy of Hapuku Lodge + Tree Houses, Courtesy of Hapuku Lodge + Tree Houses; p. 27: Courtesy of Treeful Treehouse Sustainable Resort; p. 28: Courtesy of Treeful Treehouse Sustainable Resort, Courtesy of Treeful Treehouse Sustainable Resort, Courtesy of Treeful Treehouse Sustainable Resort; p. 31: Courtesy of TreeDwellers; p. 32: Courtesy of Finn Lough / Will Archer; p. 35: Chasehunterphotos / Shutterstock, Courtesy of Clear Sky Resort Bryce Canyon, Courtesy of Clear Sky Resort Bryce Canyon; p. 36: Courtesy of Clear Sky Resort Bryce Canyon / Scott Osborne; p. 38: Courtesy of Klarhet, Jane Wooldrige, Courtesy of Klarhet, Courtesy of Klarhet; p. 41: Courtesy of Finn Lough / Christina Kruse, Courtesy of Finn Lough / Will Archer, Courtesy of Finn Lough / Christina Kruse; p. 42: Courtesy of Sun City Wadi Rum; p. 45: Courtesy of Pristine El Calafate Luxury Camp; p. 46: Courtesy of Métis Crossing / Jay R. McDonald, Courtesy of Métis Crossing / Travel Alberta, Courtesy of Métis Crossing, Courtesy of Métis Crossing / Jay R. McDonald; p. 48: Courtesy of El Silenco Lodge / Brice Ferre Studio; p. 51: Courtesy of Shinta Mani Wild Tents; p. 52: Courtesy of Shinta Mani Wild Tents, Courtesy of Shinta Mani Wild Tents, Courtesy of Shinta Mani Wild Tents / Mac Ernelson; p. 53: Courtesy of Shinta Mani Wild Tents / Krishna Adithya Prajogo, p. 54: Courtesy of Flamingo Everglades Adventures / KEVIN SNYDER PHOTOGRAPHY, GIBAN / Shutterstock, Courtesy of Flamingo Lodge / Bonnie Barnes, Courtesy of Flamingo Everglades Adventures / KEVIN SNYDER PHOTOGRAPHY; p. 57: Michal Knitl / Shutterstock, Courtesy of Awasi Iguazu / Ingrid Weyland, Courtesy of Awasi Iguazu / Luciano Bacchi, Courtesy of Awasi Iguazu; p. 58: Courtesy of Mashpi Lodge, Courtesy of Mashpi Lodge / Juan Carlos Narvaez Dobronski, Courtesy of Mashpi Lodge; p. 60: Courtesy of Mashpi Lodge; p. 61: Courtesy of Mashpi Lodge / Jack Anstey, Courtesy of Mashpi Lodge, Courtesy of Mashpi Lodge / Lucas Bustamante; p. 62: Courtesy of El Silencio Lodge, Courtesy of El Silencio Lodge / Brice Ferre, Courtesy of El Silencio Lodge; p. 65: Courtesy of Nayara Tented Camp; p. 66: Courtesy of Nayara Tented Camp / Brice Ferre, Courtesy of Nayara Tented Camp / Brice Ferre, Courtesy of Nayara Tented Camp / Brice Ferre, Courtesy of Nayara Tented Camp / Brice Ferre, Courtesy of Nayara Tented Camp / Miles Photography; p. 69: Courtesy of Anavilhanas Jungle Lodge / Felipe Castellari, Courtesy of Anavilhanas Jungle Lodge / Vitor Marigo, Courtesy of Anavilhanas Jungle Lodge, Courtesy of Anavilhanas Jungle Lodge / Felipe Castellari; p. 71: Johanna Veldstra / Shutterstock, Courtesy of Table Rock Jungle Lodge / Benedict Kim, Courtesy of Table Rock Jungle Lodge / Benedict Kim; p. 72: Courtesy of Blancaneaux Lodge; p. 74: Courtesy of Blancaneaux Lodge / Kevin W Quischan; p. 75: Courtesy of Blancaneaux Lodge / Kevin W Quischan, Courtesy of Blancaneaux Lodge, Courtesy of Blancaneaux Lodge; p. 76: Courtesy of Copal Tree Lodge / Francis Fraioli, Courtesy of Copal Tree Lodge, Courtesy of Copal Tree Lodge, Courtesy of Copal Tree Lodge; p. 79: Courtesy of BIO Habitat Hotel; p. 80: Courtesy of BIO Habitat Hotel, Courtesy of BIO Habitat Hotel, Courtesy of BIO Habitat Hotel, Courtesy of BIO Habitat Hotel; p. 81: Courtesy of BIO Habitat Hotel; p. 83: Courtesy of The FloatHouse River Kwai; p. 84: Courtesy of Soneva Kiri; p. 87: Courtesy of Islas Secas, Courtesy of Islas Secas, Courtesy of Islas Secas, Courtesy of Islas Secas, Courtesy of Islas Secas; p. 88: Courtesy of Islas Secas, Courtesy of Islas Secas, Courtesy of Islas Secas; p. 89: Courtesy of Islas Secas; p. 91: Courtesy of Saugerties Lighthouse / Anna Landewe; p. 92: Courtesy of Lizard Island / Alex Kydd, Courtesy of Lizard Island, Courtesy of Lizard Island, Courtesy of Lizard Island / Elise Hassey; p. 95: Courtesy of Misool / Shawn Heinrichs, Courtesy of Misool / Sabine Templeton, Courtesy of Misool / Shawn Heinrichs, Courtesy of Misool / Derrick Thomson; p. 97: Courtesy of Fogo Island Inn / Alex Fradkin, Courtesy of Fogo Island Inn / Iwan Baan, Courtesy of Fogo Island Inn / Iwan Baan, Courtesy of Fogo Island Inn / Alex Fradkin; p. 98: Courtesy of GoldenEye / Brie Williams / Island Outpost Images; p. 100: Courtesy of GoldenEye / Brie Williams / Island Outpost Images, Courtesy of GoldenEye / Brie Williams / Island Outpost Images, Courtesy of GoldenEye / Brie Williams / Island Outpost Images; p. 101: Courtesy of GoldenEye / Christian Horan / Island Outpost Images, Courtesy of GoldenEye / Adrian Boot / Island Outpost Images; p. 102: Courtesy of Mamula Island; p. 104: Courtesy of Soneva Kiri / Helicam, Courtesy of Soneva Kiri, Courtesy of Soneva Kiri; p. 106: Courtesy of [illegible] FotoArt, Courtesy of Jicaro Island Lodge / Jesper Anhede; p. 109: Courtesy of Jungle Bay Dominica, Courtesy of Secret Bay, Courtesy of Secret Bay; p. 110: Courtesy of Mandala Resort / Alvaro Herrero, Courtesy of Mandala Resort, Courtesy of Mandala Resort; p. 113: Courtesy of We Are Morocco Travel; p. 114: Courtesy of Xanterra Travel Collection / The Oasis at Death Valley / Mike Ver Sprill, Courtesy of Xanterra Travel Collection / The Oasis at Death Valley, Courtesy of Xanterra Travel Collection / The Oasis at Death Valley / Michel Verdure; p. 117: Givaga / Shutterstock, Courtesy of Al Moudira / Mark Anthony Fox, Courtesy of Al Moudira / Mark Anthony Fox, Courtesy of Al Moudira / Mark Anthony Fox; p. 118: Courtesy of We Are Morocco Travel, Courtesy of We Are Morocco Travel, Courtesy of We Are Morocco Travel, Courtesy of We Are Morocco Travel; p. 121: Courtesy of Orchard Canyon on Oak Creek, Courtesy of Orchard Canyon on Oak Creek / John Burcham, Wirestock Creators / Shutterstock; p. 122: Wirestock Creators / Shutterstock.com, Courtesy of Argos in Cappadocia, Courtesy of Argos in Cappadocia, Courtesy of Argos in Cappadocia / Rainer Klostermeier / Axel Kull; p. 125: Courtesy of Three Camel Lodge, Courtesy of Three Camel Lodge, Courtesy of Three Camel Lodge / Iñaki Relanzon; p. 126: Courtesy of Visit Big Bend / Jim & Lynne Weber, Courtesy of The Summit at Big Bend / Quin Schrock, Courtesy of Visit Big Bend / Kara Gerbert, Courtesy of The Summit at Big Bend / Tony Maples; p. 129: Courtesy of Real Egypt-Dahabiya Nile Sailing, Akimov Konstantin / Shutterstock, Courtesy of Real Egypt-Dahabiya Nile Sailing, Courtesy of Real Egypt-Dahabiya Nile Sailing; p. 130: Courtesy of Green Safaris Chisa Busanga Camp; p. 133: Courtesy of Xigera Safari Lodge / The Red Carnation Hotel Collection; p. 134: Courtesy of Xigera Safari Lodge / The Red Carnation Hotel Collection, Courtesy of Xigera Safari Lodge / The Red Carnation Hotel Collection, Courtesy of Xigera Safari Lodge / The Red Carnation Hotel Collection, Courtesy of Xigera Safari Lodge / The Red Carnation Hotel Collection; p. 137: Courtesy of Green Safaris Chisa Busanga Camp / Stevie Mann; p. 139: © Alex Mowat / Frontiers North Adventures; p. 141: Courtesy of Ngare Serian / Bobby-Jo Photography, Courtesy of Ngare Serian / Bobby-Jo Photography, Courtesy of Ngare Serian / TEAGAN CUNNIFFE, Courtesy of Ngare Serian; p. 142: Courtesy of Sal Salis, Courtesy of Sal Salis, Courtesy of Sal Salis, Courtesy of Sal Salis, Courtesy of Sal Salis / Emma Sweeney; p. 145: Courtesy of Safari West, Courtesy of Safari West / Ray Mabry, Courtesy of Safari West / Ray Mabry, Courtesy of Safari West / Sarah-Jane Tarr, Courtesy of Safari West / John Burgess; p. 146: Courtesy of One&Only Gorilla's Nest, Courtesy of Volcanos Safari Virguna Lodge, Courtesy of Volcanos Safari Virguna Lodge; p. 148: Courtesy of Volcanos Safari Virguna Lodge / SHAUN S RITCHIE, Courtesy of Volcanos Safari Virguna Lodge, Courtesy of One&Only Gorilla's Nest, Courtesy of One&Only Gorilla's Nest / Philip Lee Harvey; p. 149: Courtesy of One&Only Gorilla's Nest / Philip Lee Harvey; p. 151: Travel Stock / Shutterstock, Courtesy of Entamanu Ngorongoro Safari Camp, Courtesy of Entamanu Ngorongoro Safari Camp, Courtesy of Entamanu Ngorongoro Safari Camp; p. 153: Som Moulick / Shutterstock, Anshik Thakur / Shutterstock, Courtesy of Tree House Hideaway - Bandhavgarh / Thiru, Courtesy of Tree House Hideaway - Bandhavgarh / Thiru; p. 154: Courtesy of &Beyond Phinda Forest Lodge, Courtesy of &Beyond Phinda Forest Lodge, Courtesy of &Beyond Phinda Forest Lodge; p. 157: Courtesy of Hebridean Sea Safari + Glenapp Castle / Edward Braham, Courtesy of Hebridean Sea Safari + Glenapp Castle, Courtesy of Hebridean Sea Safari + Glenapp Castle, Courtesy of

Hebridean Sea Safari + Glenapp Castle, Courtesy of Hebridean Sea Safari + Glenapp Castle; p. 158: Courtesy of Leopard Trails Yala Camp, Courtesy of Leopard Trails Yala Camp, Courtesy of Leopard Trails Yala Camp / Dhanush de Costa, Courtesy of Leopard Trails Yala Camp; p. 161: Courtesy of Angama Mara, Courtesy of Angama Mara / Adam Banniste, Scott Ramsay / Scott Ramsay; p. 162: Courtesy of Angama Mara, Courtesy of Angama Mara, Courtesy of Angama Mara / Sammy Njoroge / Charlotte Ross Stewart, Courtesy of Angama Mara; p. 163: Courtesy of Angama Mara / DOOK PHOTO; p. 164: Courtesy of Hacienda el Porvenir; p. 166: Courtesy of Abbey Road Farm / Kathryn Elsesser, Courtesy of Abbey Road Farm, Courtesy of Abbey Road Farm / John Valls; p. 169: Courtesy of Lone Mountain Ranch / Heidi A Long / Longviews Studios; p. 170: Courtesy of Lone Mountain Ranch / Eric Martin, Courtesy of Lone Mountain Ranch; p. 171: Courtesy of Lone Mountain Ranch / Audrey Hall; p. 173: Courtesy of Villa Lena, Courtesy of Villa Lena, Courtesy of Villa Lena / Niklas Adrian Vindelev, Courtesy of Villa Lena, Courtesy of Villa Lena/ Julie and Uwe GbR, Courtesy of Villa Lena; p. 174: Courtesy of Hacienda el Porvenir / Dan Barham, Courtesy of Hacienda el Porvenir, Courtesy of Hacienda el Porvenir, Courtesy of Hacienda el Porvenir; p. 177: Nicholas J Klein / Shutterstock, Courtesy of Visit Big Sky, Courtesy of Visit Big Sky / Jak Wonderly; p. 178: Courtesy of Iron Creek Bay Estate / Peter Whyte Photography, Photography by Rob D / Shutterstock, Courtesy of Iron Creek Bay Estate; p. 181: Courtesy of Quinta da Pacheca / Brunastartt, Courtesy of Quinta da Pacheca / Pedro Sarmento Costa, Courtesy of Quinta da Pacheca / Brunastartt; p. 182: Courtesy of Clark Farm Silos, Courtesy of Clark Farm Silos, Courtesy of Clark Farm Silos, Courtesy of Clark Farm Silos; p. 185: Courtesy of Masseria Torre Coccaro / Mr & Mrs Smith, Courtesy of Masseria Torre Coccaro / Mr & Mrs Smith, Courtesy of Masseria Torre Coccaro / Mr & Mrs Smith; p. 186: Courtesy of Rancho Santana / Kuba Okon, Courtesy of Rancho Santana, Courtesy of Rancho Santana, Courtesy of Rancho Santana / Kuba Okon, Courtesy of Rancho Santana / Kuba Okon; p. 189: Courtesy of Triple Creek Ranch / Pam Voth, Courtesy of Triple Creek Ranch, Courtesy of Triple Creek Ranch, Courtesy of Triple Creek Ranch / MONICA BENNETT; p. 190: Courtesy of Opensky / DAVID ADAM ELLIOTT; p. 193: Courtesy of Ofland Escalante / Kim + Nash Finley; p. 194: Courtesy of Ofland Escalante, Courtesy of Ofland Escalante / Kim + Nash Finley, Courtesy of Ofland Escalante / Kim + Nash Finley, Courtesy of Ofland Escalante / Kim + Nash Finley; p. 197: Courtesy of Anaway Place, Courtesy of Anaway Place / Christina Hussey; p. 198: Courtesy of Anaway Place, Courtesy of Anaway Place; p. 199: Courtesy of Anaway Place / Christina Hussey, Courtesy of Anaway Place; p. 201: Andrew S / Shutterstock, Courtesy of Backland, Courtesy of Backland, Courtesy of Backland; p. 202: Courtesy of Eastwind Oliverea Valley / Lawrence Braun, Courtesy of Eastwind Oliverea Valley / Lawrence Braun, Courtesy of Eastwind Oliverea Valley / Lawrence Braun, Courtesy of AutoCamp Catskills; p. 205: Courtesy of GLAMP Minty; p. 206: Courtesy of ULUM Moab / Bailey Made; p. 209: Courtesy of Whitetail Woods / Brian Basham, Courtesy of Whitetail Woods, Courtesy of Whitetail Woods; p. 210: Courtesy of Huttopia Sutton / Romain Etienne; p. 213: Courtesy of Dunton River Camp / Jack Richmond, Courtesy of Dunton River Camp / Jack Richmond, Courtesy of Dunton River Camp, Courtesy of Dunton River Camp, Courtesy of Dunton River Camp; p. 214: Don Mammoser / Shutterstock, Courtesy of Under Canvas West Yellowstone, Courtesy of Under Canvas West Yellowstone; p. 217: Courtesy of Mendocino Grove, Courtesy of Mendocino Grove / Emily Nathan, Courtesy of Mendocino Grove; p. 218: Courtesy of Open Sky / Matthew Parent, Courtesy of Open Sky / DAVID ADAM ELLIOTT, Courtesy of Open Sky / Arika Bauer; p. 221: SB SHOTS / Shutterstock, Courtesy of Camp Aramoni / Matt Haas, Courtesy of Camp Aramoni / Matt Haas; p. 222: Wirestock Creators / Shutterstock, Courtesy of FireLight Camps, Courtesy of FireLight Camps / Carly Jane Underwood, Courtesy of FireLight Camps; p. 225: Courtesy of Walden Retreats, Courtesy of Walden Retreats, Courtesy of Walden Retreats / Michelle Nash Photography; p. 226: Courtesy of White Desert / Andrew Macdonald, Courtesy of White Desert / Andrew Macdonald, Courtesy of White Desert / Andrew Macdonald; p. 229: Courtesy of Treebones Resort Big Sur / Two Feathers, Courtesy of Treebones Resort Big Sur / Two Feathers, Courtesy of Treebones Resort Big Sur / Ryuji Morishita, Courtesy of Treebones Resort Big Sur / Two Feathers; p. 230: Courtesy of Gangtey Lodge Bhutan / Ken Spence; p. 232: Darryl Brooks / Shutterstock; p. 234: Courtesy of Freycinet Saffire, Courtesy of Freycinet Saffire, Courtesy of Freycinet Saffire; p. 236: Courtesy of Freycinet Lodge / RACT Destinations, Courtesy of Freycinet Lodge / Gabi Mocatta; p. 237: Courtesy of Freycinet Lodge / Melissa Findley, Courtesy of Freycinet Lodge / Alastair Bett, Benny Marty / Shutterstock; p. 239: Courtesy of The Point Resort, Courtesy of The Point Resort / Kindra Clineff, Courtesy of The Point Resort / Kindra Clineff; p. 240: Courtesy of Eden Boutique Hotel; p. 242: Courtesy of Eden Boutique Hotel; p. 243: Courtesy of Eden Boutique Hotel, Courtesy of Eden Boutique Hotel, Courtesy of Eden Boutique Hotel; p. 244: Courtesy of Urban Cowboy / Oveck, Courtesy of Urban Cowboy / Oveck, Courtesy of Urban Cowboy / Ben Fitchett, Courtesy of Urban Cowboy / Ben Fitchett; p. 247: Courtesy of Gregans Castle/ Leila Brewster; p. 248: Courtesy of Gregans Castle, Courtesy of Gregans Castle, Courtesy of Gregans Castle / Cprendergast; p. 249: Courtesy of Gregans Castle / Cprendergast, Courtesy of Gregans Castle / Leila Brewster; p. 251: Courtesy of Gangtey Lodge Bhutan / Ken Spence, Courtesy of Gangtey Lodge Bhutan / Ken Spence, Courtesy of Gangtey Lodge Bhutan / Ken Spence; p. 252: Courtesy of Gangtey Lodge Bhutan / Chris Caldecott, Courtesy of Gangtey Lodge Bhutan / Ken Spence, Courtesy of Gangtey Lodge Bhutan / Ken Spence; p. 253: Courtesy of Gangtey Lodge Bhutan / Chris Caldecott, Courtesy of Gangtey Lodge Bhutan / Ken Spence; p. 255: Courtesy of Tutka Bay Lodge / Karyn Traphagen, Courtesy of Tutka Bay Lodge / Jeff Schultz, Courtesy of Tutka Bay Lodge, Courtesy of Tutka Bay Lodge; p. 256: Courtesy of Areias do Seixo, Courtesy of Areias do Seixo, Courtesy of Areias do Seixo / Manuel Gomes da Costa, Courtesy of Areias do Seixo / Vanessa&Pascal, Courtesy of Areias do Seixo; p. 259: Courtesy of Explora Torres Del Paine, Courtesy of Explora Torres Del Paine, Courtesy of Explora Torres Del Paine; p. 260: Courtesy of Tu Tu' Tun Lodge / Liz Barclay, Courtesy of Tu Tu' Tun Lodge, CSNafzger / Shutterstock, Courtesy of Tu Tu' Tun Lodge; p. 263: Courtesy of Hotel Nafarrola / Iker Basterretxea, Courtesy of Hotel Nafarrola / Iker Basterretxea, Courtesy of Hotel Nafarrola / Iker Basterretxea; p. 264: Courtesy of Sun Mountain Lodge / Anne Young; p. 267: Courtesy of Eco Selo Nevidio / Milos Samardzic, Jennifer Lamb, Courtesy of Eco Selo Nevidio; p. 268: Courtesy of Cloud Camp; p. 271: Courtesy of Arctic Bath, Courtesy of Arctic Bath, Courtesy of Arctic Bath / Sami Laitinen, Courtesy of Arctic Bath / Sami Laitinen; p. 272: Courtesy of Amanresorts Limited, Gnomeandi / Shutterstock, Courtesy of Amanresorts Limited / SUKAMOTO; p. 273: Courtesy of Amanresorts Limited; p. 274: Courtesy of Hells' Backbone Grill & Farm / Morgan Reedy; p. 277: Courtesy of Wind Cave National Park, Courtesy of Wind Cave National Park, Courtesy of Custer State Park; p. 278: Courtesy of Locavore Farm; p. 281: Courtesy of Hells' Backbone Grill & Farm / Mary McIntyre, Courtesy of Hells' Backbone Grill & Farm / Morgan Reedy, Courtesy of Hells' Backbone Grill & Farm / Morgan Reedy, Courtesy of Hells' Backbone Grill & Farm / Morgan Reedy; p. 282: Courtesy of Tabacón Thermal Resort & Spa; p. 285: Burning Bright / Shutterstock, Courtesy of Wild Food Adventures in Armenia / Linda Hermans, Courtesy of Wild Food Adventures in Armenia / Narek Harutyunyan, Courtesy of Wild Food Adventures in Armenia / Narek Harutyunyan; p. 286: Courtesy of Turner Farm, Courtesy of Turner Farm, Courtesy of Turner Farm, Courtesy of Turner Farm; p. 288: Courtesy of South Pacific-Seabourn Pursuit / Taylor Gray; p. 291: Courtesy of Scenic Luxury Cruises & Tours / Ron Clifford; p. 292: Courtesy of Scenic Luxury Cruises & Tours / Ulli Seer, Courtesy of Scenic Luxury Cruises & Tours / Ulli Seer, Courtesy of Scenic Luxury Cruises & Tours; p. 293: Courtesy of Scenic Luxury Cruises & Tours / Pablo Bianco; p. 294: Courtesy of South Pacific-Seabourn Pursuit / Taylor Gray, Courtesy of South Pacific-Seabourn Pursuit / Taylor Gray, Courtesy of South Pacific-Seabourn Pursuit / Taylor Gray, Courtesy of South Pacific-Seabourn Pursuit / Taylor Gray, Courtesy of South Pacific-Seabourn Pursuit / Richard Sidey, Courtesy of South Pacific-Seabourn Pursuit / Taylor Gray; p. 296: PinkBlue Studio / Shutterstock; p. 297: Courtesy of Seabourn Pursuit, Courtesy of South Pacific-Seabourn Pursuit / Taylor Gray, Courtesy of South Pacific-Seabourn Pursuit / Taylor Gray; p. 299: Courtesy of Maine Windjammer Association / Fred LeBlanc, Courtesy of Maine Windjammer Association / Nick Parson; p. 300: Courtesy of Maine Windjammer Association / Fred LeBlanc, Courtesy of Maine Windjammer Association / Tracey Sheppard, Courtesy of Maine Windjammer Association / Fred LeBlanc; p. 301: Courtesy of Sail Maine Coast / Leigh Madeleine; p. 302: Courtesy of Silversea Cruises / Pablo Bianco, Courtesy of Silversea Cruises; p. 305: Courtesy of Silversea Cruises / Bruno Cazarini, Courtesy of Silversea Cruises / Kris Markovska, Courtesy of Silversea Cruises / Bruno Cazarini, Courtesy of Silversea Cruises, Courtesy of Silversea Cruises / Kris Markovska; p. 307: Courtesy of HX Expeditions / Ted Gatlin, Courtesy of HX Expeditions / Andrea Klaussner, Jane Wooldridge; p. 308: Courtesy of HX Expeditions / Clara Tuma, Courtesy of HX Expeditions / Rune Kongsro, Courtesy of HX Expeditions / Espen Mills, Courtesy of HX Expeditions / Clara Tuma; p. 310: Courtesy of Celebrity Flora, Courtesy of Celebrity Flora / Michel Verdure; p. 312: Courtesy of Celebrity Flora / Quentin Bacon; p. 313: Jennifer Lamb, Jennifer Lamb, Meghan Lamb, Courtesy of Celebrity Flora / Michel Verdure, Meghan Lamb, Jennifer Lamb; p. 315: Courtesy of Antarctic Lindblad Nat Geo / Ralph Lee Hopkins; p. 316: Courtesy of Antarctic Lindblad Nat Geo / Ralph Lee Hopkins, Courtesy of Antarctic Lindblad Nat Geo, Courtesy of Antarctic Lindblad Nat Geo / Oivind Haug, Courtesy of Antarctic Lindblad Nat Geo / David Vargas, Courtesy of Antarctic Lindblad Nat Geo / Ralph Lee Hopkins; Back cover: Courtesy of White Desert, Courtesy of Misool / Sabine Templeton, Courtesy of Finn Lough / Will Archer